International Justice and the Third World

International Justice and the Third World is a collection of essays on the philosophy of development. Contesting the view that there is no such thing as justice between societies of unequal power, and that there is no obligation to assist poor people in distant countries, it helps make good the lack of philosophical literature about global justice and the conceptual and ethical issues surrounding the idea of development.

Together, the essays affirm that a notion of global justice is both necessary and possible, and respond to theories which deny the existence of obligations to all human beings. It is variously argued that these obligations are based on human needs, on human rights or on social relations. Liberal and Marxist approaches to universal responsibilities are discussed, and their ability to manage global issues of equity assessed. As many millions of women in the Third World suffer special oppression, it is stressed that any adequate theory must respond to their plight. At the same time the presuppositions of the various economic and political models of development are explored in a chapter which argues for a democratic and participatory approach.

Another chapter argues for a convergence of the platforms of environmentalists and developmentalists. *International Justice and the Third World* thus relates Third World development to sustainability, to issues of gender, and to environmentalism, questioning throughout the sufficiency of market mechanisms to cope with these issues. The concluding chapter, building on earlier contributions, argues that current Third World indebtedness is profoundly exploitative, and that the debts of Third World countries should be unconditionally cancelled.

International Justice and the
Third World

International Justice and the Third World

Studies in the Philosophy of Development

edited by
Robin Attfield and Barry Wilkins

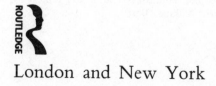

London and New York

First published 1992
by Routledge
11 New Fetter Lane, London EC4P 4EE

Simultaneously published in the USA and Canada
by Routledge
a division of Routledge, Chapman and Hall Inc.
29 West 35th Street, New York, NY 10001

Phototypeset in 10 on 12 point Bembo by
Intype, London
Printed in Great Britain by
Clays Ltd, St Ives plc

British Library Cataloguing in Publication Data
International justice and the third world: studies in
the philosophy of development.
I. Attfield, Robin II. Wilkins, Barry
179

Library of Congress Cataloging in Publication Data
International justice and the third world: studies in the philosophy
of development / edited by Robin Attfield and Barry Wilkins.
p. cm.
Includes bibliographical references and index.
1. Social justice. 2. Economic development–Moral and ethical
aspects. 3. Economic development–Environmental aspects.
4. International economic relations–Moral and ethical aspects.
5. Economic assistance–Developing countries–Moral and ethical
aspects. I. Attfield, Robin. II. Wilkins, Barry.
JC578.I58 1992
320'.01'1–dc20 91–38394

ISBN 0–415–06924–6
0–415–06925–4 (pb)

Contents

Acknowledgements

We are grateful to Kai Nielsen and to the Society for Applied Philosophy for permission to reprint 'Global justice, capitalism and the Third World', from the *Journal of Applied Philosophy*, vol. 1, no. 2, 1984.

We are also grateful to Onora O'Neill and to Oxford University Press for permission to reprint 'Justice, gender and international boundaries', from M. Nussbaum and A. K. Sen (eds), *The Quality of Life*, Oxford: Clarendon Press, 1992.

Our thanks go also to Andrew Belsey for some helpful comments on an earlier draft of the Introduction, to Geoff Boden for preparing the Bibliography and the Index, to Miles Litvinoff for helpful and constructive copy-editing and to the publishers and all the contributors for their obligingness and co-operation.

Contributors

Robin Attfield is a Reader in Philosophy at the University of Wales, Cardiff, and a member of its Centre for Applied Ethics. He has also taught in Nigeria and Kenya. His publications include *A Theory of Value and Obligation* (London: Croom Helm, 1987) and *The Ethics of Environmental Concern* (Oxford: Blackwell, and New York: Columbia University Press, 1983), of which the second (revised) edition was published recently by University of Georgia Press. With Katharine Dell he edited *Values, Conflict and the Environment* (Oxford: Ian Ramsey Centre, Oxford, and Centre for Applied Ethics, Cardiff), an interdisciplinary report on environmental decision-making, of which copies are available from Westminster College, Oxford.

Andrew Belsey is a Lecturer in Philosophy and Hon. Secretary of the Centre for Applied Ethics, at the University of Wales, Cardiff. He is Joint Editor, with Ruth Chadwick, of the Routledge series on Professional Ethics, and the author of articles on various philosophical topics, including applied philosophy, in a range of journals including *Philosophy*, *Metaphilosophy* and *Ratio*. He is the joint organizer, with Robin Attfield, of the 1993 Royal Institute of Philosophy Conference at Cardiff on Philosophy and the Natural Environment.

Andrew Collier has lectured at the universities of Warwick, Sussex and Bangor, and is now a Senior Lecturer in Philosophy at the University of Southampton. His recent publications include *Scientific Realism and Socialist Thought* (Hemel Hempstead: Harvester Press, 1989), *Socialist Reasoning* (London: Pluto Press, 1990) and 'The inorganic body and the ambiguity of freedom', *Radical Philo-*

sophy, 57, spring 1991. He is currently writing a book on Roy Bhaskar's critical realism.

Nigel Dower is a Senior Lecturer in Philosophy and in Politics and International Relations at the University of Aberdeen, and Director of its Centre for Philosophy, Technology and Society. From 1983 to 1986 he taught philosophy at the University of Zimbabwe. He has had a research interest for a number of years in the ethical aspects of international relations, world poverty, development and environmental issues. Publications include *World Poverty: Challenge and Response* (York: Ebor Press, 1983) and (as editor and contributor) *Ethics and Environmental Responsibility* (Aldershot: Gower, 1989).

Geoffrey Hunt taught Philosophy for twelve years in Lesotho and Nigeria, followed by Fellowships in the University of Wales at Cardiff and Swansea. He is presently Director of the National Centre for Nursing and Midwifery Ethics, Polytechnic of West London (based at Hammersmith Hospital). His publications include articles in *Journal of Applied Philosophy, The Philosophical Forum, Praxis International* and *Logique et Analyse*, and contributions to several books.

Kai Nielsen is Professor and Head of the Department of Philosophy at the University of Calgary, having previously taught at Amherst College, New York University, Brooklyn College, the Graduate Center of the City University of New York and the University of Ottawa. His most recent books are *After the Demise of the Tradition: Rorty, Critical Theory, and the Fate of Philosophy* (Boulder, CO: Westview Press, 1991), *Marxism and the Moral Point of View* (Boulder, CO: Westview Press, 1988) and *Equality and Liberty: A Defense of Radical Egalitarianism* (Totowa, NJ: Rowman & Allanheld, 1985).

Onora O'Neill, who was till recently a Professor of Philosophy at the University of Essex, will from 1992 be Principal of Newnham College, Cambridge. She has written on a wide variety of topics in ethics and political philosophy, including theories of international justice and development ethics. Her publications include *Faces of Hunger: An Essay on Poverty, Justice and Development* (London: Allen & Unwin, 1986), which takes a Kantian approach to development issues. More recently her work in this field has addressed the ethical significance of state boundaries and the transformation of political philosophy in the wake of the revolutions of 1989.

Barry Wilkins is a Lecturer in Philosophy at the University of Wales, Cardiff, Chair of its Board of Studies in the History of Ideas and a member of its Centre for Applied Ethics, for which he organizes annual workshops on Third World issues. He is author of articles on political philosophy and applied philosophy, is a contributor to the multi-volume series *The Communist International in Lenin's Time* (New York: Pathfinder Press) and is currently working on the relationship between the social and political thought of Rousseau and of Marx.

Introduction

While almost everyone is in favour of development, not many people could readily specify what this commits them to. And while everyone is in favour of justice for themselves, many are puzzled about whether its claims extend to global society, in a world as inequitable as our own. Yet for the poorer countries, predominantly the countries of the 'South', or (to use the now customary expression) the Third World, both development and a more equitable form of international relations are pressing matters; nor are they pressing for the poorer countries alone.

Yet till recently there has existed comparatively little philosophical discussion of the concept and the implications of development; indeed, one of the aims of this book is partially to make good this deficiency. Since the very concept of development is a site of struggle, a definition cannot yet be offered; at this stage it may suffice to point out that underdevelopment is present in a society in which a number of mutually reinforcing evils are present, such as high rates of infant mortality and morbidity, low rates of productivity, poor provision of health care and of educational opportunities, illiteracy, and (centrally) poverty. Thus whatever else development involves, it consists, minimally, in moves away from this cycle of evils. And this is already enough to show that, for hundreds of millions of people alive today, development is a requirement of the satisfaction of basic needs, and thus, we maintain, of international or global justice.

Another aim of this book is to clarify and defend the notion of global justice, and to apply it to issues of development, not least with regard to the Third World. Here the issue is not so much the concept of justice (which is at least as widely acknowledged in theory as it is disregarded in practice), controversial as it often is, as its scope and thus its significance. While considerable diversity will be found in the accounts of justice which follow, the central issues cluster around the sense in which justice is global or universal, and thus has undeniable practical significance for people worldwide.[1] The various rival accounts of justice (Kantian, Marxian, rights-based and consequentialist; objectivist, relativist and communitarian) make their appearance in answer to these issues, and are further discussed below.

While some of the current contributors have pioneered the subject of the philosophy of development (Onora O'Neill and Nigel Dower not least),[2] mention should also here be made of the important contributions of Peter Singer, with his seminal 'famine relief argument',[3] and, more particularly, of Amartya Sen. Besides his contribution to the understanding of how famine is due to inaccessibility rather than to shortage of food[4] (a crucial point underlined below by Kai Nielsen), Sen has contributed importantly to the ethical basis of justice and of development, which he locates not so much in needs, interests or rights but in human capabilities and their facilitation.[5] While the approach of the current editors turns rather on satisfying needs, a close correlation can nevertheless be maintained between needs and capabilities, at least where human beings are concerned. Thus much of Sen's work can be regarded as complementary to the positions upheld both in this introduction and in many of the contributions which follow, whether grounded in interests (as with Nielsen and with Andrew Collier), in needs (as with Andrew Belsey) or in rights (as with Dower). Meanwhile Sen's recent work linking the elimination of hunger with participation and democracy[6] coheres well with the participatory accounts of development here from O'Neill and from Geoffrey Hunt, while the contributors to this volume would without exception support Sen's advocacy of the role of public action in overcoming poverty, 'against the current' of the orthodoxies of the 1980s as that may be.[7]

In the current collection, the subject of global justice is ably introduced by Kai Nielsen, who first presents in a challenging manner some of the key facts about global malnutrition and its social and political background. This enables him to counter the neo-Malthusian claim that a massive redistribution of resources would only cause greater harm through the insufficiency of food and the growth of population. Hunger, malnutrition and famine depend not on food supply but on distributions of income and on entitlements to food. The basic causes of famine are poverty, the world economic system and associated western policies. While this chapter was written in the early 1980s, and while Nielsen's remarks about the political sociology of food may be open to qualification, the passage of time has in no way detracted from the contemporary relevance of his conclusions.

Turning to global justice, Nielsen effectively refutes the belief that justice among societies only applies to relations between societies of similar power which co-operate to mutual advantage. The requirement of reciprocal advantage is far too strong. The Kantian conception of moral equality in which all people are to be treated as persons calls, instead, for a willingness to ask whether we should be willing for roles to be reversed with those on the receiving end of the relation wherever there is interdependence or interaction. In view of the nature and extent of current inequalities, this conception of the moral equality of people already shows the current international food order to be fundamentally unjust. Global justice is a plain extension of domestic justice, granted that in the international as well as the national arena we stand in conditions of interdependence, of moderate scarcity and of interests which sometimes conflict.

Further, the injustice is so great that extensive redistributions are in place. Those who believe in moral equality have to accept that the interests of everyone matter, and matter equally; this much is common to many liberal as well as socialist thinkers. To those right-wing liberals who take respect for equal interests to issue mainly in rights to non-interference, Nielsen replies that the current system very deeply harms many people in the Third World, and further that moral equality also issues in rights to fair co-operation and to non-subordination, rights which can conflict with non-interference. Thus people's very liberty to guide their own lives in accordance with their own 'unmystified preferences' often calls for public interventions; and to put an end to the conditions of immiseration of people in the South, which for them nullify this liberty, requires significant intervention and redistribution.

In the matter of priorities between rights of non-interference in matters of property and other rights, Nielsen argues for a hierarchy of interests. Bodily integrity, and also the kind of moral integrity associated with the intactness of one's civil liberties, are much more vital than property interests; and it is the latter rather than the former which would sometimes be overridden by moves to collective ownership, which Nielsen takes to be necessary to 'overcome starvation, malnutrition, domination, subordination and great poverty and ignorance' on a global scale.

Here, in a confessedly outspoken concluding section, Nielsen spells out what he takes to be the practical implications. As no adequate redistribution can take place within the present socio-economic order, which allows at best of lessening the severity of injustice, a necessary condition of global justice is the shedding of capitalism, unclear as it may be how this is to be done. The alternative is 'reformist tinkering inside bourgeois parameters'. Some of the other contributors are more disposed to regard efforts at amelioration of the system as consistent with the moral serious-ness to which Nielsen appeals. But all would support the essential moral case for changes of structure on a global scale.

The case for universal obligations with far-reaching global implications is independently argued by Andrew Belsey, who buttresses it against a range of familiar objections. With Nielsen, he points out that poverty is the product of the current global system of power relations; and this system, being traceable to human choices, is therefore open to challenge, not least from advocates of justice. But the applicability of talk of justice to these matters is resisted by those who make justice in one way or another local or particular.

Belsey first tackles the view that there are no obligations with-out reciprocity, meaning by this not the moral reciprocity on which much of Nielsen's case is based, but the power to recipro-cate. This view miscarries partly because the very power relations which deny poor countries any appreciable power over rich ones can themselves be challenged, and partly because in the modern world peoples are all in many ways interdependent.

Another objection to the universality of morality claims that the special obligations which we owe to our kin relegate obli-gations to people in distant continents to insignificance. The loyalties arising from special relations are among the grounds sometimes cited for this view; such accounts of morality are further discussed below by Onora O'Neill. For his part Belsey robustly charges unqualified arguments of this kind with being rationalizations of selfishness. At the same time the position is different where special obligations are conditional, as they are with John Stuart Mill, on the interests of others not being imperilled; in the interdependent modern world, preference for family or friends frequently harms distant people, and thus forgoes whatever support (let alone immunity) acceptance of the conditional status of such obligations might have seemed to afford.

Belsey then turns to the claim, representatively put forward by James Fishkin, that people are not morally obliged to give up institutionalized ways of life to which they have become accustomed. Fishkin's appeal to the optional nature of sacrifice fails, however, as there is no moral sacrifice in giving up what you have no right to, or what you hold in consequence of exploitation; as Northern affluence is based on exploitation, its forfeiture might be a psychological blow, but, far from being a sacrifice, is morally obligatory.

Global justice, however, does not call for an abandonment of 'our' way of life (an ideological distortion of morality, this), but calls for the moral bases of this very way of life (such as care and concern for others and belief in human equality) to be taken seriously. What global justice involves is a network of relationships between people who are equal in their needs – equal not mathematically but in that similar needs must be met before any worthwhile life can be lived. The vision which comes when our moral blinkers are removed discloses the moral equality of 'the observed and the observers', of 'the sufferers and those who are in a position to provide assistance'. Justice thus involves equality of consideration, under which basic needs are trumps, whoever's they may be.

Belsey's argument is not based on existing relationships (as is Collier's), but instead brings out something of the character which just relationships would have. Nor is it Kantian, unlike the arguments of Nielsen from respect for personal liberty or of O'Neill from sharability (see below), or, come to that, rights-based, like Nigel Dower's. Its basis is rather an enlightened version of consequentialism, in which not happiness but the satisfaction of needs is the criterion of morality. Consistently harnessed to a Kantian-like belief in moral equality, it generates principles which are both forceful and difficult to resist. But are such principles too abstract, as Collier for one would hold? These are among the issues tackled both by O'Neill and later implicitly by Dower.

Reflecting on the debate about development, Onora O'Neill

insists that, when principles of justice and of the relations between members of different societies are in question, the predicament of 'impoverished providers' in the Third World should not be overlooked. Abstract principles all too easily assume an idealized form, for example as if agents were always, or typically, both rational and independent. Such principles are prone to be so framed as to fail to provide for people who are seen as dependent and whose options in life are severely constrained by social structures and by the power of others, people who include countless millions of Third World women.

As O'Neill points out, it is often claimed by feminists that gender bias is integral to liberal justice. Some go so far as to reject talk of justice as 'male', as neglectful of 'the actualities of human difference' and as if it devalued the virtues of love and care. To this she rightly replies that justice and care should not be presented as alternatives, nor either of them as complete approaches to moral issues. Justice and care are virtues of different (if overlapping) spheres; and where social structures are defective, talk of justice is likely to be indispensable.

Yet liberal justice still confronts the objection of being too abstract and unrooted in social reality. This can be a point of entry for relativized theories, which seek to derive justice from 'history, tradition or local context'. Sensitive as such communitarian approaches may be to context, however, they tend to relegate women's lives to a private sphere, and to validate the weakness of the weak and their oppression by the strong; within such theories the critical role of appeals to justice is thus liable to disappear. Thus theories of justice need to retain their universal scope (something which requires abstraction), but to abstract without adopting ideals biased towards one gender, nation or race.

O'Neill proceeds to lay the foundations of such a theory, a theory abstracting from cases without idealizing the individual, and framed so as to apply to interacting parties. (Here there is an echo of Andrew Collier's claim that peoples who seldom interact bear only the most marginal of obligations towards one another.) It is also intended to be sensitive to local contexts and to real differences of capacity and of opportunity, and to avoid that uniformity with which universal theories are sometimes charged. One criterion of such a theory (and here O'Neill's Kantianism emerges) is held to be sharability. Principles unable to be universally adopted are indefensible; and this rules out, to say the least, deception and the kinds of coercion which undercut other people's independence. Further, structures will be just if and only if those affected by them are free alike to consent to them, to refuse them or to renegotiate them; or so O'Neill maintains.

At this point some would want to point out that people's perceptions are often so moulded by disinformation and by ideology that their consent is insufficient to legitimate what they consent to – and may not be necessary for legitimation either, in that structures neither consented to nor even dreamed of may still be more just. Justice, it might be held, is concerned with need rather than with consent. But to dwell on such an objection would obscure something crucial: the kind of theory defended by O'Neill already requires a radical restructuring of social and inter-societal arrangements on a global scale, and in the interests of the poor and the vulnerable. The restructuring required adds a further and vital dimension to that required by Nielsen, in that it calls for a change of power relations between genders as well as between economic classes.

While it is liberal theory which O'Neill seeks to apply to international justice, Andrew Collier attempts the like with regard to Marxist theory. Can a Marxist who holds that obligations arise out of historically specific shared interests and shared motivations uphold universal interests and obligations, extensive enough to include the emancipation of the proletariat on a global scale? On the face of it, the flow of wealth to the Third World which would be required is contrary to the interests of western workers. Moreover, historical materialism requires loyalties to be based on actual ties, and not on merely possible ones, nor again on abstract ethics such as utilitarianism or Kantianism, which, in common with F. H. Bradley, Collier dismisses as utopian.

Collier thus undertakes the task of rescuing a communitarian ethic from the conservatism and the narrowness to which, as O'Neill points out, such theories are prone. Existing roles, he claims, can be criticized on the basis of values implicit in other roles in which people participate within the network of relationships which comprise society. (Even Bradley, holds Collier, could in principle support such criticism, despite both his conservatism and his justified rejection of abstract ethics.) Thus we need a 'social ontology' richer than social atomism, the view which

regards society as constituted by nothing but individuals, and
which Collier associates with utilitarianism and Kantianism. (But
note that O'Neill, a Kantian, rejects such an atomistic posture.)
The relational ontology of Marx allows us to see how the lattice
of social relationships, which makes us what we are and which
will nowhere be wholly corrupt, allows of dissent from a corrupt
state or even a corrupt society.

The worlds by which people define themselves are importantly
shared worlds, naturally generating obligations towards other
beings. Furthermore, universal obligations arise from there being
one shared world, constituted as such by the facts of economic
and ecological interdependence. Emancipation for workers in
these circumstances means taking power collectively over the
interlocking global system; and the ties of global interdependence,
which make us what we are, supply for this both a natural
motivation, and the grounds of a matching universal obligation.

Some, however, consciously choose a different option, the preservation of a neo-imperialist system of oppression; and there are,
according to Collier, no arguments whatever available to Marxists
to persuade them of contrary obligations. The obligations of
proletarians as proletarians are universal in that they are obligations *to* all; but, since obligations arise from historical ties which
make people what they are, there are no obligations incumbent
on oppressors. Genuinely universal obligations depend on sharing
in the aim of class emancipation.

Anyone who believes that even oppressors have obligations to
desist from cruelty, injustice or despotism will find difficulty
with this close association of obligation, motivation and material
interests. In face of such criticism, Collier falls back on the mul-
tiple roles which agents usually occupy; non-oppressive roles may
generate humanitarian scruples even in those prone to connive in
oppression, and therewith a conflict of obligations. This move
would seem to allow for the emergence of a sense of universal
obligation in virtually anyone; and, undeniably, it supplies a
ground for belief in such possibilities.

Yet Collier would still have to say that for an agent lacking
relationships liable to generate such motivations, there is no obligation to resist oppression or to desist from oppressing the weak
and the powerless. Readers unable to accept this must, it seems,
reject his communitarian belief that obligations arise solely out of
ties and relationships. A potential chasm opens up between, on

the one hand, communitarian systems of ethics and, on the other, belief in global obligations – global both as to their beneficiaries and as to the agents and agencies to whom they apply. Many Marxists, however, would allow of no exceptions to the universality of obligations, appealing either to a common human nature and common human needs or to the hoped-for future world community as the basis of their claims.

Nigel Dower, too, upholds belief in universal ('cosmopolitan') obligations, grounding them on human rights; rights which, for the poor, underpin a right to development. Avoiding the pitfalls of abstract generalization, he argues for a right to development which is significantly qualified, yet strong enough to generate obligations to realize it on the part of everyone in a position to do so. It is also a right to sustainable development, since no other kind is worthy of the name.

This right may, however, seem problematic, even if the existence of human rights is granted. The case for the corresponding global obligations has to be made out, and the case for governments being subject to them; nor are these tasks left unshouldered. There are also questions about what can count as development, and problems about whether self-determining countries, having decided their own path to development, are morally entitled to assistance from others in pursuit of whatever path they have chosen. There are problems too about the right to aid for development where the beneficiaries are not primarily the deprived or the disadvantaged. Yet tackling the objections to belief in development rights serves to bring out how difficult it is to deny such rights in cases of unacceptable poverty and of the deprivation of basic needs.

Dower's appeal here is ultimately to universal human rights, which are argued to include positive rights of subsistence if negative rights such as rights to liberty are also admitted. These rights are held to involve a claim upon the rest of humanity, and are shown to require much more of governments than the norms of the existing international order recognize. While there is no right of richer countries to aid for the sake of continued development, the subsistence rights of the poor and of the exploited vindicate the right to development of countries in which these rights cannot be exercised without it.

Yet not every change which those in power favour is recognizable as development. While development consists in the kind of socio-economic change which ought to happen, general economic growth can easily fail to deserve this accolade; and unsustainable processes invariably fall short of it. Sustainability, indeed, concerns not just processes which can be sustained but ones which deserve to be sustained; and thus it excludes both exploitation and environmental destruction, whether domestic or exported. It thus also excludes practices (like the emission of carbon dioxide at current levels) which would undermine sustainable conditions globally even if pursued by no more than those countries currently in a position to pursue them.

Indeed, the only way to discover whether processes which are domestically sustainable are justifiable is to consider whether they are sustainable globally and from the point of view of world development. Only those policies and practices which could fit into a sustainable global package are genuinely sustainable and justifiable. These include some forms of economic growth for poorer countries, but not perpetual economic growth for rich countries, even though the need to realize basic rights exists there too. The requirements of sustainability thus clarify the nature of the right to development, which is a right to sustainable development if it is anything; at the same time the global perspective makes sustainability of development something which everyone has a right to claim of all agents and agencies, governments included.

Geoffrey Hunt's distinctive claims are that people interested in development need to get clear about the theoretical framework which they knowingly or unconsciously adopt, and that there are five current types of framework, to one or another of which all such people are more or less affiliated. The key role for a philosopher is to bring these frameworks to consciousness; to claim impartiality for one's approach is to bear an unacknowledged allegiance, almost invariably, to one or another liberal model. Hunt makes clear his own allegiance to a Marxist model of the participatory kind; he also argues for it as both explaining and rising above the others. (So it is possible to step back and compare models, at least in point of explanatory adequacy.)

In describing the models, Hunt also draws out the characteristic attitude of their holders towards environmental protection. Thus among liberal frameworks the Market Model regards the unalloyed free market system as capable of coping with environmental problems, and environmentalist demands for intervention as ideological ploys of critics of this system. By contrast the Regulation Model recognizes imperfections in both national and international markets, ascribes environmental problems to misallocation of resources and favours interventions by states and by international agencies to remedy poverty, to rectify the consequent environmental damage and to stabilize the global system.

According to the Green Model, by contrast, environmental problems are due to industrialism, overconsumption and the pursuit of economic growth, and development would involve moves towards 'small-scale self-sufficient ecologically benign co-operative and communalistic production' (p. 124), albeit within a social-democratic, capitalist framework. Moves away from world-scale industrialization involve countries delinking from world markets and opting for self-reliance. (Already internationalist advocates of sustainability such as Dower seem to bestride the Regulative and Green frameworks.)

According to Hunt, both Marxist models involve a deeper understanding of growth. According to the Statist Model underdevelopment results from colonialism and subsequently from the structural inequalities of neo-colonialism, and the growth necessary for independent development can only be ensured by state control and the replacement of small-scale communal production with production which is centrally planned. The solution to environmental problems is accordingly better planning. Without deviating from the underlying economic analysis of this model, the Participatory Model advocates a different approach to development, through participatory democracy and industrialization of a kind suited to the needs of Third World peoples. Environmental problems are caused by globally divisive social relations of production, and not by ecological factors, and they can only be resolved through the democratic, participatory control of production at local, national and ultimately global levels, to foster the 'collective human good'. This form of growth, in which 'the development of the free creative powers of each' is, at last, 'the condition of the freedom and welfare of all' (p. 144), would employ ecologically benign technology, protect or restore the environment (e.g. retrieving deserts with newly engineered species of plants) and promote harmony both ecologically and within human society.

This model combines an understanding of some of the structures underlying both underdevelopment and environmental problems with the participatory elements of Green solutions. Hunt is also able to show how the other four models plausibly embody distorted reflections of the social relations of various historical phases; and could also claim that the Participatory Model has in no way been discredited by recent events, unlike the Statist Model. Yet this would not immunize the Participatory Model from criticism itself. Criticisms might comprise the charges of technological optimism, or of the irresponsible rejection of piecemeal ameliorative measures which might avert localized hardship or save lives. Alternatively the Participatory Model might be accused of virtually ignoring the beneficial role which could be played in promoting development by a Third World state genuinely committed to meeting the needs and aspirations of its people; or, as will shortly emerge, of ignoring the collective good of everything *but* humanity – the charge of anthropocentrism. The possibility of yet other models should also be mentioned, such as O'Neill's vision of a restructured world economy (defended on a Kantian basis), or Dower's of a world restructured for globally sustainable development (grounded in human rights, which Hunt admits to be decreasingly controversial); socio-economic elaborations of these visions might easily bestride two or three of Hunt's models. Yet a human-centred bias might be discerned in these approaches too.

Robin Attfield argues that in view of the problems of underdevelopment environmentalists are obliged by consistency, as well as by morality, to support sustainable development in the Third World; or rather that this is so to the extent that their own principles are themselves morally defensible, as the principles of misanthropic environmentalism are shown not to be. These obligations apply to environmentalists of the 'deeper' as well as of the 'shallower' kinds. Thus where environmentalism is grounded on a rejection of unjustified discrimination, or on egalitarianism, or again on the liberation of oppressed creatures, the same grounds require support for resistance to injustice and oppression in inter-human relations, both within and between human societies.

This in turn means that critiques of current evils which ascribe them to a single source such as anthropocentrism need to be broadened. Echoing Warwick Fox's criticism of unidimensional critiques which either over-inclusively or over-selectively ascribe all the problems to (say) capitalism or to (say) patriarchy, Attfield maintains that environmentalist critics of anthropocentrism should target their protests at economic oppression, sexism and racism too. By the same token, developmentalists who ascribe current problems to oppressive inter-human relations and structures should also take into account 'a plurality of seats of power and sources of oppression', including anthropocentrism, and thus support one or other of the 'deeper' kinds of environmentalism.

Further arguments are presented in support of this broader view of both the problems and the principles required to combat them. One is the argument that it is inconsistent to oppose unjustified human suffering but to connive at comparable unjustified suffering among non-human animals. Additionally it is argued that the very hierarchy of power relations in which advocates of development often locate the source of world problems, far from being exhausted by inter-human relations, extends also to inter-species relations. These relations are often no better justified (and no more inevitable) than inter-human exploitation, and thus constitute exploitation themselves. Thus critiques of capitalism, sexism and racism must be supplemented so as to include anthropocentrism and human chauvinism.

This discussion is exemplified by reference to a proposal to preserve a portion of Indonesian rainforest and at the same time facilitate the social and economic development of local people through the systematic farming (with a view to export) of the butterflies which live there. Objections to this developmentally promising scheme include not only the subversion of the environment on which local humans depend, but also the good of the forest community, butterflies included. While butterfly ranching could be less bad than the clear-felling of the forest for timber and therewith the total loss of the environment required by local people for their way of life, this extension of the global economic system could easily undermine both local development and the local ecosystem. This in turn suggests that development, to be worthy of the name (as well as to be sustainable), must be ecologically sensitive and resist anthropocentric policies, natural as it might seem to gear development to human interests only.

Questions of the practical forms which this kind of development might assume are not here addressed. Yet to the extent that some of the relevant principles of value and obligation are brought to light, together with an enhanced critique of the sources of current problems, that is itself potentially of considerable practical significance. The principles here adduced, which involve consideration being paid to the full range of interests which are at stake, plausibly support both piecemeal measures of amelioration, at least in cases where nothing better is feasible or sustainable, and also strategies of global change and restructuring. They also support self-help and participation, and are consistent with increasing democracy, which, as Drèze and Sen have argued, is also crucial to development.[8] Indeed, to revert to Hunt's allusive remark, the development of the free creative powers of each person is the condition of the freedom and welfare of all.

In the final chapter, Barry Wilkins tackles a practical issue where, arguably, the ethical case for restructuring is both urgent and compelling: that of Third World debt. While they remain burdened by indebtedness and by the supposed obligation to service current debt, poor countries have little or no prospect of significant development, however enlightened or imaginative their strategies may be. Like Nielsen, Wilkins surveys the empirical facts of his chosen area, facts which disclose that for a number of countries the possibility of debts being repaid is non-existent.

In depicting and explaining the growth of Third World debt over the last thirty years, Wilkins concludes that Third World countries occupy a position of structural weakness in the world economic and political system, and that this weakness benefits the institutions of the advanced capitalist world. The shortcomings of some Third World leaders have counted for little alongside these structural factors, and it is factors such as these which have engendered the debt crisis. There is a convergence here with Nielsen's and Hunt's structural explanations of growing global inequalities.

Turning to the consequences of indebtedness for the people of the Third World, Wilkins finds that the burden of debt servicing is effectively carried by the poor majority, and particularly by Third World women (as stressed by O'Neill) and by the children of the poor, 'the most vulnerable human beings in the entire world' (p. 179). This is because debt servicing swallows up a large proportion of earnings and resources, diverting them from being spent on development, and because of the austerity programmes imposed on debtor countries by bodies such as the International Monetary Fund.

Surveying the various solutions proposed for coping with indebtedness, it is shown that there is no possibility of Third

World countries continuing to service all their debts. The policies of limited debt relief so far introduced are argued to be too limited themselves; while debt-for-equity swaps are rejected as being an economic means of advanced capitalist countries exercising power over Third World countries, or, in the precise sense of the word, neo-colonialist. As for debt-for-nature swaps, they sometimes oppress local peoples, and even in the absence of oppression they have a negligible impact on debt, distracting attention meanwhile from persisting economic problems.

Susan George's proposals are also rejected. Repayment in local currency is still repayment; and concessions conditional on democratization and on development are coercive, and presuppose a moral authority to coerce on the part of governments whose record makes any claim to such authority ridiculous. Debt renunciation by single governments could be hazardous in the extreme; collective renunciation, morally justified as it may be, carries substantial risks of retaliation; and what has been called 'conciliatory default' (p. 187), while plausibly avoiding these risks, would bring only partial relief from the burden of debt. Much the best solution would be for western governments to cancel Third World debts unconditionally, a policy which in the light of the earlier conclusions is in any case morally obligatory. Neither the economic nor the ethical objections to such debt cancellation succeed in undermining it.

While Wilkins does not elaborate a normative ethic to substantiate his conclusions concerning the moral obligation to cancel Third World debt, these conclusions are in large measure substantiated by the arguments of previous contributors, even if this is clearer in the cases of Latin American, African and South Asian economies than for those of the Pacific rim. The moral case for global obligations, however, whether liberal or Marxist, and whether grounded in rights (as with Dower) or interests (as with Nielsen) or needs (as with Belsey), overwhelmingly upholds a restructuring of international relations of the kind which Wilkins's conclusions exemplify. Indeed, it upholds much more, steps towards participatory democracy and sustainable development included, as argued in several contributions here. Much work, however, remains to be done in further sifting alternative accounts of global justice, and in identifying their (often convergent) applications, not least their applications to development. The editors' hope is that this volume of essays will help to stimulate further reflection, and action too, in this field.

Robin Attfield
Barry Wilkins

NOTES

1 See further Steven Luper-Foy (ed.), *Problems of International Justice*, Boulder, CO: Westview Press, 1988. The existing literature on development ethics is well surveyed in David A. Crocker, 'Toward development ethics', *World Development*, 19, 5, 1991, pp. 457–83.

2 Onora O'Neill, *Faces of Hunger: An Essay on Poverty, Justice and Development*, London: Allen & Unwin, 1986, also 'The moral perplexities of famine and world hunger', in Tom Regan (ed.), *Matters of Life and Death: New Introductory Essays in Moral Philosophy*, 2nd edn, New York: Random House, 1986, pp. 294–337; Nigel Dower, *World Poverty: Challenge and Response*, York: Ebor Press, 1983.

3 Peter Singer, 'Famine, affluence and morality', *Philosophy and Public Affairs*, 1, 1971–2, pp. 229–43; 'Reconsidering the famine relief argument', in P. G. Brown and H. Shue (eds), *Food Policy*, New York: Free Press, 1977, pp. 36–53; 'Rich and poor', ch. 8 of his *Practical Ethics*, Cambridge: Cambridge University Press, 1979, pp. 158–81.

4 Amartya Sen, *Poverty and Famines: An Essay on Entitlement and Deprivation*, Oxford: Clarendon Press, 1981; see Nielsen, p. 22 below.

5 Amartya Sen, *Resources, Values and Development*, Oxford: Blackwell, and Cambridge, MA: Harvard University Press, 1984, pp. 513–15.

6 Jean Drèze and Amartya Sen, *Hunger and Public Action*, Oxford: Oxford University Press, 1989.

7 See ibid., pp. 257–9, a section entitled 'Against the current?'.

8 See ibid.

Poverty, Famine, War, Four Horsemen of the Apocalypse, Statute of limitations.

Chapter 1

Global justice, capitalism and the Third World

Kai Nielsen

1. Malthusian argument was to prevent harm but,
2. Neo Malthusian got too caught up in

(for 200 years Malthusian theory has been proved wrong because people have not out shipped production)

ABSTRACT: *Reflecting on the North–South dialogue, I consider questions of global justice. I argue that questions of global justice are just as genuine as questions of domestic justice. A too-narrow construal of the circumstances of justice leads to an arbitrary forestalling of questions of global justice. It isn't that we stand in conditions of reciprocal advantage that is crucial but that we stand in conditions of moral reciprocity. I first set out concerning the conditions in the North and the South and the relations between them something of the facts in the case coupled with some interpretative sociology. Such investigations show massive disparities of wealth and condition between North and South and further show that these disparities have been exacerbated by the interventionist policies of the west. I then, while remaining mindful of the strains of commitment, argue that justice requires extensive redistribution between North and South but that this can be done without at all impoverishing the North, though to do so would indeed involve a radical reordering of the socio-economic system of the North.*

SOME FACTS ABOUT FAMINE

Let us start with some stark empirical realities. Approximately 10,000 people starve every day. There was a severe drought last year (1983) in Africa and about 20 million people, spread through eighteen countries, face severe shortages of food: shortages that will in some instances bring on starvation and in others, for very many people, will bring about debilitating malnutrition – a malnutrition that sometimes will permanently and seriously damage them. The Brandt Report of 1980 estimates that 800 million people cannot afford an adequate diet. This means that millions are constantly hungry, that millions suffer from deficiency diseases and from infections that they could resist with a more adequate diet. Approximately 15 million children die each year from the combined effects of malnutrition and infection. In some areas of the world half the children born will die before their fifth birthday. Life for not a few of us in the industrially developed world is indeed, in various ways, grim. But our level of deprivation hardly begins to approximate to the level of poverty and utter misery that nearly 40 per cent of the people in the Third World face.

As Robert McNamara, who is surely no spokesman for the left, put it, there are these masses of 'severely deprived human beings struggling to survive in a set of squalid and degraded circumstances almost beyond the power of sophisticated imaginations and privileged circumstances to conceive'.[1] Human misery is very much concentrated in the southern hemisphere (hereafter 'the South') and by any reasonable standard of justice there is a global imbalance of the benefits and burdens of life – the resources available to people – that calls for an extensive redistribution of resources from the industrial countries of the northern hemisphere ('the North') to the South.

This, of course, assumes that there is something properly called global justice and this, in certain quarters, will be resisted as a mirage or as being an incoherent conception. We can properly speak of justice within a society with a common labour market, but we cannot speak of justice for the world community as a whole. We cannot say, some claim, of the world community as a whole that it is just or unjust. Justice is only possible, the claim goes, where there are common bonds of reciprocity. There are no such bonds between a Taude of Highland New Guinea and a farmer in Manitoba. In general there are no such bonds between people at great distances from each other and with no cultural ties, so, given what justice is, we cannot correctly speak of global justice. I think this is a mistaken way of construing things and I shall return to it in a moment.

The call for a massive redistribution of resources also assumes, what neo-Malthusians will not grant, namely that we can carry this out without still greater harm resulting.[2] Part of the demand for the redistribution of resources is in the redistribution of food and in the resources (including the technology and the technological know-how) to realize agricultural potential. Neo-Malthusians

believe that this redistribution, at least for the worst-off parts of
the Third World, is suicidal.

It is a moral truism, but for all of that true, that it would be
better, if no greater harm would follow from our achieving it, if
we had a world in which no one starved and no one suffered
from malnutrition. But, some neo-Malthusians argue, greater
harm would in fact follow if starvation were prevented in the
really desperate parts of the world, for with the world's extensive
population-explosion resulting from improved medicine and the
like, the earth, if population growth is not severely checked, will
exceed its carrying capacity. An analogy is made with a lifeboat.
Suppose the sea is full of desperate swimmers and the only available lifeboat can only take on a certain number. It has, after all,
a very definite carrying capacity. If too many are taken on the
lifeboat it will swamp and everyone will drown. So the thing is
not to go beyond the maximum carrying capacity of the lifeboat.

We are, neo-Malthusians claim, in a similar position vis-à-vis
the earth. It is like a lifeboat and if the population goes out of
control and gets too large in relation to the carrying capacity of
the earth there will be mass starvation and an unsettlement bringing on a suffering vastly exceeding the already terrible suffering
that is upon us. Sometimes our choices are between evils and,
where this is so, the rational and morally appropriate choice is
to choose the lesser evil. It may be true that we may never do
evil that good may come, but faced with the choice between two
certain evils we should choose the lesser evil. Better four dead
than twenty. But, some neo-Malthusians claim, vis-à-vis famine
relief, this is just the terrible situation we are in.

Parts of the earth have already, they claim, exceeded their
carrying capacity. The population there is too great for the region
to yield enough food for its expanding population. Yet it is in
the poorer parts of the world that the population continues to
swell and, it is terrible but still necessary to recognize, it is the
above horrendous situation that we are facing in many parts of
the world.

Neo-Malthusians maintain that if we do not check this population explosion in a rather drastic way the whole earth will in
time be in the desperate position of the Sahel. Redistributive
reform is soft-hearted and soft-headed, encouraging the poor to
increase their numbers and with that to increase the sum total of
misery in the world.

I shall talk about neo-Malthusianism first and then, after I have considered the International Food Order, turn to a consideration of whether we have a coherent conception of global justice. Neo-Malthusianism, I shall argue, is a pseudo-realism making dramatics out of a severe and tragic morality of triage when the facts in the case will not rationally warrant such dramatics – will not warrant in these circumstances a morality of triage.

In the first place, while lifeboats have a determinate carrying capacity, we have no clear conception of what this means with respect to the earth. What population density makes for commodious living is very subjective indeed; technological innovations continually improve crop yield and could do so even more adequately if more scientific effort were set in that direction.

Second, for the foreseeable future we have plenty of available fertile land and the agricultural potential adequately to feed a very much larger world population than we actually have.[3] Less than half of the available fertile land of the world is being used for any type of food production. In Africa, for example, as everyone knows, there are severe famine conditions and radical underdevelopment, but African agriculture has been declining for the last twenty years.[4] Farmers are paid as little as possible; masses of people have gone into the large urban centres where industrialization is going on. Domestic food production is falling while a lot of food is imported at prices that a very large number of people in the Third World cannot afford to pay. Yet Africa has half the unused farm land in the world. If it were only utilized, Africa could readily feed itself and be a large exporter of food.[5] The principal problem is not overpopulation or even drought but man-made problems, problems on which I will elaborate in a moment when I discuss the Postwar International Food Order.

Third, the land that is used is very frequently used in incredibly inefficient ways. The latifundia system in Latin America is a case in point.[6] In Latin America as a whole, and by conservative estimates, landless families form 40 per cent of all farm families. One per cent of all farm families control, again by conservative estimates, 50 per cent of all farm land. This landed elite has incredible power in Latin America and they use this power to keep the peasantry poor, disorganized and dependent. The latifundia system is an autocratic system, but – and this is what is most relevant for our purposes – it is also a very inefficient system of agricultural production. The landowner, not infrequently through his farm manager, has firm control over the running of the farm and over the destinies of his farm labourers. The *latifundios* are very large estates and the land on them is underworked. Much of it is used for pasture. Only 4 per cent of all the land in large estates is actually in crops. There is more fallow land, that is land not even used for pasture but held idle, than there is land in crops. If the *latifundia* land were redistributed to peasants and they were allowed to work it intensively and particularly if they formed into peasant co-operatives, the food production would be increased enormously. Again, it isn't the lack of land or the size of the population that is the problem but the way the land is used.

Fourth, there is the problem of cash crops: crops such as peanuts, strawberries, bananas, mangoes, artichokes, and the like. Key farm land, once used by local residents for subsistence farming, is now used for these cash crops, driving subsistence farmers off the best land into increasingly marginal land and, in many (4) instances, forcing them to purchase food at very high prices, prices they often cannot afford to pay. The result has been increasing malnutrition and starvation and impoverishment. Previously in New Guinea most of the tribal peoples had a reasonably adequate diet. Now, with the incursion of the multinationals and the introduction of cash crops, severe malnutrition is rife. The good land is used for cash crops and the farming for local consumption is on the marginal land. Mexican peasants, to take another example, did reasonably well on a staple diet of corn and beans. With the advent of multinational food producers, they became a rural, but typically underemployed, proletariat, in one not atypical instance, planting, harvesting and processing in freezing plants strawberries for export and importing food to replace the staple food they had previously grown themselves.[7] The catch was that the food they purchased was typically less nutritious and was at prices they could hardly afford. Again, in those Mexican communities malnutrition is rife but the principal cause here, just as in New Guinea, is in the socio-economic system and not in droughts or population explosion.

In fine, against neo-Malthusians, it is not the case that the basic cause of famine is the failure of the food supply relative to the population. Rather the basic cause of famine is poverty and certain economic policies. People who are not poor are not hungry. We look at North–South imbalance and it is plain as anything can be that this is the result of the workings of the world economic system and a clear indicator of that is the food economy. A stark difference between North and South is in the vast malnutrition and starvation which are principally a phenomenon of the South. But these famine conditions result from the working of the economic system in allocating the ability of people to acquire goods.[8] As Amartya Sen has shown for the great Bengal famine of 1943–4, a famine in which around 3 million people died, it was not the result of any crop failure or population explosion.[9] In 1942 there had been an extraordinary harvest but the 1943 crop was only somewhat lower and was in fact higher than the crop of 1941 which was not a famine year. Sen's figures show that the 1943 crop was only 10 per cent less than the average of the five preceding years. Yet 1943 was a famine year of gigantic proportions. Why? The answer lies in people's economic position.[10] People have entitlements to a range of goods that they can acquire. Whether they have such entitlements, whether they can command the goods they need, depends on the workings of the economic system. Given – to take a current (1983) example – the minimum wage in Brazil (something for which approximately a third of the workforce labours), if that situation persists, many workers will not have the entitlement to the food they need to survive. In fact, right now a day's wage enables them only to command a kilo of beans. They can, that is, only purchase a kilo of beans for a day's work at the minimum wage. So people in such circumstances, understandably, reasonably and indeed rightly, take considerable risks to loot supermarkets and the like. People starve when their entitlements are not sufficiently large to buy the food necessary to keep them alive. That, to return to Sen's example of the great famine in Bengal, is precisely what happened in Bengal in 1943–4 and is happening again in Brazil and, with greater severity, in a not inconsiderable number of other places.

The food available to people is a matter of income distribution and that, in the capitalist system, is fundamentally rooted in their ability to provide services that people in the economy are willing to pay for. In poorer countries for many people about two-thirds of their total income goes for expenditures on food. Where there is some rapid industrialization newly employed workers are likely, with increased entitlements, to spend more on food. This, under a capitalist system, will force food prices up and it is very likely as a result that the entitlements of very poor agricultural labourers – labourers who own no land and have only their labour power to sell – will fall, until, even with a constant supply of food in their environment, they will no longer be able to purchase food to meet their minimum needs. Where people are on the margin of sustainable life, a famine may be created by such an increase of demand with little or no decline in the food supply.[11] What we need to recognize is that hunger, malnutrition and famine are fundamentally questions of distribution of income and the entitlements to food. And here, of course, we have plainly questions of justice and, I shall argue below, questions of global justice. But in trying to achieve a moral assessment of what should be done in the face of such extensive starvation and malnutrition, neo-Malthusian accounts are very wide of the mark, principally because of their failure to understand what causes and sustains such misery.

THE POLITICS OF FOOD

In order to make more perspicuous my discussion of global justice and to make even clearer why we should *not* regard the starvation and malnutrition facing the South as a matter of actual food shortages caused by or at least exacerbated by population explosion, I want to do a bit of political sociology and describe – an interpretative description if you like – the rise and fall of the Postwar International Food Order.[12] Since the early 1970s the perception of scarcity and disaster because of that scarcity has been a popular refrain of much of our discussion of the world food economy. But this, as I in effect indicated in the previous section, is more ideology than fact. To understand what is going on, we need to come to understand the political economy of food as it was developed after the Second World War in the capitalist world. The capitalist world, after the last great war, went from the gold standard to the dollar standard with the United States clearly becoming the preponderant world power. In the 1950s and 1960s, the American state, reflecting plainly the interests of its capitalists, developed a policy of food aid to Third World countries. These were countries which were often trying rapidly to industrialize. This food aid, at one and the same time, provided a lot of cheap food for their new and very inexpensive industrial labour force and a respite for the American farmers with their, relative to the market, overproduction. (We must remember that since the Roosevelt years the farmers had come to be a powerful lobby.) But it should also be noted that this food aid programme helped turn self-sufficient agrarian countries into economically dependent countries dependent on food aid. It led to a commodification of food and to placing structurally these Third World countries in the commodity exchange system of the capitalist order.

The easiest way to see how the postwar food order developed and declined is to chart the fate of wheat in the world economy. In the 1950s and 1960s the surplus in wheat in the United States was sustained both for domestic political reasons and to pull the newly emerging Third World countries firmly into the capitalist orbit. It was an astute way to help make the world safe for the flourishing of capitalism. Cheap food exported and subsidized from America encouraged in Third World countries the growth, in the process of industrialization, of urban populations. It encouraged, that is, the formation of a proletariat and a lumpenproletariat from a previously peasant population – a proletariat and a lumpenproletariat dependent on cheap food sold to them principally as a commodity. A previously self-sufficient agriculture in Third World countries radically declined and ceased to be self-sufficient. Much of the rural population, in a state of impoverishment, as a huge reserve industrial army, was in effect driven into the cities and in tandem with that, as rural production declined, rural life became ever more impoverished.

Though there were in the 1950s and 1960s great hardships for both the new urban workers and the peasants in the countryside, none the less the system based on the export of cheap food from America worked in some reasonable fashion until the early 1970s. Then it began to come apart. This International Food Order 'encouraged a massive increase in the numbers of people in all countries separated from direct ties to agriculture'.[13] In such a situation an increase in grain prices will trigger an increase in scarcity, though the scarcity is not rooted in what 'can technically be produced but in what people with constant or declining real monetary incomes can buy'.[14] What we had facing us in the 1960s was an 'extraordinary growth of urban populations – an aspect of proletarianization – and agricultural underdevelopment'.[15] The capitalist rationale for this activity was plain; food aid was intended to assist capitalist development in the Third World while appeasing the farm lobby in America. The thing was to integrate these Third World societies into the capitalist economic system: a system which was becoming a world system. Cheap foreign wheat facilitated this by facilitating the growth of urban populations, but it also contributed to underemployment and poverty in the countryside in these very same countries. But in the 1970s the International Food Order began to break down. Grain surpluses dwindled, prices rose, food aid was cut back. The food aid programme gradually ceased to have a capitalist rationale. What had happened was that the food aid programme had in the course of time made commercial markets work. By virtue of its very success, food aid became increasingly superfluous from a capitalist perspective. Some of the urban workers could now afford to buy food under market conditions, though many in the urban centres (those marginally employed or unemployed) had the *need* for the food but in a market system no longer had the *entitlement*. Similar things obtained for rural farm labourers rotting in the countryside where agricultural production had been cut back. The difficulty for Third World countries in continuing to get cheap food was exacerbated by the huge Russian–American grain deals of 1972 and 1973. Consumerism and a meat diet American-style became a goal in the Soviet Union and in eastern Europe. And even though *détente* is now a thing of the past, or at least temporarily shelved, the grain sales to the Soviet Union still go on. But food aid to the Third World has almost vanished, the western agricultural sector continues to decline, farmers become fewer, now pitted against consumers, and food prices continue to rise so that the many poor in Third World countries lose their entitlements. Capitalism, of course, needs a workforce that can reproduce itself but with newly developed industrial enterprises in the Third World a little starvation and malnutrition will not hurt, will not affect the efficiency of capitalist production, as long as they have, as they indeed have, a huge labour pool to draw upon. Individual workers can starve as long as there are plenty of replacements. Things like this happened with the industrialization of the western world under capitalism in the nineteenth century. It is now being repeated in the Third World in the twentieth century.

- famine result from distn. rather than lack
- structures prevent people to have access to food

GLOBAL JUSTICE AND THE THIRD WORLD

With this sketch of political sociology before us, we can now
return to the topic of global justice. There are some who would
maintain that talk of justice can only coherently be applied within
particular societies or at best between societies similarly situated
and in a condition of mutual co-operation. I want to show why
this doctrine is false and why it is quite morally imperative for
us to speak of global justice and injustice and to characterize these
notions in a perspicuous fashion.

Those who would argue against extending justice arguments
into a North–South context, and into the international arena generally, will argue that when we talk about what is to be done
here we need to recognize that we are beyond the circumstances
of justice. For considerations of justice coherently to arise there
must, between the people involved, (a) be a rough equality in
the powers and capacities of persons, (b) be a situation where
people do co-operate but largely on the basis of reciprocal advantage and (c) be a situation where all parties are in a condition
of moderate scarcity.[16] It is, many have argued, only in such
circumstances that issues of justice are at home. Only in such
circumstances, the claim goes, can we appeal to principles of
justice to adjudicate conflicting claims on moderately scarce
goods. For principles of justice to function, there must be enough
reciprocity around for people to find some balance of reciprocal
advantage. If they cannot find that, they have no basis for regulat-
ing their conduct in accordance with the principles of justice.

However, if these really are the circumstances of justice, it
looks at least as if we can have no global justice, for the richest
nations do not seem to be related to the poorest ones in such a
way that the rich nations secure a reciprocal advantage if justice
is done. It very likely makes more sense for them to go on cruelly
exploiting the poor nations as they have done in the past. There
is, in short, in most circumstances at least, little in it for them if
they would do what, in circumstances of greater equality, we
would uncontroversially say is the just thing to do.

The mistake here, I believe, is in sticking with the existence
of a skein of actual co-operative reciprocity as essential for the
circumstances of justice. The world is certainly not a co-operative
scheme. We do not have in place internationally schemes for
mutual support. It is even rather far-fetched, given the class nature

of our own societies, to regard discrete societies as co-operative partnerships, but certainly the world is not. We do not have in place there the co-operative reciprocal interdependency which, some say, is essential for justice.

However, this condition for the very possibility of justice is too strong. That this is so can be seen from the following considerations. There is a worldwide network of international trade; poor countries stand to rich countries in complex relations of interdependence, indeed in an interdependency relation that places poor countries in a position of dependence. The rich nations, functioning as instruments for gigantic capitalist enterprises, have dominated and exploited underdeveloped countries using their resources and markets on unfair terms. Between North and South – between rich and poor nations – there are conflicts of interest and competing claims under conditions not so far from moderate scarcity such that conditions giving scope for arguments of justice obtain. In intra-state situations we do not need conditions of actual reciprocity of mutual advantage for issues of justice to be in place. The Australian Aborigine population could be too small, too weak and too marginal to mainstream life in Australia for the non-Aboriginal population to gain any advantage from *not* seizing their lands and driving them from them without any compensation. But such an action would not only be plainly wrong; it would be grossly unjust. Yet it is quite possible that the non-Aboriginal population would stand to gain rather than lose from such an action. Still, that would not make such an action one whit the less unjust. What we need to invoke instead is a *moral reciprocity* not resting on actual schemes of co-operation for mutual advantage but instead on a broadly Kantian conception of moral equality in which justice requires that we all treat each other as equals, namely, we are to treat all people as persons and in doing so treat them as we would reasonably wish to be treated ourselves.[17] In other words, we must, in reasoning justly, be willing to universalize and to engage in role reversal. It does not take much moral imagination for us, if we are relatively privileged members of the so-called First World, to realize that we would not wish to live the marginal existence of many people in the Third World. We would, that is, not wish to starve or have our children starve or to be in one way or another crippled by malnutrition or live, where this could be avoided, without anything like an adequate education or without adequate housing and the like. We would not accept role reversal here. If our feet, that is, were in their shoes, we would not take as morally tolerable, where such conditions could be avoided, such conditions of life for ourselves. But there is no relevant difference here between ourselves and them. If, in such circumstances, we would not will it for ourselves, we cannot will it for them either.

In the light of our conception of the moral equality of people, we could not accept such inequalities as just. Yet it is just such inequalities that the International Food Order, a deliberate policy objective of the United States, acting for the capitalist order, has brought about in the postwar years. Even given Nozickian notions of justice in rectification, it would be correct to say that many people in Third World countries are not being treated justly. However, the injustice of such an order is even more evident if we develop a conception of justice as fair reciprocity. People, through conquest, domination and exploitation, have been made worse off than they were before these relations were brought into place. They have been driven into bargains they would not have made if they had not been driven to the wall. They are plainly being coerced and they are surely not being treated as moral equals.

If we start with an idea of moral reciprocity in which all human beings are treated as equals, we cannot accept the relations that stand between North and South as something that has even the simulacrum of justice. But any tolerably adequate understanding of what morality requires of us will not allow us to accept anything less than a commitment to relations of moral equality. Starting from there we can see that global justice is a plain extension of domestic justice when we remember that in the international arena as well as in the domestic arena we stand (a) in conditions of interdependence, (b) in conditions of moderate scarcity (if we pool our resources) and (c) in conditions where our interests sometimes conflict. Moreover, by any plausible principles of global justice we might enunciate, the relations between North and South are so unjust that extensive redistributions of resources are in order. Whatever critical standards we use to regulate conflicting claims over scarce goods, we cannot, if we have any tolerably good knowledge of the facts in the case and a sense of fairness, but think the present relations are unjust and require rectification. There is not even in the various states of the North a fair access to basic natural and cultural resources, but viewed globally to speak of anything like a fair access to basic natural and cultural resources, where people are being treated as equals, can be nothing but a cruel and rather stupid joke.

If we start from a premise of *moral* equality as the vast majority of social theorists and moral philosophers right across the political spectrum do, from Robert Nozick to G. A. Cohen, we will believe that the interest of everyone matters and matters equally. There is no not believing in that, if we believe in *moral* equality.

For liberal egalitarians, such as Ronald Dworkin, this will involve a commitment to attain, not equality of condition but equality of resources, while for a radical egalitarian it will involve, as well, under conditions of productive abundance, a commitment to try to move as close as we reasonably can to an equality of condition. While rejecting all such egalitarian readings of *moral* equality, Nozick, with most other philosophers and economists on the right, thinks of moral equality as consisting most essentially in protecting individual rights to non-interference. Individuals in a just social order must be protected in their rights peacefully to pursue their own interests without interference from government, church or anyone else. Even if the kind of redistribution from North to South I am advocating did not bring about financial hara-kiri for people in the North, it would still involve an interference with their right peacefully to pursue their own interests where they are not harming anyone. Thus such a redistribution would still be wrong.

There are at least two responses that should be made here. The first is to assert that such capitalist behaviour has in fact harmed people. Sometimes this has been intentional, often not. But in any event, harm has been done. This is a factual issue, but if the factual descriptions I have given are near to the mark, and particularly if I have accurately described the workings of the International Food Order, the capitalist order centred in the west has indeed harmed, and continues to harm, very deeply many people in the Third World. (I do not mean to imply that it only harms people in the Third World.) But in our historical circumstances this is unnecessary for we could have an economic system whose underlying rationale was production to meet human needs and which was controlled democratically. Moreover, we now have the technical capacity to develop our productive powers so that the needs of people could be met. But the capitalist order has been massively supported in a very large part of the North and a not inconsiderable number of people in the North have been the beneficiaries of a socio-economic order that did so exploit. (Of course, there are others in the North who are just victims of that order.) This being so, even Nozickian notions of justice in rectification would require redistribution between North and South.

However, a second response seems to me more fundamental, less puritanical and less concerned with blaming people. To see best what is at issue we should proceed rather indirectly. We not only have rights to non-interference, we also have rights to fair co-operation and these rights can conflict. A very important liberty is the liberty to be able to guide one's own life in accordance with one's own unmystified preferences. Central to liberty is the capacity and opportunity to make rational choices and to be able to act on those rational choices.[18] This is much broader than to construe liberty as simply the absence of restrictions or interference, though it certainly includes that. What is vital to see here is that liberty will not be adequately protected if we limit our rights to the protection of rights to non-interference. We must also give central weight to the rights of fair co-operation. If the right of all to effective participation in government and, more generally, to effective direction of their lives is to be attained, there must be in place in our social organizations a respect for the right of everyone to fair co-operation. It is, of course, evident that respect for this right is not very widespread in the world. It will not only not be in place where there is subordination and domination, it will also not be effective where there is widespread starvation, malnutrition, exploitation and ignorance. What is unavoidable is that in class-based societies rights to fair co-operation and rights to non-interference will conflict. To move towards correcting the imbalances between North and South, we will have to move to a collective ownership and control of the means of production, for otherwise economic power becomes concentrated in the hands of a few and they will dominate and exploit others. But moving to collective ownership will in turn have the effect of overriding the rights to non-interference of Horatio Alger types who, capitalistically inclined, seek to acquire productive property through hard work and honest bargains. (It is hardly accurate or fair to say that there are no capitalists like that, particularly small capitalists.) In following their entirely peaceful interests – they have no wish to dominate or impoverish anyone – they wish to invest, buy and sell, and own productive property. If we are to protect their rights to non-interference, these activities can hardly be stopped, but if they are allowed to go on, the institutional stage is set, whatever the particular agent's own inclinations may be, for the undermining of rights to fair co-operation. So we have a fundamental clash of rights: rights of non-subordination with rights to non-interference.

To overcome the great disparities between North and South, even to put an end to the conditions of immiseration in the South – starvation, malnutrition, lack of work, extreme poverty – there would have to be significant and varied redistribution from North to South. In doing this we would have to give rather more weight to the rights of fair co-operation than to rights of non-interference. But – and here is what is alleged to be the catch – there is no significant consensus concerning which rights are to be overriding when they conflict.

I think that there would be a consensus if we came to command a clear view of these rights and their relations, along with some other powerful moral considerations, and came, as well, to command a clear view of the relevant social realities. Surely people have a right to pursue their interests without interference. But there are interests and interests. (Indeed, rights are most paradigmatically linked to our vital interests.) There is, among these interests, our interest in maintaining our bodily and moral integrity. To require, for example, that a person (say, a quite ordinary person), quite against her wishes, donate a kidney to keep someone alive whose value to the society is extensive is, that fact notwithstanding, still an intolerable intrusion on that involuntary donor's bodily integrity; to require a person to give up her religion or political convictions to enhance social harmony or even peace is another intolerable intrusion in that person's life – it simple runs roughshod over her civil liberties. But the interference with the peaceful pursuit of a person's interests that would go with a collective ownership of the means of production would not touch such vital interests. Rather what would be touched is her freedom to buy and sell, to invest and to bequeath *productive* property. But these interests are not nearly as vital as the above type of interests which genuinely are vital for our personal integrity. When the price for overriding those less vital interests is, as it is in the North–South situation, the overcoming of starvation, malnutrition, domination, subordination, great poverty and ignorance (certainly vital interests for any person), there is no serious doubt about in which direction the trade-offs should go. That there is not a massive consensus about this results, I believe, not from deeply embedded moral differences between people but from disputes or at least from different beliefs about what is in fact the case and about what in fact can come to be the case.[19] Ideological mystification leads us to believe that there is nothing significant that could be done about these matters or nothing that could be done short of impoverishing us all or undermining our civil liberties. But that is just ideological mystification.

REDISTRIBUTION VERSUS CAPITALISM

So we know that from the moral point of view, justice, or at least humanity, requires an extensive redistribution between North and South. We also know, if we have anything of a sense of *realpolitik*, that nothing like this is going to happen within the present socio-economic order. We can, as I have tried to indicate, know something of what morality requires here, but what is far more important to know, and much less obvious, is what are the mechanisms by which this conception of moral requiredness can become a reality in the lives of people so that our societies can be turned around. You may think that what I am about to say is too *parti pris* or perhaps you will even believe it to be vulgar, but it seems to me to be plainly true all that notwithstanding. And, even if it is vulgar, it is better to say something which if true is importantly true than to be evasive out of a sense of nicety or out of fear of saying something obvious.

What I think is plainly true is this: our capitalist masters, in principal control of the consciousness industry, have a plain interest in maintaining something not very different from the present North–South state of affairs.[20] To stabilize things they might, in certain circumstances, where they envisage a threat, favour some minor redistribution of wealth, but it would be very much against their interests, and that of a tiny stratum beholden to them, to make any extensive redistributions – redistributions that would touch their secure power base. Capitalism requires, and indeed can accept, at most a somewhat improved and more efficient version of the present and that, in turn, requires great injustice and inhumanity. It could only marginally improve our lot. A necessary but not a sufficient condition for attaining the end of such global injustice and inhumanity is the shedding of capitalism. As long, that is, as we live in a capitalist system, we are going to have such injustices. At most we might lessen their severity a bit.

eliminate capitalism

If we are morally serious and not ideologically blinkered, we will realize that it is our central social task to get rid of capitalism. But concretely how this is to be done, given capitalist dominance in western industrial societies, is anything but obvious. (This is exacerbated by the technological sophistication of these societies – by their awesome means of surveillance and control.) However, that the way or the ways are not obvious does not mean, if our efforts are over the long haul, that it cannot be done or that we should settle, as many do, for some reformist tinkering inside bourgeois parameters. We are not going to get justice or even a reign of common humanity that way. Recognizing that there are no quick fixes, we need to continue to struggle, without hiding from ourselves the sobering and indeed depressing recognition that things are probably going to get much worse before they get better.

NOTES

Reprinted from *Journal of Applied Philosophy*, 1, 2, 1984, pp. 175–86, by permission of the Society for Applied Philosophy and of the author.

1 Robert McNamara as cited by Peter Singer, *Practical Ethics*, London: Cambridge University Press, 1979, p. 159.
2 Garrett Hardin, 'Lifeboat ethics: the case against helping the poor', and Joseph Fletcher, 'Give if it helps, but not if it hurts', both in William Aiken and Hugh La Follette (eds), *World Hunger and Moral Obligation*, Englewood Cliffs, NJ: Prentice-Hall, 1977, pp. 11–21 and 103–14 respectively.
3 Harriet Friedmann, 'The political economy of food: the rise and fall of the Postwar International Food Order', in Michael Burawoy and Theda Skocpol (eds), *Marxist Inquiries*, Chicago, IL: University of Chicago Press, 1982, pp. 248–86.
4 ibid.
5 ibid.
6 Ernest Feder, 'Latifundia and agricultural labour in Latin America', in Teodor Shanin (ed.), *Peasants and Peasant Societies*, Harmondsworth: Penguin, 1971, pp. 83–102.
7 Frances Moore Lappé and Joseph Collins, *Food First: Beyond the Myth of Scarcity*, Boston, MA: Houghton Mifflin, 1977, pp. 256–8, 278–81; Ernest Feder, *Strawberry Imperialism: An Enquiry into the Mechanisms*

of Dependency in Mexican Agriculture, The Hague: Institute of Social Studies, 1978.

8 Amartya Sen, *Poverty and Famines: An Essay on Entitlement and Deprivation*, Oxford: Clarendon Press, 1981; Kenneth J. Arrow, 'Why people go hungry', *New York Review of Books*, XXIX, 12, 15 July 1982, pp. 24–6.

9 Sen, op. cit., pp. 52–83.

10 ibid.

11 ibid., pp. 24–37.

12 My account here is indebted to Harriet Friedmann's masterful account of this order. See Friedmann, op. cit., pp. 248–86.

13 ibid., p. 250.

14 ibid.

15 ibid., p. 268.

16 David Hume, *A Treatise of Human Nature*, ed. L. A. Selby-Bigge, Oxford: Clarendon Press, 1964, pp. 485–95; John Rawls, *A Theory of Justice*, Cambridge, MA: Harvard University Press, 1971, pp. 126–30; Brian Barry, 'Circumstances of justice and future generations', in R. I. Sikora and Brian Barry (eds), *Obligations to Future Generations*, Philadelphia, PA: Temple University Press, 1978, pp. 204–48.

17 David A. J. Richards, 'International distributive justice', in Roland J. Pennock and John W. Chapman (eds), *Nomos*, XXIV, New York: New York University Press, 1982, pp. 275–95; Thomas Nagel, *Mortal Questions*, Cambridge: Cambridge University Press, 1979, pp. 111–12.

18 Richard Norman, 'Liberty, equality, property', *Aristotelian Society*, supplementary volume, LV, 1981, pp. 199–202.

19 This is powerfully argued by Andrew Collier in 'Scientific socialism and the question of socialist values', in Kai Nielsen and Steven Patten (eds), *Marx and Morality*, Guelph, Ontario: Canadian Association for Publishing in Philosophy, 1981, pp. 121–54.

20 Hans Magnus Enzensberger, *The Consciousness Industry*, New York: Seabury Press, 1974, pp. 3–25.

PL 470 (law for food aid)

Chapter 2

World poverty, justice and equality

Andrew Belsey

All social inequalities which have ceased to be considered expedient, assume the character not of simple inexpediency, but of injustice, and appear so tyrannical, that people are apt to wonder how they ever could have been tolerated; forgetful that they themselves perhaps tolerate other inequalities under an equally mistaken notion of expediency, the correction of which would make that which they approve seem quite as monstrous as that which they have at last learnt to condemn.[1]

Millions of people in the world live in poverty, not the relative poverty of the poor who live in wealthy societies but the absolute poverty of the poor in the Third World, the South, whose basic needs are unmet. The absolute poor can live, after a fashion, but they lack adequate food, clean water, sanitation, access to medical services and other material necessities, and for those who live such lives death is a frequent visitor. But when the fragile and unstable equilibrium of the systems that support people in absolute poverty breaks down, then hunger and malnutrition give way to famine and starvation, and death takes up residence. The situation is worst in parts of Africa, where drought and civil war have combined to jeopardize the lives of millions whose existence was already precarious.

In the 1980s television acted as a global eye-opener, bringing the tragedy of African famine into the living rooms of the affluent and stirring their consciences into donating generously to various special appeals and projects. Yet in a new decade little has changed – unless things have actually got worse – and the media still have grim news to report. 'At least 16 million people living in four African countries could be facing starvation today,' said the

Guardian in December 1990, and the harrowing message is echoed in many other stories.[2]

However, it is a truth, though a depressing one, that even if the immediate and desperate crisis of famine and starvation could be solved, the underlying problem of widespread absolute poverty would remain, and with it the constant threat of breakdown into further famines. Famine relief is of course vital, but because it is treating the symptoms rather than tackling the underlying causes it is only amelioration and not a cure.

So beneath the eye-catching, heart-rending crisis of famine is the persistent, day-to-day tragedy of absolute poverty and its consequences. It is estimated that one billion people live below the World Bank's poverty line of $370 a year – hardly a generous amount. This is about 33 per cent of the population of the Third World and 20 per cent of the total world population. The number of people living in absolute poverty is falling as a proportion of world population but still rising in total numbers. Furthermore, the gap between these poorest people and the rest is widening.

The hunger that follows from absolute poverty is so established, so institutionalized, so much part of daily experience for millions of people that it has been called 'silent' to distinguish it from clamorous emergencies that produce famine.[3] The term implies no acceptance or complacency, of course, but is employed to draw attention to the shocking invisibility of persistent hunger. It is shocking because the invisibility hides the fact that it is completely unnecessary.

For why is there such widespread hunger and malnutrition in the world? Because of poverty: people are too poor to buy the food they need or are dispossessed of the land on which they could grow it. And poverty exists within a country because its economic, political and social structures are unable to deliver what is required to meet people's basic needs. If individual countries are considered, there is usually a problem of both production and distribution: insufficient resources are available and they are unequally distributed. But on a global scale the problem is one of distribution, not production. For example, there is sufficient food produced in the world to feed everyone adequately. People are hungry not because there is not enough food to go round; they are hungry because it does not in fact go round, because they are unable to get access to it. (Even in famines there is food for those who can buy it.) A response to the problems of poverty and hunger therefore requires a global foundation. Poverty is a characteristic not simply of this country or that country but of a system, that is to say a structure of relationships between countries, especially the unequal relationships, economic and political, that exist between the Third World countries of the South and the industrialized countries of the capitalist North.[4]

The idea that poverty is the product of systemic, exploitative power relations between countries is one that became central to a critical analysis of world poverty. Thus Robin Jenkins wrote in 1971 that 'In modern times there is one dominant reason why some states are rich and others poor, why the rich states grow richer and the poor states stay poor: because the world system is inherently exploitative.'[5] This exploitative world system is not, however, something given as a fact of nature, something inevitable and unchangeable. It must ultimately be traceable to human activity and to human choices, and thereby be challengeable, both practically and morally. The case has been eloquently stated by Bennett:

> If human poverty and hunger are so persistent, their causes must be found in the institutions, policies and ideologies which serve to widen the gap between rich and poor. People die of hunger because they are poor, because they cannot afford to buy what food is available. They lack access to basic resources. In short, they are powerless within a system of injustice.[6]

In 1988 the then president of the World Bank, Barber Conable, expressed his concern about the economic inefficiencies of world poverty. But he also had no doubt about its (im)moral status:

> Poverty on today's scale prevents a billion people from having even minimally acceptable standards of living. To allow every fifth human being on our planet to suffer such an existence is a moral outrage. It is more: it is bad economics, a terrible waste of precious development resources. Poverty destroys lives, human dignity and economic potential.[7]

The correct response to the existence of such moral outrage is to search for justice. As Susan George has put it: 'the relevant virtue for fighting hunger . . . is justice, because charity can never be more than a stop-gap – it does not and cannot change unjust structures. Injustice and inequalities are structural, and have firm foundations.'[8]

To search for justice is the appropriate response because it is a practical response, bringing together moral concern and political action. But is it possible to combine this search for justice with the requisite global outlook? The difficulties are considerable. First there is the enormity of the task, the hubristic nature of the challenge. For it is the world that needs shifting, and the problem is that there is no firm point on which anyone can stand, Archimedes-like, to lever the world back into a just balance. This is connected to the second difficulty, the argument, found in both the history of moral thought and contemporary moral thinking, that acts of justice, obligation or concern for others can be performed only on a local stage and never in a global environment.

Consider just a few fairly random historical examples of this line of thought. At the start of the western philosophical tradition Plato suggested that it was wrong for Greek to enslave Greek, implying that there was no objection to the enslavement of non-Greeks.[9] In the seventeenth century Locke casually dismissed the idea that anyone could have concern for 'the happiness or misery of a man in the Indies, whom he knows not'.[10] And in the nineteenth century Sidgwick put the point rather more reflectively when he reported (rather than endorsed) what 'common-sense morality' would say about the duties of benevolence:

> We should all agree that each of us is bound to show kindness to his parents and spouse and children, and to other kinsmen in a less degree: and to those who have rendered services to him, and any others whom he may have admitted to his intimacy and called friends: and to neighbours and to fellow-countrymen more than others: and perhaps we may say to those of our own race more than to black or yellow men, and generally to human beings in proportion to their affinity to ourselves.[11]

In each case there is a claim, unargued, that moral concern, duty or obligation is entirely or primarily local or particular. But some present-day moralists and philosophers have supposed that the claim is correct, and have provided arguments to support it. Some of these arguments will now be examined in the next four sections, before it is suggested in the final section that they are not in the end adequate.

NO ONE IS OUTSIDE THE SYSTEM

One argument is based on the idea that morality is a matter of reciprocal obligations, and that therefore where there is no reciprocity there are no obligations.[12] A crude variety of this is represented by the childhood principle of 'I-won't-hit-you-if-you-don't-hit-me'. This is also the reciprocity of Mafia mobs – hardly a paradigm of the moral! A less crude variety is a version of social contract theory: people agree out of self-interest to enter a social group providing mutual protection and support; obligations exist between members of the group but those outside are not owed anything. Thus, just as animals that cannot reciprocate are owed nothing by human beings, so inhabitants of the Third World who cannot reciprocate are owed nothing by inhabitants of the affluent countries.

This argument gets its surface credibility from the analogy, but it is a highly misleading one. For there are actually two different arguments mixed up here, and they must be separated. The strong version makes it a necessary truth that some categories of individuals cannot enter a reciprocal contract with existing normal adult human beings, though there could be considerable discussion about where to draw the line: candidates for necessary exclusion include future people, non-human animals, infants, children and mentally handicapped adults. The weak version trades on the plausibility of the strong version, but quite illegitimately, for it is based on contingent and empirical facts about international relationships, such as (to use Singer's example) that 'the power of people in, say, Chad to reciprocate either good or evil that is done to them by, say, citizens of the United States is very limited'.[13] If there is a necessary lack of reciprocity between human beings and animals then it cannot be changed or challenged. But the actual relationship between Chad and the United States can be challenged and changed.

Furthermore, any claim that people in the Third World lack the power to reciprocate would not meet with total agreement. For, on the one hand, there is Heilbroner's lurid scenario, according to which lack of action by the affluent North to alleviate Southern poverty will lead to insurrection by the poverty-stricken masses of the South and their expropriation of the North's wealth through nuclear blackmail.[14] Then, on the other hand, there is the more moderate version of this tale put forward by the Brandt

Commission, which argued that it was in the interests of the North for it to bring about a more just world economic order.[15] The point, then, is that the people, and the countries, of the world are linked in a network of relationships, a system. And it is reciprocal because anyone's future is inseparably linked to everyone's. Reciprocity need not be contractual, either explicitly or implicitly. Whatever conceptual difficulties that might prevent reciprocity between human beings and other animals or between the present generation and future human generations are irrelevant to a bnnrhddr'thnn nf tnd'x&r htl'n world. No one is outside the system; everyone is in the same boat.

MORALITY AS SELFISHNESS?

A popular objection to the existence of global morality is based on the claim that morality (like charity) begins at home. (Leave aside the point that those who claim that charity begins at home usually mean that it ends there as well.) What is being claimed is that human beings have special and particular obligations to those other human beings who are emotionally, genetically or geographically close. These obligations arise from and within socially constituted role relationships which provide the only meaningful links between people, and therefore these obligations are the only or the overriding obligations that people have. Something like the basic claim here has already been met in Sidgwick's report of nineteenth-century common-sense morality, above, but the idea has continued in use in recent times in discussions of world poverty and the obligations of the affluent. Those who take this line to argue for the existence of only limited obligations towards the Third World commonly refer for support to an essay by Bernard Williams, so his influential ideas require examination.[16]

Actually, Williams provides surprisingly little argument, proffering instead the persuasive power of an example, which is: if you can save only one of two people in peril, and one is your wife and the other a stranger, which one should you save? (Note the sexist assumption in the construction of this example.) Williams says that to regard this as a problem for which we must seek an answer is inappropriate, or even repugnant. Of course you save your wife, but to suppose that there could be any further justification for this (some higher-order moral principle) is, according to Williams, 'one thought too many'.[17]

This is an intuitionist rather than a rationally based position, but why should these sorts of intuitions be accepted? They are derived from an equally intuitive vision of society as constituted by bonds of loyalty created by immediate and emotionally powerful relationships between particular people. In such a society the central core of obligation is unchallenged and unchallengeable, being the product of a mystical union which can emerge in human consciousness only in feeling and not in rational discourse.

But does such an atavistic vision convey a morality? Does it suggest why you should save your wife rather than the stranger? The first fragment of argument that could be extracted from the picture is that you should save your wife because she is *your* wife. This, however, seems not so much a moral argument as a feeble rationalization of selfishness: it's for your sake, not hers, that you save her. A second argument is that you should save your wife because you have a special obligation to her because she is your *wife*. But again, far from this being a noble principle, it is, when seen in the light of the sexist assumption on which the original example was based, another rationalization of selfishness. You save her not because of your special obligation to her but because of her special obligation to you. To put it crudely but clearly, if you save the stranger, who will wash your socks?

A variation on this second argument is that your relationship with your wife is constituted by a morally based institution (i.e. marriage), and that far from there being any question about it, morality requires you to give priority to your wife. But this is entirely question-begging. The morality of institutions such as marriage and the family and the roles they prescribe is highly questionable. Such institutions are ideological and moral minefields, and any suggestion that morality is embedded in existing social institutions requires a most thorough critique. The point, however, is important, as it shows that, among moral philosophers at least, there is a link between arguments about special obligations and arguments that institutionalized forms of life set limits on what one ought to do.

To return to Williams. He does have a wider argument. *You* as a being are (at least partly) constituted by the relationships you have with others, and the more intimate the relationship, the more central it is to your identity. If then you save your wife, the reason is not for her sake, but for your sake, because her loss would destroy you, would destroy your very identity and so would make your life not worth living. This argument is simply another rationalization of selfishness. For consider: presumably the death of the stranger will destroy someone else's identity, make someone else's life not worth living. In believing that you ought to save your wife you are giving your interests priority over those of this someone else. No doubt people do behave in this way, but to dignify such behaviour with the name of virtue is to put on the mask of hypocrisy.

MILL'S SENSIBLE EMPIRICISM

So the arguments that you should save your wife are rationalizations of selfishness. But what is selfishness? To be unselfish is to follow the Benthamite principle that everybody is to count for one and nobody for more than one. (This is not of course advocating altruism in the sense of self-sacrifice, for among those who count for one is yourself. Benthamite impartiality does not require you to discount yourself.) But the arguments that you should save your wife breach this principle: they privilege the interests of *you*. You count for more than one.

So the claims in these arguments that there are special obligations collapse into selfishness. But the notion that there are special obligations is liable to lead more generally into selfishness. For if it is true that you have special obligations to certain individuals, then presumably one such individual can be yourself. For with whom can you have a closer relationship; with whom is your identity more closely bound up? Once special obligations are allowed, the road to egoism is wide open, unless a block can be found which permits special obligations to others but not to yourself. It is not clear what such a block could be.

Nevertheless, there could still be further arguments, and indeed the argument for special obligations might be thought to receive support from someone usually considered to be one of the classic expositors of impartial utilitarianism, John Stuart Mill. It is a widespread misapprehension, says Mill, to suppose that utilitarianism requires concern with 'so wide a generality as the world, or society at large'. It is 'particular persons' who (Mill says here) normally are the objects of utilitarian concerns, and these individuals are elsewhere identified as 'family or friends' and are contrasted with 'strangers'.[18]

But it is clear that any such obligations are not special, for they must conform to, not override, utilitarian considerations. In benefiting particular individuals, the utilitarian agent must 'assure himself . . . that he is not violating the rights . . . of anyone else'.[19] Rights are 'legitimate and authorized expectations', and since Mill was no upholder of natural rights, these rights that he refers to must be constituted and conferred by a utilitarian calculation. So the correct action is always determined not by special obligations but by utility.

Mill believed that in most cases the rights of others would not be violated. Being a good empiricist, Mill based his argument on what he took to be the facts that the great majority of actions could affect only particular individuals, and that very few actions could affect wider interests. In these few cases all wider interests involved must, of course, be included. But, being a good empiricist, Mill would surely have accepted that as the world changed, as it (metaphorically) shrank, as its parts became interdependent within a global system, this fact about the extent of an action's influence would no longer hold, and more and more actions would be concerned with even 'so wide a generality as the world'. And therefore concern for the world on a wider scale, once confined to a minority of actions, would become the norm. So Mill's preference for family and friends over strangers was based on what he took to be empirical circumstances, circumstances which surely no longer hold. There is no support for special obligations, and certainly no support for global selfishness, in Mill.

MORALITY AS SACRIFICE?

Another argument used to limit the obligations of the affluent to the Third World is based on the claim that people are not morally obliged to give up institutionalized ways of life to which they have become accustomed and within which they shape their purposes and plans.

An argument of this type has been put forward by James Fishkin, who begins by making a plausible-sounding general point: 'Certain levels of sacrifice cannot be morally required of any individual.'[20] But this is then given a more concrete, less plausible and, it could be suggested, thoroughly complacent interpretation:

> For any of us to give up virtually *all* of the normal activities whose appropriateness we take for granted and replace them with actions determined by duties or obligations would constitute a very substantial sacrifice, a sacrifice of the sort that might be characterized as 'beyond the call of duty'. It would constitute a substantial sacrifice precisely because it would require us to give up an entire way of life. More particularly, if we were each to give up our present activities and replace them entirely with actions prescribed by duty or obligation, our particular interests would be sacrificed in that our present projects, our plans of life, would have to be relinquished or abandoned.[21]

The rhetoric of this piece cries out for thorough analysis. For a start, who are 'us'? Presumably the affluent inhabitants of the North. It may very well be true that many of them take for granted the appropriateness of their normal activities and way of life, but it should hardly need pointing out that this in no way shows that they are right to do so. Terms like 'normal', 'appropriate' and 'taken for granted' are morally question-begging and should be viewed with suspicion by a moral philosopher, not used as foundations for a claim. It is not appropriate for philosophers to take for granted what passes for normal in a society, nor to assume that what is normal is, *ipso facto*, acceptable or justifiable. Even meta-ethicists who are unconvinced that there is a 'naturalistic fallacy' ought to be startled by the suggestion that actual ways of life and actual plans and projects are, just by existing, morally worthy.

Not that Fishkin explicitly claims moral worthiness for the Northern affluent way of life. It is not clear whether this way of life is, in his view, *morally* justified, or whether it is simply *justified* – by existing, by being 'ours', etc. Nevertheless, in spite of this ambiguity it seems clear that Fishkin's position is based on what is surely an absurd duality, between, on the one hand, what he calls 'the way of life we commonly take for granted in modern, secular, Western moral culture',[22] and, on the other, morality as constituted by duties and obligations reserved for special occasions. It is difficult to think of a more immoral foundation for moral philosophy.

The point is simple in relation to the issue of Third World poverty. If the plans, projects and way of life of the affluent require the acquisition of more than their just share of the world's resources then they ought to be abandoned. But doesn't Fishkin have an argument to bring to bear here, namely that to abandon one's way of life is a 'sacrifice'?

But this is the most question-begging term of all, especially when it trades on an ambiguity. To give up something you are used to could be a psychological blow, but this does not mean that it is a sacrifice in the morally relevant sense, and it is only this sense that makes sense in the context of world poverty and the distribution of global resources. Consider food. There is sufficient food produced in the world for everyone to have an adequate diet. If it were distributed to produce this result there would be no sacrifice by the affluent – not unless gluttony has been elevated from a vice to a virtue. To give up what you do not need is no sacrifice.

But more importantly, to give up what you have no right to is no sacrifice. The affluent way of life of the North requires more than the acquisition of a disproportionate share of the world's resources; it is based on expropriation, made possible by the exploitative power relations between North and South. The fact that there is an existing pattern of distribution in no way shows that it is justified. If it is based on exploitation the opposite conclusion must be drawn. However much the affluent take their way of life for granted, they have no right to the excessive resources on which it is based. To give up the resources and the way of life is, therefore, no sacrifice but a requirement of morality and justice.

HUMAN NEEDS, EQUALITY AND JUSTICE

The arguments examined and criticized so far are clearly ideological, in the sense that they serve the interests of those who are on the more powerful side of the unequal power relations and who do not wish to see this inequality subverted. They are arguments which seek to draw boundaries, emotional, cultural, geographical, around the very notion of a moral relationship, and thus to disqualify global concern and the ideals of global justice. More concretely the arguments serve to turn the hearts and eyes of the affluent away from the moral enormity of world poverty and hunger and from the tragedy of suffering that they engender.

Some reasons for believing the arguments to be inadequate and therefore to fail in their ideological task have been indicated already. But rather than continue with the critique it would be more advantageous (and, it is to be hoped, more inspiring) to turn to a more positive approach, and try to sketch an alternative account of people and the moral relations that should exist between them in the unequal world of today.

A start can be made by reversing Fishkin's claim – made in the context of a discussion of global inequalities – that unbounded obligation 'would require us to give up an entire way of life'. This is wrong because the demand for global justice is based on ideals of care and concern for others which are common to both the religious and the secular ethical traditions of the societies of the North. Furthermore, these ideals are foundational, in contrast to what *would* have to be given up in the name of global justice: not an entire way of life but merely the excessive consuming of resources, activities which are, in the pejorative sense, materialistic excrescences, and therefore morally superficial. Overconsumption of food, of fuel, of minerals – these are not what animate the moral interiors of people who currently 'enjoy' an affluent standard of living, as the guilt which accompanies and often overwhelms the enjoyment makes clear. People are troubled by the global inequalities that the media bring home to them, and seeing no difference between themselves and the hungry in the capacity to suffer they know that the suffering lacks both justification and justice.

So far from calling for an abandonment of 'our' way of life, global justice is a demand to take its moral bases seriously, and to rectify its present decrepitude by rebuilding it on its original, genuine foundations. The heavily ideological distortion of morality, the 'ordinary morality' criticized by Kagan among others,[23] hides from sight the alternative moral ideals of global justice. To overcome this lack of vision Kagan recommends strengthening the 'vividness' of the recognition of the suffering of others,[24] while in somewhat similar vein Sprigge finds moral blindness to be caused by a failure at the conceptual level, a lack of imaginative sympathy in the presence of suffering.[25]

What underlies the enhanced insight available when the moral blinkers are removed is an egalitarian insistence on seeing more clearly the sameness of the observed and the observers, the absence, already alluded to, of any morally relevant difference between the sufferers and those who are in a position to provide assistance. To argue thus is to take the idea of equality – human equality, global equality – seriously.[26]

Sprigge's egalitarian seriousness is located within a holistic, somewhat mystical metaphysics, which involves each of us 'having a sense of union with a great spiritual whole to which we belong'.[27] There is one advantage in such a position. Like those whose views were criticized above as selfish, Sprigge takes the self and those near and dear to the self as important, but his final position is quite distinct because his universal holism is completely incompatible with selfishness. Moral argument might start from the self or those close to the self but it ends there only through the lack of imagination that Sprigge deplores. To privilege one's own self is to fail to recognize, in addition to the individuality, the fundamental similarity and equality of selves; to remedy this 'may sometimes go somewhere to quench our petty egoisms'.[28]

But perhaps this is too modest a conclusion. Sprigge's egalitarianism is based on the equal distribution of morally relevant faculties, capacities and abilities within (and indeed beyond) the human species. It is this common humanity as the basis for insight and action which is the source and origin of global morality. As Sprigge puts it: 'for there to be full recognition of the reality of another's suffering, humanity in me must recognize itself as present equally in [the other]'.[29]

An alternative way of emphasizing common humanity, shorn of mystical overtones, is to concentrate on the notion of needs. To claim that everyone is equal in their needs is not to commit oneself to the falsehood that everyone needs the same amount of food, or anything else. It simply means that everyone has similar needs that must be met before any sort of worthwhile life can be lived.

Global justice is the encapsulation of an ideal of a network of relations between people who are equal in their needs. At present these needs are not equally met, as the barest glance at the actual poverty and hunger in the world reveals, and it is this inequality that is the glaring injustice. Of course, in the face of hunger and starvation both development aid and relief aid should be provided, but the cause of justice is best served by a structural transformation, away from unequal global relations based on exploitation and towards equality based on recognition of common similar needs.

A just global distribution of resources involves equality, in two ways. The aim should be the overall result which is best for everyone, in the sense that everyone's interests are to be considered equally, but in this consideration equal needs are trumps, and the more basic the need the greater its trumping force.[30] Thus justice and equality, globally conceived, are inseparable as the twin foundations of the moral response to the tragedy of unmet needs which is the concrete, everyday reality of world poverty.

NOTES

1 John Stuart Mill, *Utilitarianism*, ch. 5, in *Utilitarianism, On Liberty, Essay on Bentham*, London: Collins/Fontana, 1962, p. 320.

2 *Guardian*, EG supplement, 11 December 1990, p. 1. See also Victoria Brittain, 'Fighting brings grim harvest of despair', *Guardian*, 2 January 1991; John Vidal, 'Long shadows over a parched land', *Guardian*, 18 January 1991.

3 Jon Bennett, *The Hunger Machine: The Politics of Food*, Cambridge: Polity Press, 1987, p. 12.

4 Kai Nielsen, 'Global justice, capitalism and the Third World', *Journal of Applied Philosophy*, 1, 2, 1984, pp. 175–86, reprinted in this volume, pp. 17–34.

5 Robin Jenkins, *Exploitation*, London: Paladin, 1971, pp. 42–3.

6 Bennett, op. cit., p. 13.

7 Barber Conable, speech at the opening of the 1988 World Bank and IMF joint annual meeting, reported in the *Guardian*, 28 September 1988.

8 Susan George, in Bennett, op. cit., p. 1. See also Onora O'Neill, *Faces of Hunger: An Essay on Poverty, Justice and Development*, London: Allen & Unwin, 1986, esp. chs 7 and 8.

9 *Republic*, 469 b–c. Cf. MacIntyre's comment on early Greek thought: 'Those who fall outside the system fall outside the moral order. And this is indeed the fate of slaves' (Alasdair MacIntyre, *A Short History of Ethics*, London: Routledge & Kegan Paul, 1967, p. 8).

10 John Locke, *An Essay Concerning Human Understanding*, ed. Peter Nidditch, Oxford: Clarendon Press, 1975, 2.1.11, p. 110.

11 Henry Sidgwick, *The Methods of Ethics*, 7th edn, London: Macmillan, 1907, p. 246; first pub. 1874. The passage is quoted by Peter Singer, *The Expanding Circle*, Oxford: Oxford University Press, 1981, p. 23, but Singer does not quote a further passage from the same page which seems to be an important addition to what has just been said: 'those who are in distress or urgent need have a claim on us for special kindness'.

12 As argued (for the case of future people) by Martin Golding, 'Obli-

gations to future generations', in Ernest Partridge (ed.), *Responsibilities to Future Generations*, Buffalo, NY: Prometheus Books, 1981, pp. 61–72. See also the critical discussion in Peter Singer, *Practical Ethics*, Cambridge: Cambridge University Press, 1979, pp. 68–71.

13 Singer, *Practical Ethics*, op. cit., p. 70.

14 Robert Heilbroner, *An Inquiry into the Human Prospect*, London: Calder & Boyars, 1975.

15 Brandt Commission (the Independent Commission on International Development Issues), *North–South: A Programme for Survival* (the Brandt Report), London: Pan Books, 1980.

16 Bernard Williams, 'Persons, character and morality', in his *Moral Luck*, Cambridge: Cambridge University Press, 1981, pp. 1–19. This is mentioned by James Fishkin in 'Theories of justice and international relations: the limits of liberal theory', and used by Brian Baxter in 'The self, morality and the nation–state', both in Anthony Ellis (ed.), *Ethics and International Relations*, Manchester: Manchester University Press, 1986, pp. 1–12 and 113–26 respectively.

17 Williams, op. cit., p. 18.

18 Mill, op. cit., pp. 270, 300.

19 ibid., p. 270.

20 Fishkin, op. cit., p. 4.

21 ibid., p. 5.

22 ibid., p. 5.

23 Shelly Kagan, *The Limits of Morality*, Oxford: Oxford University Press, 1989, p. 3.

24 Kagan, op. cit., p. 394.

25 T. L. S. Sprigge, *The Rational Foundatinns of Ethics*, London: Routledge, 1988, esp. pp. 178, 255.

26 See John Baker, *Arguing for Equality*, London: Verso, 1987.

27 Sprigge, op. cit., p. 270.

28 ibid., p. 270.

29 ibid., pp. 265–6.

30 See Robin Attfield, *A Theory of Value and Obligation*, London: Croom Helm, 1987, pp. 140–3.

What is the argument?

Chapter 3

Justice, gender and international boundaries

Onora O'Neill

Employment opps for women being population down.

ABSTRACT: *Discussions of international and of gender justice both legitimately demand that principles of justice abstract from differences between cases and that judgements of justice respond to differences between them. Abstraction and sensitivity to context are often treated as incompatible: abstraction is taken to endorse idealized models of individual and state; sensitivity to human differences is identified with relativism. Neither identification is convincing: abstract principles do not entail uniform treatment; responsiveness to difference does not hinge on relativism. These points are used to criticize discussions of international and gender justice by liberals, communitarians and feminists. An alternative account of justice is sketched, which combines abstract principles with consideration of human differences in the application of principles. The case of poor women in impoverished economies – a hard case both for gender and for international justice – illustrates how universal, abstract principles of justice may not only permit but mandate differentiated application.*

JUSTICE FOR IMPOVERISHED PROVIDERS

Questions about justice to women and about international justice are often raised in discussions of development. Yet many influential theories of justice have difficulty in handling either topic. I shall first compare some theoretical difficulties that have arisen in these two domains and then sketch an account of justice that may be better suited to handling questions both of gender and of international justice.

I begin by distinguishing *idealized* from *relativized* theories of justice. *Idealized* accounts of justice stress the need to abstract from the particularities of persons. They paint justice as blind to gender and nationality. Its principles are those that would regulate the action of idealized 'abstract individuals', hence take no account of differences between men and women and transcend international boundaries. *Relativized* accounts of justice not only acknowledge the variety and differences among humankind but ground principles of justice in the discourse and traditions of actual communities. Since nearly all of these relegate (varying portions of) women's lives to a 'private' sphere, within which the political virtue of justice has no place, and see national boundaries as limits of justice, appeals to actual traditions tend both to endorse institutions that exclude women from the 'public' sphere, where justice is properly an issue, and to insulate one 'public' sphere from another.

Both idealized and relativized accounts of justice look inadequate from the perspective of those whom they marginalize. Women, in particular poor women, will find that neither approach takes account of the reality of carrying both reproductive and productive tasks, while having relatively little control over the circumstances of one's life. Women's lives are not well conceived just as those of idealized individuals. A world of such individuals assumes away relations of dependence and interdependence; yet these are central to most lives actually available to women. Nor are women's lives well conceived solely in terms of traditions that relegate them to a 'private' sphere. The productive contributions and the cognitive and practical independence of actual women are too extensive, evident and economically significant to be eclipsed by ideologies of total domesticity and dependence.

The awkward fit of theory to actuality is most vivid for poor women in poor economies. These women may depend on others but lack the supposed securities of dependence. They are impoverished but are often providers. They are powerless, yet others who are yet more vulnerable depend on them for protection.[1] Their vulnerability reflects heavy demands as much as slender resources. They may find that they are relegated to and subordinated within a domestic sphere, whose separate and distinctive existence is legitimated not by appeals to justice but by entrenched views of family life and honour. They may also find that this domestic sphere is embedded in an economy that is subordinate to distant and richer economies. They not only raise children in poverty; they raise crops and do ill-paid and insecure work, their rewards fluctuating to the beat of distant economic forces. This second subordination too is legitimated in varied discourses which endorse an internationalized economic order but only national regimes of taxation and welfare. A serious account of justice cannot gloss over the predicaments of impoverished providers in marginalized and developing economies.

PREVIEW: ABSTRACT PRINCIPLES AND CONTEXT-SENSITIVE JUDGEMENT

Both idealized and relativized approaches to justice make seemingly legitimate demands. Idealized approaches insist that justice must *abstract* from the particularities of persons. Blindness to difference is a traditional image of justice and guarantees impartiality. Yet principles of justice that are supposedly blind to differences of power and resources often seem to endorse practices and policies that suit the privileged. Hence a demand that justice take account of *context* can seem equally reasonable. Justice, it is argued, needs more than abstract principles: it must guide judgements that take account of actual contexts and predicaments and of the differences among human beings. Relativized principles of justice meet this demand: but since they are rooted in history, tradition or local context, they will endorse traditional sexism or nationalism. Any relativism tends to prejudice the position of the weak, whose weakness is mirrored and partly constituted by their marginalization in received ways of thought and by their subordination and oppression in established orders. Yet idealizing approaches do no better. Where relativist approaches are uncritical of established privilege, idealized approaches are uncritical of privileges from which they abstract.

If accounts of justice had to be either idealized or relativized, we would have to choose between demands for abstraction from difference and for sensitivity to difference. If there are other possibilities, an account of justice may be able to meet demands both for abstract principles and for context-sensitive judgements. I shall try to sketch a third possibility, which gives both abstraction and sensitivity to context their due – but only their due. This can be done by meeting the demands for abstraction from and sensitivity to context in two distinct, successive moves.

The first move is to argue for abstract principles of universal scope, while rejecting the supposed link between abstraction and positions that not merely abstract but (in a sense to be explained) idealize. Much contemporary moral reasoning, and in particular 'abstract liberalism' (whether 'deontological' or utilitarian), handles issues of gender and international justice badly not because it abstracts (e.g. from sex, race, nationality), but because it also almost always idealizes specific conceptions of the human agent and of national sovereignty, which are often admired and are more (nearly) feasible for men rather than women and for developed rather than developing societies. However, abstraction itself, without idealization, is the route rather than the obstacle to broad scope and is unobjectionable in *principles* of justice.

The second move answers demands that we take account of the context and particularities of lives and societies, but does not built culturally specific ideals of gender and of national sovereignty into the *principles* of justice. The second move insists that judgements of justice take account of *certain* differences by applying abstract principles to determinate cases without tacitly reintroducing restricted ideals (e.g. of gender and national sovereignty), so relativizing principles of justice to accepted beliefs, traditions or practices. Abstract principles can guide context-sensitive judgement without lapsing into relativism.

ABSTRACT JUSTICE AND HUMAN DIFFERENCES: FEMINIST DEBATES

Discussions of gender justice have been structured by disagreements over the extent and import of differences between men and women. For liberals who defend abstract principles of justice it has been embarrassing that the Rights of Man were taken for so long and by so many of their predecessors as the rights of men and that liberal practice failed for so long to end male privilege.[2] (Socialist feminists suffer analogous embarrassments.) Starting with Wollstonecraft and J. S. Mill, liberal feminists argued against women's difference and claimed that women's like rationality entitled them to equal rights.

More recent liberal feminists have noted that even when women had equal political and legal rights, their political participation and economic rewards remained less than those of men and less than those of men whose qualifications and labour-force participation women matched. Supposedly gender-neutral and neutralizing institutions, such as democratic political structures and markets, did not eliminate gender differentials.[3] Many have concluded that approximations to political and legal justice in various domains of life evidently cannot close the radical gap between men's and women's paths and prospects.[4]

In response some liberal feminists argued that justice demands more thorough equal treatment. For example, it may require forms of affirmative action and reverse discrimination in education and employment, as well as welfare rights to social support for the poor and those with heavy family responsibilities. *Some* differences are to be acknowledged in principles of justice. This move has two difficulties. First, many liberals deny that justice demands compensatory redistribution, especially of positional goods. They think these should be allocated by competitive and meritocratic procedures. This debate is of particular importance in the developed world.

The second problem arises even where the goods to be distributed are not positional, and is particularly significant in the Third World. Where resources are scarce, non-positional goods such as basic health care or income support or children's allowances or unemployment insurance may be unfundable out of a slender national tax base. If social justice demands basic welfare provision, justice *must* reach across boundaries. An account of gender justice would then have to be linked to one of international distributive justice.[5]

This liberal debate continues, but its terms have been increasingly questioned by feminists in the last decade, many of whom claim that, despite its aspirations, gender bias is integral to liberal justice.[6] Their suspicions focus on the very abstraction from difference and diversity which has been the hallmark of liberal justice. Some of these 'post-liberal' feminists criticize abstract liberalism by highlighting respects in which particular supposedly gender-neutral theories covertly assume or endorse gendered accounts of the human subject and of rationality. Many aspects of these critiques are convincing.

However, the most fundamental contemporary feminist challenge to abstract liberalism ostensibly impugns reliance on abstraction itself. Gilligan's influential work claims that an emphasis on justice excludes and marginalizes the 'other voice' of ethical thought. 'Abstract liberalism' simply and unacceptably devalues care and concern for particular others, which are the core of women's moral life and thought, seeing them as moral immaturity.[7] The voice of justice is characterized as 'male' for its refusal to grasp the actualities of human difference, for its supposed agnosticism about the good for man and its resulting disregard of the virtues, and specifically of love and care. On this account the problem is not to secure like treatment for women, but to secure differentiated treatment for all.

In locating the distinction between justice and care (and other virtues) in a disagreement over the legitimacy of relying on abstract principles, feminist critics of abstract liberalism often view concern for care as not merely different from but opposed to concern for justice. They can end up endorsing rather than challenging social and economic structures that marginalize women and confine them to a private sphere. Separatism at the level of ethical theory can march with acceptance of the powers and traditions that be. A stress on caring and relationships to the exclusion of abstract justice may endorse relegation to the nursery and the kitchen, to purdah and to poverty. In rejecting 'abstract liberalism' such feminists converge with traditions that have excluded women from economic and public life. An appeal to 'women's experience', 'women's traditions' and 'women's discourse' does not escape but rather echoes ways in which women have been marginalized or oppressed. Some who celebrate the other 'voice' risk being thought to insist that differences are taken seriously only when actual differences are endorsed.[8]

The disputes that now divide liberal feminists and their contextualist critics ostensibly pose an unwelcome dilemma about gender justice. If we adopt an abstract account of justice, which is blind to differences between people, and so to the ways in which women's lives in the developed and in the undeveloped world differ from men's lives, we commit ourselves (it is said) to uniform treatment regardless of difference. But if we acknowledge the ethical importance of human differences, we are likely to endorse traditional social forms that sustain those differences, including those that subordinate and oppress women.

ABSTRACT JUSTICE AND NATIONAL DIFFERENCE: COMMUNITARIAN DEBATES

This dilemma recurs in certain discussions of international justice. Abstract liberalism proclaims the Rights of Man. As Burke was quick to complain, this is quite a different matter from proclaiming the traditional rights of Englishmen, or of Frenchmen, or of any coherent group. Abstraction was the price to be paid for ethical discourse that could cross the boundaries of states and nations and have universal appeal; and Burke found the price unacceptable. The internationalist, cosmopolitan commitments that were implicit in the ideals of liberalism have repeatedly been targets of conservative and communitarian criticism.

Liberal practice has, however, once again been quite different. It has not been universalistic, but clearly subordinated to the boundaries and demands of nation-states. This is evident in relations between rich and poor states. Like treatment for like cases is partially secured by laws and practices within many democratic states; only a few enthusiasts argue for world government, or think that rights of residence, work and welfare, as well as burdens of taxation, should be global. Such enthusiasm is often dismissed by practical people who hold that a plurality of national jurisdictions provides the framework(s) within which liberal ideals can be pursued. Liberals may not be generally willing to take differences seriously; but they have taken differences between sovereign states remarkably seriously.

The communitarian critics want to take differences and boundaries seriously in theory as well as in practice.[9] When boundaries are taken wholly seriously, however, international justice is not just played down but wiped off the ethical map. Walzer's work is a good case in point. He holds that the largest sphere of justice is the political community and that the only issues not internal to such communities are about membership in them and conflicts between them. The issues of membership concern the admission of individual aliens; rights and duties do not go beyond borders.[10] A commitment to community is a commitment to the historical boundaries of political communities, whatever these happen to be and whatever injustices their constitution and their preservation cost. Communitarians cannot easily take any wider view of ethical boundaries since their critique of abstraction is in part a demand for ethical discourse that takes 'our' language, 'our' culture and 'our' traditions seriously.[11]

Like current debates on gender justice, discussions of international justice apparently pose an unwelcome choice. Either we can abstract from the reality of boundaries and think about principles of justice that assume an ideal, cosmopolitan world, in which justice and human rights do not stop at the boundaries of states; or we can acknowledge the reality of boundaries and con-

strue the principles of justice as subordinate to those of national
sovereignty. Cosmopolitan ideals are evident in the discourse of
much of the human rights movement; but some recent liberal
theorists have shifted towards the relativism of their communitarian critics and even view liberal principles of justice as no more
than the principles of liberal societies. Rawls in particular now
hinges his theory of justice not on an abstract and idealized construction of an original position but on the actual ideals of citizens
of liberal democratic societies.[12] Here we see a surprising and
perhaps unstable convergence between abstract liberal theorists
and their communitarian critics.

ABSTRACTION WITH AND WITHOUT IDEALIZATION

Debates about gender and international justice are not merely
similar in that each is structured by a confrontation between
advocates of abstract principles and of context-sensitive judgements. In each debate the two parties depict these demands as
incompatible. However, the reason for the incompatibility may
be that many advocates of abstraction and of sensitivity to context
are making other, stronger claims that are indeed incompatible.
What these debates term 'abstraction' is often a set of specific,
unargued *idealizations* of human agency, rationality and life and
of the sovereignty and independence of states. And in each debate
what is described as attention to actual situations and contexts in
judging in fact often extends to building recognition of differences
into fundamental *principles* – and so amounts to *relativism*. These
conflations are avoidable.

Abstraction, taken strictly, is simply a matter of detaching
certain claims from others. Abstract reasoning hinges nothing on
the satisfaction or non-satisfaction of predicates from which it
abstracts. All uses of language must abstract more or less: the
most detailed describing cannot dent the indeterminacy of language. Indeed, it is not obvious that there is anything to object
to in very abstract principles of justice. Highly abstract ways of
reasoning are often admired (mathematics, physics) and frequently
well paid (accountancy, law). What is different about abstract
ethical reasoning? When we look at objections to 'abstract' ethical
principles and reasoning in detail it appears that they are often
objections not to *detachment* from certain predicates, but to the

inclusion of predicates that are false of the objects of the domains to which a theory is then applied. Reasoning that abstracts from some predicate makes claims that do not hinge on the objects to which the reasoning is applied satisfying that predicate. Reasoning that idealizes makes claims that hinge on the objects to which it is applied satisfying certain predicates. Where those predicates are unsatisfied the reasoning simply does not apply.

The principles and theories of justice to which the critics of 'abstract liberalism' object are indeed abstract. They take no account of many features of agents and societies. However, these principles and theories not only abstract but idealize. They assume, for example, accounts of rational choice whose claims about information, coherence, capacities to calculate and the like are not merely not satisfied by some deficient or backward agents, but are actually satisfied by no human agents (perhaps they are approximated, or at least admired, in restricted shopping and gambling contexts!). They also assume idealized accounts of the mutual independence of persons and their opportunities to pursue their individual 'conceptions of the good', and of the sovereignty and independence of states, that are false of all human beings and all states. Such idealizations no doubt have theoretical advantages: above all they allow us to construct models that can readily be manipulated. However, they fail to apply to most, if not all, practical problems of human choice and foreign policy.

If idealized descriptions are not simply abstracted from descriptions that are true of actual agents, they are not innocuous ways of extending the scope of reasoning. Each idealization posits an 'enhanced' version of the objects of the domain to which the model is applied. Idealizations may privilege certain sorts of human agent and life and certain sorts of society by covertly presenting (enhanced versions of) their specific characteristics as true of all human action and life. In this way covert gender chauvinism and an exaggerated view of state sovereignty can be combined with liberal principles. Idealization masquerading as abstraction yields theories that appear to apply widely, but which covertly exclude those who do not match a certain ideal, or match it less well than others. Those who are excluded are then seen as defective or inadequate. A reconsideration of debates about gender and international justice shows that the feminist and communitarian critics of liberal justice could legitimately attack spurious idealizations without impugning abstraction that eschews idealization.

GENDER AND IDEALIZED AGENTS

Liberal discussions of justice ostensibly hinge nothing on gender differences. They apply to individuals, considered in abstraction from specific identities, commitments and circumstances. Recent critics insist that liberal theories of justice are far from being as gender blind as their advocates claim. An instructive example is Rawls's *A Theory of Justice*. Rawls was particularly concerned to avoid an extravagant view of human agents. His principles of justice are those that would be chosen by agents in an 'original position' in which they know *less* rather than *more* than actual human agents. He conceives his work as carrying the social contract tradition to 'a higher level of abstraction'. In particular, agents in the original position do not know their social and economic position, their natural assets or their conceptions of the good.[13] The original position operationalizes the image of justice as blind to difference.

However, Rawls has at a certain point to introduce grounds for those in the original position to care about their successors. He suggests that we may think of them as heads or at other times as representatives of families, 'as being so to speak deputies for an everlasting moral agent or institution',[14] and that some form of family would be just. In doing so, he pre-empts the question of intra-familial justice. He pre-empts the question not by crude insistence that heads of families must be men, but by taking it as read that there is some just form of family which allows the interests of some to be justly represented by others. The shift from individuals to heads of families as agents of construction is not an innocent abstraction: it *assumes* a family structure which secures identity of interests between distinct individuals. It takes for granted that there is some just 'sexual contract',[15] that justice can presuppose a legitimate separation of 'private' from 'public' domains. This is idealization indeed: it buries the question of gender justice rather than resolving it. Rawls's text leaves it surprisingly obscure whether some (women?) are to be relegated to a 'private' sphere and represented by others (men?) in the construction of justice, whether both 'public' and 'private' realms are to be shared by all on equal terms or whether some (women?) alone are to carry the burdens of both spheres.[16]

The more radical feminist critique of abstract liberalism refuses not merely the suppressed gendering of the subject which Pateman and Okin detect in classical and contemporary liberal writers, but abstraction itself. In advocating an ethic of care these critics come close both to traditional misogynist positions and to ethical relativism. When the 'voices' of justice and of care are presented as alternatives between which we must choose, each is viewed as a complete approach to moral issues. However, the two in fact focus on different aspects of life. Justice is concerned with institutions, care and other virtues with character, which is vital in unmediated relationships with particular others (and perhaps also important in mediated relationships). The central difference between the 'voices' of justice and of care is not that they demand that we reason in different ways. Justice requires judgements about cases as well as abstract principles; care is principled as well as responsive to differences. Justice matters for impoverished providers because their predicament is one of institutionally structured poverty, which cannot be banished by idealizing an ethic of care and insisting on its place in face-to-face relationships.

IDEALIZED BOUNDARIES

A comparable slide from unavoidable abstraction to suspect idealization can be found in discussions of international justice. Discussions of global economic and political issues often take it for granted that the principal actors are states. Traditionally, the main divide in these discussions has been between realists, who contend that states, although agents, are exempt from moral obligations and criticism, and idealists, who insist that states are not merely agents but accountable agents, who must meet the demands of justice.[17]

However, in discussions of distributive justice, the salient issue has not been the conflict between idealists and realists but their agreement that state boundaries define the main actors in international affairs. These shared terms of debate endorse an exaggerated, idealized view of the agency and mutual independence of sovereign states, which is increasingly criticized as obsolete. The common ground on which realists and idealists traditionally debated international relations is being eroded as other actors, including international agencies, regional associations and above all transnational corporations, play a more and more significant role in world affairs.[18] A world that is partitioned into discrete and mutually impervious sovereign states is not an abstraction from our world, but an idealized version of it, or perhaps an idealized version of what it once was. Realists as well as idealists idealize the sovereignty of states.

Idealized conceptions both of state sovereignty and of state boundaries limit discussions of international distributive justice. Although long subject to theoretical questioning from advocates of human rights, who deny that states can be sovereign in determining the fates of individuals, many liberals are coy about criticizing rights' violations beyond boundaries. They limit criticism to violations of liberty rights and offer little account of the agency or responsibilities of institutions; they find it hard to see how justice could require that state boundaries be breached to reduce poverty that lies beyond them. We still speak of *international* rather than of *transnational* justice. Even those liberals who defend welfare rights are often concerned with welfare in one (rich) country. It is common to classify economic development of poorer regions as optional 'aid', not obligatory justice. Those who have tried to argue for global welfare rights within a liberal framework have to show who bears the obligations that correspond to these rights, and this has proved an uphill task.[19] Meanwhile liberals, like communitarians, confine justice within national boundaries. Liberals do so self-consciously and provisionally, communitarians on principle and unapologetically, others tacitly and without discussion.

ABSTRACTION WITHOUT IDEALIZATION

The only way to find theories that have wide scope is to abstract from the particularities of agents; but, when abstraction is displaced by idealization, we are not led to theories with wide scope but to theories that apply only to idealized agents.

This suggests that if we are interested in international or in gender justice we should resist the temptation to rely on idealizing models of human agency or national sovereignty. We should instead consider what sort of theory of justice we would have if we abstract but refuse to idealize any one conception of rationality or independence, and so avoid marginalizing or excluding those who do not live up to specific ideals of rationality or of independence from others. Abstraction without idealization may allow us to consider a wide range of human agents and institutional arrangements without hinging anything on the specific features of agents' traditions, ideologies and capacities to act. If we could do this, we might avoid idealized accounts of agency and sovereignty without following feminist and communitarian critics of abstract liberalism into relativism.

Recent discussions may simply have been mistaken in treating appeals to idealized and to relativized standards of rationality and agency as the only options. There are other possibilities. We do not have to hinge liberal arguments for rights or for the limits of government power either on the *hypothetical* consent of those who meet some *ideal* standard of rationality and mutual independence or on the *actual* acceptance of an outlook and its categories that *relativizes* consent to an established order. We could instead begin simply by abstracting from existing social orders. We could consider what principles of action must be adopted by agents who are numerous, diverse and *neither* ideally rational *nor* ideally independent of one another and yet avoid specific assumptions about these agents. We can bracket both idealizations and the status quo. The issues then becomes: how powerful and convincing an account of justice can we offer if we appeal neither to fictions of ideal rationality and independence nor to the contingencies of actual agents and institutions? What happens if we abstract without idealizing?

PLURALITY AND JUSTICE: WHO COUNTS?

Let us begin with the thought of a plurality of potentially interacting and diverse agents. This rules out two cases. First, it rules out the case where justice is not a problem because there is no plurality, or no genuine plurality, of agents, hence no potential for conflict between agents. (The action of agents in such a degenerate plurality might be automatically or necessarily co-ordinated, e.g. by instinct or by a pre-established harmony.) Second, it rules out hinging an account of justice on an assumed, contingent and determinate limit to the diversity of its members, which provides a common ground between them and permits a contingent, socially guaranteed convergence and co-ordination. The two cases that are ruled out are once again those that would base principles of justice on an assumed ideal convergence or an assumed actual historical or social convergence.

What does justice require of such a plurality? At least we can claim that their most basic principles must be ones that *could* be adopted by all. If they were not, at least some agents would have to be excluded from the plurality for whom the principles can hold, the boundaries of which would have to be drawn more narrowly.

Such a redrawing of boundaries is, of course, the very move often used to exclude women and foreigners, let alone foreign women, from the domain of justice. Those who exclude simply refuse to count certain others as members of a plurality of potentially interacting human agents. The universalist aspirations of an account of justice that hinges on the sharability of principles can easily be derailed by excluding some from the domain of justice without argument. So it is important to see the move for what it is. This can best be done by asking *who* makes the move.

The move is not made by idealized genderless theorists who live outside state and society. It is made by people who generally expect women to interact with them, to follow language and reason, to understand and take part in elaborate traditions and institutions, perhaps even to love, honour and obey. It is made by people who expect ordinary processes of translation, trade and negotiation to work with foreigners. To deny the agency of others with whom we interact in complex ways reeks of bad faith. Bad faith can be avoided only by counting as members of the plurality for whom principles of justice are to hold *anybody* with whom interaction is to be undertaken or held possible. The question then becomes: are there any principles which must be adopted by all members of a plurality of potentially interacting agents? We cannot simply stipulate that such principles are irrelevant for interactions with certain others on whose (no doubt imperfect) capacities to reason and (no doubt limited) abilities to act independently we know we depend.

If women were all transported to Betelgeuse, and so beyond all interaction with the remnant men on earth, neither men nor women would have to see the other as falling within the domain of justice. Less fancifully, since the ancient inhabitants of the Andes and their contemporaries in Anglo-Saxon England could not and did not interact, neither would have acted in bad faith if they excluded the other from the domain of justice. Neither of them could practise either justice or injustice to the other. Things are different for the actual men and women who inhabit the earth now: the potential for interaction cannot be assumed away, and others cannot be arbitrarily excluded from the domain of justice. We rely on global economic and political processes, so cannot consistently insist that justice (conveniently for the developed world) stops at state frontiers, any more than we can rely on women's rationality and their productive contribution and then argue that justice (conveniently for some men) stops at the edge of a supposed 'private' sphere, whose existence and demarcation are in fact presupposed in defining a 'public' sphere.

PLURALITY AND JUSTICE: WHAT PRINCIPLES?

Justice is then in the first place a matter of keeping to principles that can be adopted by any plurality of potentially interacting beings. But if we eschew both idealization and relativism, and rely on mere abstraction, will we have strong enough premises to identify those principles? Does a universalizability test cut any ice? Granted that universalizability is not uniformity (as some critics of abstract liberalism suppose), is it not too weak a demand on which to ground an account of justice? In particular, will not any internally coherent principle for individual action be a universalizable principle?[20]

We have, however, to remember that we are considering the case of a plurality of *potentially interacting* beings, that is of beings who share a world. Any principle of action that is adopted by all members of such pluralities alters the world that they share and becomes a background condition of their action. This is why certain principles of action which can coherently be held by one agent cannot be coherently proposed as principles for all. Examples of non-universalizable principles can illustrate the point. A principle of deception, which undermines trust, would, if universally adopted, make all trusting, hence all projects of deception, incoherent. Selective deception is on the cards: universal deception is impossible. Since nobody who hopes to deceive can coherently will that a principle of deception be fundamental to the practice of any plurality, justice requires that it be rejected. Equally, a policy of coercion, which seeks to destroy or undercut others' agency and independence, cannot (without incoherence) be universally prescribed by one who seeks to coerce, since its universal adoption puts any coercer's agency and plans to coerce at risk. Those who are victims of coercion cannot (while victims) also act on the principles on which their coercers act.[21] Equally, a principle of violence which damages the agency of some others cannot be universally acted on. Put quite generally, nobody whose own principles of action hinge on victimizing some, and so on destroying, paralysing or undercutting their capacities for action, can be committed to those same principles holding universally.[22]

To keep matters under control, let us imagine only that justice demands (at least) that action and institutions not be based on principles of deception and victimization. (There may be other principles of justice.) Still, we are far from showing just what justice demands, since we do not know what refusing to deceive or to coerce may demand in specific circumstances. These guidelines are highly indeterminate. We seem to have paid the classic price of abstraction. Highly abstract principles do not tell us what to do in a specific context.

However, abstract principles are only part of practical, or specifically of ethical, reasoning. Principles never determine their own applications; even the culturally specific principles that relativists favour do not determine their own applications. All practical reasoning requires judgement and deliberation by which principles are applied to particular cases. An account of gender and international justice is no exception. We need in particular to be able to judge what specific institutions and action are needed if poor women in poor economies are to be accorded justice.

PLURALITY AND JUSTICE: DELIBERATION WITHOUT RELATIVISM

Two background issues must be dealt with summarily before considering moves from abstract principles to determinate judgements. First, we have no reason to expect that principles of justice will provide any algorithm of rational choice. Nor do we need any algorithm for principles to be important. Even principles that provide only a set of side constraints on action may make exigent demands. Second, we have no reason to think that principles of justice are relevant only to the action of individuals. A full account of the agency of institutions would be a complex matter. I shall not go into it here, but will assume that it can be given and that institutions and practices, like individuals, must meet the demands of justice.

These moves, however, are preliminary to the main task of giving a more determinate account of what may be required if principles of deception or victimization are rejected. How, for example, can we judge whether specific types of family or economic activity are based on deception or victimize some people? Are all forms of hierarchy and subordination coercive? If not, how do we discern the boundaries of deceit and coercion in actual contexts? It is not hard to see that certain categories of individual action – for example, fraud or wife burning or battering – deceive or victimize, but other cases of deception and coercion by individuals are hard to adjudicate. It is also hard to judge whether social traditions that isolate or exclude women, or economic and familial arrangements that ensure their acute economic vulnerability, amount to modes of deceit and coercion.

In this chapter the task cannot be to reach determinate judgements about particular cases, but only to see whether reasoned moves from very abstract principles towards more specific principles, whose relevance and application to particular cases may be easier to assess, may be possible. It will not be enough to lean on the received criteria by which 'our' tradition or nation picks out ethically significant 'cases' or 'options' for approaching them. We beg questions if we assume that categories of thought that have been hospitable to male dominance and to imperialism can be decisive for discerning or judging justice to those whose problems have been marginalized and whose agency and capacities have been formed, perhaps deformed, by unjust institutions. We cannot rely uncritically on the categories of established discourse, including the discourse of social scientists and of the 'helping' professions, to pick out the significant problems. These categories are themselves matters for ethical concern and criticism.[23] We have, after all, no more reason to trust relativized discussions of justice, gender or boundaries than to trust idealized approaches unequivocally. Those discussions are no more free of theory and ideology than are idealized discussions of justice. Their ways of individuating typical problem cases may be familiar; but familiarity may mask contentious and unjust delimitations. If the received views of a society or tradition are taken as defining the domain of problems to which abstract principles of justice are applied, unvindicated ideals will be introduced and privileged, just as they are in idealized approaches to justice.

Some confirmation of the ways in which received descriptions of social relations reflect larger and disputed ideals is suggestive. Consider, for example, how issues of gender can be passed over as if invisible. We often find an enormous amount of shifting around in the choice of basic units of social analysis. In the shifts between descriptions that focus on individuals, wage-earners and heads of families, there is enough flexibility for the blunt facts of economic and other subordination of women to be veiled. Women's low wages can seem unworrying if the women are wives for whom others provide; their dependence on husbands and fathers can seem acceptable if they are after all wage-earning individuals, so not invidiously dependent. Reproductive labour may (with convenient ambiguity!) be thought of as priceless.[24] Wage-earning women's low pay can be seen as fitting their low skills and vindicating their domestic subordination to wage-earning men, who as 'heads of families' are entitled to discretionary expenditure and leisure that wage-earning women must do without because they (unlike men!) have family commitments. The gloomy evidence of social structures and habits of thought that classify women's contributions as less valuable, even when more onerous or more skilled, are evident enough. We continually find ourselves 'thinking about men as individuals who direct households and about women as family members'.[25]

There are equally serious reasons to mistrust the move from abstract principles to determinate judgements in discussions of individual motivation. These too are shaped by received views, and in milieux which are strongly individualist are easily diverted into attempts to pin blame for injustices on individuals. Women, after all, commonly acquiesce in their social and economic subordination. Are they then to be blamed for servility? Or are men to be blamed for oppressing or exploiting women?[26] Or do these individualist approaches to assigning blame lead no further than the higher bickering? It can seem that we have reasons to mistrust not only relativist approaches to gender justice but even the attempt to apply abstract, non-idealized principles of justice. But we do not inhabit an ideal world. Idealized conceptions of justice simply do not apply to international relations, social relations or individual acts in a world in which states, men and women *always* lack the capacities and the opportunities of idealized agents. States are not really sovereign; even superpowers have limited powers; and men and women are always more or less vulnerable, ignorant, insecure, lacking in confidence or means to challenge or oppose the status quo. In a world of agents with finite capacities and opportunities, poor women in poor economies differ not in kind but in degree in their dependence on others and in others' demands on them.

JUST DELIBERATION IN A WORLD OF VULNERABLE AGENTS

If we are to apply principles of justice that are neither idealized nor merely relative to actual societies to vulnerable lives and their predicaments, we must see how to move towards determinate judgements about actual cases. The principles of justice for which I have argued take us in this direction because they focus neither on the arrangements to which ideally rational and mutually independent beings would consent nor on the arrangements to which others in possibly oppressive situations do consent. Rather they ask which arrangements a plurality of interacting agents with finite capacities *could* consent to. I have suggested, provisionally, that this non-idealizing construction identifies the rejection of deception, coercion and other ways of victimizing others as principles of justice.

But principles are not enough. Non-idealizing abstraction avoids some problems but not others. If we are to move from abstract principles to determinate judgements we need to operationalize the idea of avoiding acting on unsharable principles, without subordinating it to the categories and views of the status quo. One reasonable way of doing so might be to ask to what extent the variable aspects of any arrangements that structure vulnerable lives are ones that *could have been refused or renegotiated by those whom they actually constrain*. If those affected by a given set of arrangements that could in principle be changed can in fact refuse or renegotiate them, their consent is no mere formality, but genuine, legitimating consent. If they could not but 'accept' those institutions, their 'consent' will not legitimate. The point of this way of operationalizing the notion of possible consent is that it neither ascribes ideal reasoning capacities and ideal independence from others to agents nor hinges legitimation on an actual 'consent' that may reflect injustice. On this account, justice requires that institutions, like acts, allow those on the receiving end, even if frail and dependent, to refuse or renegotiate any variable aspects of the roles and tasks assigned to them.

Dissent becomes harder when capacities to act are less developed and more vulnerable and when opportunities for independent action are restricted. Capacities to act are constrained both by lack of abilities and by commitments to others. Institutional arrangements can disable agency both by limiting capacities to reason and act independently and by increasing the demands to meet the needs and satisfy the desires of others. Apparent consent to such arrangements does not show that they are just. Whenever 'consent' reflects lack of capacity or opportunity to do anything but 'consent', it does not legitimate. Thinking in this way about justice we can see that *it demands more, not less, to be just to the vulnerable.* The vulnerable are much easier to deceive and to victimize than the strong: their 'consent' is all too easily elicited. If we are to judge proposals for action by seeing whether they involve serious deception or victimization (coercion or violence), *more* will be demanded when others are vulnerable than when they are secure and *most* when they are most vulnerable.[27] By contrast both idealized and relativized accounts of justice tend to conceal the fact that justice to the weak demands more than justice to the strong. Idealized accounts of justice tend to ignore vulnerability and relativized accounts tend to legitimate it.

ACHIEVING JUSTICE FOR IMPOVERISHED PROVIDERS

The lives of poor women in poor economies illustrate these points well. Consider, for example, daily commercial transactions and practices. Their justice, it is usually said, lies in the fact that arrangements are mutually agreed. But where there are great disparities of knowledge and vulnerability between agents, the 'agreement' of the weak may be spurious. They may have been duped by offers they did not understand or overwhelmed by 'offers' they dared not refuse. Within national jurisdictions these facts are well recognized and commercial practice is regulated to prevent pressure and fraud. Contracts can be voided for fraud; there are 'truth in lending' provisions; debt and bankruptcy will not lead to starvation; those with dependants can rely on a safety net of welfare rights. International economic transactions take place in a far less regulated space yet link agents with far greater disparities in power and resources. The weak can suffer both from particular others, who take advantage of their ignorance and vulnerability, and because nothing informs them about, or shields them from, the intended or unintended consequences either of distant or of local economic forces. The poor, and above all those who are impoverished providers, cannot refuse or renegotiate their role in economic structures or transactions which hurt them, even when these structures and transactions could in principle be changed. They are vulnerable not only to low wages, low standards of industrial safety, endemic debt and disadvantageous dependence on those who provide credit,[28] but also to disadvantageous patterns of entitlement within the family. For example, debtors who need further loans for survival cannot make much fuss about the terms creditors offer for purchasing their crops.[29] In many societies, the position of certain women – daughters-in-law, for example, and younger girls – is acutely vulnerable. Vulnerable agents on whom others depend are at the mercy both of market forces and of more powerful kin.

Idealized pictures of justice have tended to overlook the import of economic power: by idealizing the capacities and the mutual independence of those involved in market transactions, they obscure why the weak may be unable to dissent from arrangements proposed by the strong. They also tend to distinguish sharply between intended and unintended consequences and to view the latter as unavoidable 'forces'. Yet these forces are themselves the outcome of institutional arrangements and could be changed or modified, as they have been within many jurisdictions. The problem of shielding the weak from these forces is nothing to do with 'natural' processes and everything to do with the weakness of the voices that call for change. This is hardly surprising. Market institutions magnify the security and so the voices of the 'haves'. Formal democracy provides only slender and partial redress for the weak, and is often lacking.

Typical family structures also illustrate the gulf between ideally independent agents (whom market structures might suit) and actual powerlessness. These structures often draw a boundary between 'public' and 'private' domains, assign women (wives and daughters) to the 'private' domain and leave them with slender control of resources but heavy commitments to meet others' needs. They may lack adequate economic entitlements, effective enfranchisement or access to sources of information or debate by which to check or challenge the proposals and plans of more powerful family members. Women in this predicament lack security and must meet the demands of others (often fathers and husbands) who dominate them. Family structures can enable, even impose, forms of deception and domination. Where women are isolated, secluded, barred from education or wage earning, or have access to information only via the filter of more powerful family members, their judgement is weakened and their independence stunted. Often this vulnerability may be shielded by matching concern and restraint; often it will not. A rhetoric of familial concern and protective paternalism can easily camouflage callous lack of concern and legitimate deceptive acts and practices.

Similar points can be made about victimization. A principle of refusing coercion, for example, basically demands that action not undercut others' agency. If agents were all ideally independent of one another, they might find little difficulty in dissenting from many forms of attempted domination. However, family structures always limit independence and usually limit women's independence more. A woman who has no adequate entitlements of her own and insecure rights to a share in family property or income will not always be coerced, but is always vulnerable to coercion.[29] When her independence is also restricted by family responsibilities, she will be even easier to coerce. In these circumstances ostensible consent reveals little; it certainly does not legitimate forms of domination and subordination. Relations of dependence are not always or overtly coercive; but they provide structures of subordination within which it is all too easy to silence or trivialize the articulation of dissent. To guarantee that action is not based on principles which others cannot share, it is necessary to ensure that proposals that affect others are ones from which *they* can dissent. Institutionalized dependence tends to make dissent hard or impossible. Those who cannot secure economic independence or who cannot rely on others to take a share in caring for genuine dependants (children, the elderly) cannot easily say 'no' or set their own terms. They must go along with the proposals of the more powerful.

Genuine, legitimating consent is undermined by the very institutions which most readily secure an appearance of consent. The more relations with others are ones of structural dependence, the more the weak have to depend on trusting that the (relatively) strong will not exercise the advantages which proximity and relations of dependence give them. When the strong reliably show this restraint, there may *in fact* be no injustice within relationships which institutionalize dependence. However, institutions that rely too heavily on the self-restraint of the stronger cannot reliably avoid injustice. Whether the proposals of the strong are economic or sexual, whether they rely on the ignorance and isolation of the weak to deceive them, on their diminished opportunities for independent action or on the habits of deference and appeasement which become second nature for the weak, they ride on unjust social practices. *The weak risk recurrent injustice unless institutions are structured to secure the option of refusal or renegotiation of variable arrangements for those whose capacities and opportunities are limited.*

A woman who has no entitlements of her own lives at the discretion of other family members who have them, so is likely to have to go along even with proposals she greatly dislikes or judges imprudent. If she were an ideally independent agent, or even had the ordinary independence and opportunities of those who have entitlements adequate for themselves and their dependants, she could risk dissent from or at least renegotiate variable aspects of proposals that are put by those who control her means of life. Being powerless and vulnerable she cannot readily do either. Hence any consent that she offers is compromised and does not legitimate others' proposals. Just as we would find it absurd to hinge legitimating consent to medical treatment on procedures geared to the cognitive capacities and independence of a notional 'ideal rational patient', so we should find it absurd to hinge legitimating consent to others' plans on the cognitive capacities and independence of a notional ideal rational impoverished and dependent provider for others.

This is not to say that impoverished providers are irrational or wholly dependent or cannot consent. However, it is a matter of taking seriously the ways in which their capacities and their opportunities for action constrain their possibilities for refusal and negotiation. If they are to be treated with justice, others who interact with them must not rely on these reduced capacities and opportunities to impose their will. Those who do so rely on unjust institutional structures that enable deceit, coercion and forms of victimization.

In applying abstract, non-idealizing principles we have to take account not indeed of the actual beliefs, ideals or categories of others, which may reflect unjust traditions, but of others' actual *capacities* and *opportunities* to act – and their incapacities and lack of opportunities. This move does not lead back to relativism: no principle is endorsed because it is actually accepted. Put in general terms, we can use modal notions to identify principles but indicative ones to apply them. The principles of justice can be determined for any possible plurality: for they demand only the rejection of principles that cannot be shared by all members of a plurality. Judgements of the justice of actual situations are regulated but not entailed by these principles. The most significant features of actual situations that must be taken into account in judgements of justice are the security or vulnerability that allow actual others to dissent from and to seek change in variable aspects of the arrangements which structure their lives.

NOTES

This chapter is reprinted from Martha Nussbaum and Amartya Sen (eds), *The Quality of Life*, 1992, by permission of Oxford University Press; it is a revised version of a working paper originally prepared for the Quality of Life Conference of the World Institute for Development Economics Research (WIDER) of the United Nations University held in July 1988. I would particularly like to thank Deborah Fitzmaurice, James Griffin, Barbara Harriss, Martha Nussbaum and Sara Ruddick for help in writing this chapter.

1 Cf. Sara Ruddick, 'Maternal thinking', in her *Maternal Thinking: Towards a Politics of Peace*, Boston, MA: Beacon Press, 1989, pp. 13–27. Her account of women's predicament stresses that it reflects heavy demands as much as meagre resources. It is to be preferred, I think, because it does not take for granted that lack of resources is significant because 'public' while the press of others' demands is less so because merely 'private'.

2 See Susan Moller Okin, *Women in Western Political Thought*, Princeton, NJ: Princeton University Press, 1979; John Charvet, *Feminism*, London: Dent, 1982; Carole Pateman, *The Sexual Contract*, Cambridge: Polity Press, 1988; Alison Jaggar, *Feminist Politics and Human Nature*, Brighton: Harvester Press, 1983.

3 Alison Scott, 'Industrialization, gender segregation and stratification theory', in Rosemary Crompton and Michael Mann (eds), *Gender and Stratification*, Cambridge: Polity Press, 1986, pp. 154–89.

4 The differences run the gamut of social indicators. Most dramatically in some Third World countries women and girls do worse on a constellation of very basic social indicators: they die earlier, have worse health, eat less than other family members, earn less and go to school less. See Amartya K. Sen, 'Gender and co-operative conflicts', Working Paper of the World Institute for Development Economics Research (WIDER), Helsinki: United Nations University, 1987; and Barbara Harriss, 'Differential female mortality and health care in South Asia', Oxford: Queen Elizabeth House, Working Paper, 13, 1989, and 'Intrafamily distribution of hunger in south Asia', in Jean Drèze and Amartya K. Sen (eds), *The Political Economy of Hunger*, vol. I, *Entitlement and Well-being*, Oxford: Clarendon Press, 1991, pp. 351–424.

5 The problem is not merely one of resources. Where funds have been adequate for publicly funded welfare provision, this too has been

inadequate to eliminate the differences between the economic and political prospects of men and of women. For example, many women in the socialist countries find that they have secured greater equality in productive labour with no reduction in reproductive tasks. This is a reason for doubting that arguments establishing welfare rights – e.g. a right to food – take a broad enough view of disparities between men's and women's prospects.

6 E.g. Pateman, op. cit.; Susan Moller Okin, 'Justice and gender', *Philosophy and Public Affairs*, 16, 1987, pp. 42–72.

7 Carol Gilligan, *In a Different Voice: Psychological Theory and Women's Development*, Cambridge, MA: Harvard University Press, 1982; Eva Feder Kittay and Diana T. Meyers (eds), *Women and Moral Theory*, Totowa, NJ: Rowman & Littlefield, 1987; Genevieve Lloyd, *The Man of Reason: 'Male' and 'Female' in Western Philosophy*, London: Methuen, 1984; Carol McMillan, *Women, Reason and Nature*, Oxford: Blackwell, 1982; Sara Ruddick, 'Remarks on the sexual politics of reason', in Kittay and Meyers, op cit., pp. 237–60; Nell Noddings, *Caring*, Berkeley, CA: University of California Press, 1984; Nancy Chodorow, *The Reproduction of Mothering*, Berkeley, CA: University of California Press, 1978.

8 Many of those who urge respect for the 'other' voice insist that they do not reject the demands of justice, and that they see the two 'voices' as complementary rather than alternative. The positions taken by different writers, and by the same writers at different times, vary. The protests must be taken in context: those who appeal to 'women's experience' or 'women's thinking' appeal to a source that mirrors the traditional relegation of women to a 'private' sphere, and cannot readily shed those commitments. It is important to remember that those who care have traditionally been thought to have many cares.

9 Such approaches can be found in Michael Walzer, *Spheres of Justice: A Defence of Pluralism and Equality*, Oxford: Martin Robertson, 1983; Michael Sandel, *Liberalism and the Limits of Justice*, Cambridge: Cambridge University Press, 1982; Alasdair MacIntyre, *After Virtue*, London: Duckworth, 1981, and *Is Patriotism a Virtue?*, Lawrence, KA: Philosophy Department, University of Kansas, 1984; Bernard Williams, *Ethics and the Limits of Philosophy*, London: Fontana, 1985; and, perhaps most surprisingly, John Rawls, 'Justice as fairness: political not metaphysical', *Philosophy and Public Affairs*, 14, 1985, pp. 223–51. For some discussion of the implications of these works for international justice, see Onora O'Neill, 'Ethical reasoning and ideological pluralism', *Ethics*, 98, 1988, pp. 705–22.

10 Walzer acknowledges that this means that he can 'only begin to address the problems raised by mass poverty in many parts of the globe' (op. cit., p. 30). Critics may think that his approach in fact pre-empts answers to questions of global justice.

11 Communitarians can, however, take lesser loyalties seriously: where a state is divided into distinct national or ethical communities, those distinct traditions may in fact be the widest boundaries within which issues of justice can be debated and determined. They could argue

for secession from a multinational state; but they can say nothing
about what goes on beyond the boundaries of 'our' community. Cf.
Walzer, op. cit., p. 319.

12 Rawls, op. cit.

13 John Rawls, *A Theory of Justice*, Cambridge, MA: Harvard University
Press, 1971, pp. 11–12.

14 ibid., p. 128.

15 Cf. Pateman, op. cit.; Linda Nicholson, 'Feminism and Marx: integrating kinship with the economic', in Seyla Benhabib and Drucilla
Cornell (eds), *Feminism as Critique*, Cambridge: Polity Press, 1987.

16 See Okin, 'Justice and gender', op. cit., pp. 46–7. She considers
whether the original position abstracts from knowledge of one's sex.
Even if she is right in thinking that Rawls relies on a covertly
gendered account of the subject, this idealization may have little effect
on his theory of justice if the thought experiment of the original
position has so relentlessly suppressed difference that the supposed
plurality of voices is a fiction. In that case, we should read the work
as taking an idealized rather than a merely abstract view of rational
choice from the very start and so virtually appealing to a single,
ideally informed and dispassionate figure as the generator of the
principles of justice.

17 See Charles Beitz, *Political Theory and International Relations*, Princeton, NJ: Princeton University Press, 1979, for an account of debates
between realists and idealists.

18 Robert O. Keohane and Joseph S. Nye (eds), *Transnational Relations
and World Politics*, Cambridge, MA: Harvard University Press, 1970;
Steven Luper-Foy (ed.), *Problems of International Justice*, Boulder, CO:
Westview Press, 1988.

19 See Henry Shue, *Basic Rights: Subsistence, Affluence and US Foreign
Policy*, Princeton, NJ: Princeton University Press, 1980, 'Exporting
hazards', in Peter G. Brown and Henry Shue (eds), *Boundaries:
National Autonomy and Its Limits*, Totowa, NJ: Rowman & Littlefield,
1981, pp. 107–45, and 'The interdependence of duties', in Philip
Alston and K. Tomasevski (eds), *The Right to Food*, Dordrecht:
Nijhoff, 1984; Luper-Foy, op cit.; Onora O'Neill, *Faces of Hunger:
An Essay on Poverty, Justice and Development*, London: Allen & Unwin,
1986.

20 This is the hoary problem of formalism in Kantian ethics. For recent
discussions of aspects of the problem see Rüdiger Bittner, 'Maximen',
in G. Funke (ed.), *Akten des 4. Internationalen Kant-Kongresses*, Berlin:
De Gruyter, 1974; Otfried Höffe, 'Kants kategorischer Imperativ als
Kriterium des Sittlichen', *Zeitschrift für Philosophische Forschung*, 31,
1977, pp. 354–84; and Onora O'Neill, *Constructions of Reason: Exploration of Kant's Practical Philosophy*, Cambridge: Cambridge University
Press, 1989, pt II.

21 It does not follow that every coercive act is unjust – some coercion,
e.g. the use of sanctions to enforce law – may be the condition of
any reliable space for uncoerced action. In such cases, the appropriate
expression of an underlying principle of rejecting coercion is,

surprisingly and crucially for political argument, one that, taken out of context, might express an underlying principle of coercion.

22 I have put these matters briefly. For more extended treatment see the references in note 20 above.

23 Murray Edelman, 'The political language of the helping professions', in Michael J. Shapiro (ed.), *Language and Politics*, New York: New York University Press, 1984.

24 Nicholson, op. cit.

25 Judith Hicks Stiehm, 'The unit of political analysis: our Aristotelian hangover', in Sandra Harding and Merrill B. Hintikka (eds), *Discovering Reality: Feminist Perspectives on Epistemology, Metaphysics, Methodology and Philosophy of Science*, Dordrecht: Reidel, 1983, pp.31–43; Scott, op. cit.; Sen, op. cit.

26 Thomas Hill, 'Servility and self-respect', *Monist*, 57, 1973, pp. 87–104; Sen, op. cit.; Raymond Pfeiffer, 'The responsibility of men for the oppression of women', *Journal of Applied Philosophy*, 2, 1985, pp. 217–29; B. C. Postow, 'Economic dependence and self-respect', *The Philosophical Forum*, 10, 1978–9, pp. 181–201.

27 I focus here on the obligations of the strong rather than the rights of the weak. This is not to deny that agitation and resistance by the weak can help remind and persuade the strong of their obligations and make it more difficult for them to repudiate them. However, to focus primarily on rights falsifies the predicament of the weak, who are in no position to ensure that others meet their obligations.

28 Shue, 'The interdependence of duties', op cit.; Barbara Harriss, 'Merchants and markets of grain in south Asia', in Teodor Shanin (ed.), *Peasants and Peasant Societies*, Oxford: Blackwell, 1987, '*Differential female mortality and health care in south Asia*', op. cit., and 'Intrafamily distribution of hunger in south Asia', op. cit.

29 See Amartya K. Sen, *Poverty and Famines: An Essay on Entitlement and Deprivation*, Oxford: Clarendon Press, 1981, and 'Gender and co-operative conflicts', op. cit., for an account of entitlements.

Chapter 4

Marxism and universalism: group interests or a shared world?

Andrew Collier

UNIVERSAL OBLIGATION AS A PROBLEM FOR MARXISM

A contemporary humanitarian critic of Marxism might well argue thus: Marxism misplaces its concern for human emancipation and well-being; it is concerned with the self-emancipation of the industrial proletariat, which may have been the overriding moral issue in the nineteenth century, but is so no longer. The proletariat of the industrialized countries is a privileged class in world terms, and even if it were to emancipate itself the greater evil of Third World poverty would not be touched. The urgent task is to stop the transfer of wealth from the Third World to the richer nations, and start to reverse the flow. That is contrary to the interests of western workers as well as capitalists. We must transcend self-interest, collective as well as individual, and recognize that people have claims on us not by virtue of their class position, but by virtue of their needs as human beings.

On several empirical points, the Marxist may fault this commonly heard argument. It can be pointed out that so far from the proletariat belonging only to the richer countries, it now for the first time forms the majority of humankind; that the proletariat – north, south, east and west – has a common enemy in international capital, and shares this enemy with the world peasantry; that for long-theorized reasons, the proletariat is in a better position to defeat that enemy than the peasantry. But the moral core of this anti-Marxist case survives these replies: that Marxism does not appeal to altruism or to any universal values independent of time, place and social position; that it can therefore give no account of obligations outside the context of common interests within a collective; and that its attempt to show, without tacit appeal to altruism, or at least something larger than collective egoism, that it is 'really' in the interests of workers to sacrifice some of their prosperity for the sake of distant people, is implausible. Pushed into a corner, the Marxist may appear to be either a shamefaced altruist or a shameless collective egoist.

This is, of course, a dilemma for socialists (and workers' movements generally) only in the developed countries. The problems confronting Third World socialists are of a different nature: how to end their exploitation by multinationals and local oligarchies, and their oppression both by local despots and by bloody imperialist interventions. This struggle for self-emancipation may involve heroic self-sacrifice, and also moral dilemmas enough. But there can be no question here of any conflict between self-emancipation and human emancipation in general. They require one and the same struggle, the aim of which is that the Third World peoples may own and control their own lands and economies.

But the success of these struggles depends also on events in the richer nations. It is to socialists in these nations that the above criticisms are addressed. There is a serious case to answer here, but before it can be tackled, a preliminary issue needs to be cleared up. Marxism does not repudiate altruism in the way Hobbes does – by asserting egoism. Its argument is rather that both egoism and altruism are historical products; pre-capitalist humankind, and to a large degree capitalist humankind outside of market situations, is motivated by a complex mix of emotions, few of which could be called either egoistic or altruistic. In market situations, where every economic agent's survival depends on competitive success, egoism becomes a socially imposed necessity; and at the same time, demands for self-denial, the ideal of 'the *ascetic* but *rapacious* skinflint and the *ascetic* but *productive* slave',[1] become prominent. All non-egoistic motives then become assimilated to these in the moral ideology of the epoch.

I am fully committed to this repudiation of the egoism/altruism problematic, and my attempt to resolve the problem of universal obligations in a Marxist context is meant to avoid any appeal to either of these unnatural motives. But this change of conceptual terrain does not by itself resolve the problem. When Colletti praises Rousseau for contrasting the 'particular but real' social tie in the ancient republics with the universal but otherworldly ties in Christianity,[2] he sets up an opposition which, of course, he and every other Marxist would like to transcend in a humankind united by ties at once real and universal. But it is by no means easy to incorporate such an idea into the materialist conception of history. This is one of the unresolved problems of Milton Fisk's systematic attempt to base an ethics on that theory in his *Ethics and Society*.[3] In the name of naturalism, he makes all obligations rest on membership of classes and other real or supposed collectivities. But (aside from other criticisms which I have made elsewhere)[4] he (a) fails to show why loyalties to wider collectivities should prevail over those to narrower ones, and (b) fails to account for the 'good Samaritan' aspect of ethics, except in terms of anticipating the future unity of humankind under international socialism. But in so far as historical materialism is a non-teleological account of history, it is impossible to base present loyalties on future unities within its framework. They must be based on existing ties or give up the claim to be naturalistic. The characteristic problem of the Marxist position seems to stem from its combination of the Hegelian heritage which sees moralities as historically specific and institution-based, with a rejection of that teleology by which Hegelian ethics imparted a universalistic ideal to that view. A brief look at Bradley's version of Hegelian ethics will bring out the similarities with Fisk's version of Marxist ethics, and some inadequacies of both.

THE SOCIAL BASIS OF MORALITY: GROUPS OR RELATIONS?

First let me say that I believe Bradley's cases against both utilitarianism and Kantian ethics are broadly correct. I shall not reiterate them here. They take us to the point from which his chapter 'My station and its duties' sets out: that since we are social beings through and through, our fulfilment can only be through active participation in the historically specific institutions that make us what we are. The good for me is to do well those things that are enjoined on me by what I am: since I am a citizen, a husband, a father, a philosophy lecturer, a friend of this, that and the other person, a trade unionist, etc., I can live a good life only by being a good citizen, husband, etc.

One obvious point against this position is that it suppresses the question: ought I to be these things? Perhaps philosophizing is futile, marriage oppresses women, trade unions are against the public interest, etc. But I don't think this point is too damaging. For if I am to judge any of these roles to be unworthy, I must do so on the basis of its conflict with values which I have learnt somewhere, and where if not in the *other* institutions which have made me what I am?

Another objection is that this account gives no place for the 'moral reformer' or dissenter. It is true that Bradley says: 'to wish to be better than the world is already to be on the threshold of immorality'.[5] And what follows this remark is a polemic against moral dissenters (of a certain type) who want to change the world. In part, though, this polemic is justified – that is, in so far as it is directed against a Utopian type of moral reform which is not rooted in current life. And Bradley does go on to qualify his idea of 'my station and its duties' by saying that we can't simply take our morality from the moral world we are in, since

> That moral world, being in a state of historical development, is not and cannot be self-consistent; and the man must thus stand before and above inconsistencies, and reflect on them. This must lead to the knowledge that the world is not altogether as it should be, and to a process of trying to make it better.[6]

Bradley does not say much about this, no doubt because of his conservative temperament. But the point here is that one *could* say more about it, without departing from Bradley's main positions. To do so one would need to write a chapter 'My station and its contradictions'. This would make it possible to draw the dividing line between the moral Utopian of whom Bradley's criticisms are just, and the person whose dissent is based on sensitivity to real contradictions in existing institutions.

In addition to these points, Bradley touches on an issue which shows a more fundamental inadequacy in his theory, at least in so far as he tends to see the 'society' which makes us what we are as most fully bodied forth in the state. He notes, in passing, that 'the community in which he is a member may be in a confused or rotten condition, so that in it right and might do not always go together'.[7] It is tempting for the socialist to say: 'but might and right have *never* gone together', but this would miss a serious point. While the bourgeois state obviously protects the bourgeoisie from classes which would supplant it, it also *usually* acts as a restraint and corrective to the predatory drive of the other powerful agencies of bourgeois society, and we socialists often find ourselves co-operating with it against them – and rightly so. We support nationalization and oppose privatization even while recognizing that state ownership under capitalism is a form of capitalism, not an alternative to it; many socialists find their 'station and its duties' in state education, health or other public service institutions, and would be loath to work for private enterprise in these areas; and we do not in practice (though some do in theory) regard the police consistently as enemies: we would give them all the assistance we could in catching a rapist, or even (in many cases) a burglar. The sort of state to which Bradley's remark applies is an exceptional (though not uncommon) one even within class societies. It is one in which the state machine aggravates rather than limits the oppression inherent in most societies. This would apply to fascism and military dictatorship, and to governments such as Mrs Thatcher's, which, while retaining the forms of liberal democracy, make the liberation of the big predators the aim of government.

The problem which the recognition of such states makes for Bradley is that, assuming them to be long-lasting, the 'moral man' in them ought to be not merely unfulfilled, but non-existent. For if, in accordance with the old anecdote, the way to make your son a good man is to make him a citizen of a good state, the person born and bred in a corrupt state can only be corrupt. The prospect of reforming corrupt states would then be very bleak indeed. But it is not so: the peoples of Cuba, Portugal, Nicaragua and Romania overthrew generations-long corrupt regimes.

How does Bradley's ethics need to be modified to accommodate these points? One obvious modification will not do the job. I mean the substitution of *classes* for *states* as the dominant form of moral organism. In many ways, this view is inferior to Bradley's, since it narrows the content of morality in contrast to the extremely rich notion of the good life presented by Bradley. It does so because, while we *are* made what we are by our 'society' (in some sense of that word – though this should not be confused with the nation-state), and part of what we are is members of classes (and other social groups), we are not, and could not be, made what we are by our class (or other social group). Just as, according to Marx, people make one another but do not make themselves,[8] so classes, sexes, ethnic groups, etc. – at least 'in the first place and for the most part' – make each other but not themselves. This, as I have argued elsewhere, is the fatal flaw in Milton Fisk's ethics, which in many ways is close to Bradley's, with classes (and other oppressed groups) replacing nations, though Bradley is doubtless not the source of Fisk's ideas – his name is not even in the index of *Ethics and Society*.

To begin to resolve both Bradley's and Fisk's problems, we should take our starting point from Marx's dictum that 'society does not consist of individuals, but expresses the sum of the relations within which individuals stand'.[9] Society is not a group – nor, strictly speaking, is it an organism: it is a network of relations. For Bradley, societies as organisms are in the foreground, rather than the relations which make up society (even though he is not *here* arguing the unreality of relations). Organisms with their own teleology make us what we are for both Bradley and Fisk – with nation-states foregrounded by Bradley, classes by Fisk. There is a fundamental difference between the relational social ontology of Marx and this 'organicism'. Not that Marx's language is not organicist – it often is, but organisms are defined in terms of relations rather than vice versa. Marx thus presents a genuine 'third way' between atomism and holism. Two points will make this clearer, and forestall interpretations which would make Marx's relational ontology collapse back into atomism or holism.

(1) It is not an 'atomism of relations'; the relations themselves can exist only in the context of other relations, forming an interconnecting network.

(2) Such a network – 'society' – is not a count-noun. It does not make sense to ask how many societies there are in the world – nor is there only one society. There is society – not societies or a society. Society is an open-textured network, which can be divided in various ways for the purposes of description and analysis, but these divisions are always more or less artificial.

Every ethics presupposes a social ontology. Hegel's organicism rescued Marx from the temptations of social atomism and its ethical theories (utilitarianism, Kant, subjectivism); when Marx broke with Hegel's social ontology and developed his own, he said little about its ethical corollaries. Today, many socialists have the social atomists' suspicion of institutions larger than the individual and smaller than humankind. They see in them *alien-*

ation, rather than that *objectification* without which we would be condemned to solipsism. As a result, much socialist writing on e.g. education or the family is really liberal individualism projected to a Utopian extreme: more like Godwin than Marx. A retrieval of idealist ethics – Hegel, T. H. Green, Bradley – is a valuable corrective to this. However, it is not the last word.

What, then, are the implications of Marx's relational ontology of society for ethics? It suggests that the source and locus of values/virtues/duties are not the *telos* of a whole, nor the rights or interests of individuals, but the lattice of relations in which we are enmeshed. Says Sartre: 'in this world in which I engage myself, values spring up like partridges'; except that we don't, in the first place and for the most part, engage ourselves: we are, in Heidegger's phrase, thrown into the world.

On this view, the possibility of dissent from a corrupt society is no longer surprising, for though the 'totality' as represented by the state may be corrupt, the relations which make individuals what they are will hardly be corrupt through and through. We are what we are, not primarily through our participation in the state as citizens, but through our participation in e.g. trade unions, families, friendships, neighbourhoods, baby-sitting circles, churches, learned societies, pubs, women's groups, political parties. The prevalence of membership organizations in this list should not mislead us: it is not membership but relating that is crucial. Relating, however, not primarily as something that we *do*, but as what makes us what we are.

At this point, it may be helpful to say something about the 'rational kernel' of two notions that I have criticized rather severely elsewhere:[10] 'pre-figurative politics' and 'personal politics'. This rational kernel can be extracted, in the time-honoured Marxist way of extracting rational kernels, by *inversion*. It is not the case that we will bring socialism nearer by acting as if it were already here, nor by transforming our personal relationships in the light of as yet unrealized social values. But it is only because we have relationships – personal and otherwise – which generate non-market and non-oppressive values, that we can conceive a desire for socialism, or come under an obligation to work for it. If the institutions just listed became thoroughly reconstituted along purely market lines, as some evil people seem to wish, the basis in existing life for a socialist project would be destroyed – along with the recognizably human character of our species which, mercifully, could not survive long under these conditions. This means that socialists are certainly beholden to conserve, reproduce and develop such non-market and non-oppressive relations and institutions – though it is important that the conservative, non-Utopian nature of this duty is recognized.

THE SOCIAL BASIS OF MORALITY: SHARED WORLDS

Where has this got us so far? I am assuming that underlying every ethics there is a social ontology. I have distinguished Marx's relational social ontology from, on the one hand, 'abstract individualism', the social ontology that underlies the idea that egoism is self-explanatory, and rules us except in so far as it is overridden by some imperative or ideal external to the individual's desires – altruism or justice or the categorical imperative; and, on the other hand, from holistic or collectivist social ontologies such as those of post-Hegelian idealism, or some Marxists such as Milton Fisk, which form the foundation of theories of obligation as obligation to groups of which one is a member.

It remains to say what moral theory corresponds to Marx's relational social ontology, and how it accounts for *universal* obligation, going beyond group egoism and hence national or class or hemispheric narrowness. I shall take a slightly zigzag path to get to this destination.

First, let us look at one paradigm of ethics 'beyond egoism and altruism': that of the early Sartre.[11] He claims that, phenomenologically, as a general feature of unreflective desires, the quality of desirability attaches to what is desired, rather than the quality of desirousness attaching to the desirer. He cites the example of running for a bus; one is conscious, not of oneself as having to catch a bus, but of the bus as having to be caught. Likewise, to take a morally non-trivial example (Sartre's example, though I extend it a bit), if I see that Pierre has fallen into the lake, I am aware, at the unreflective level, of Pierre-needing-to-be-helped. Only if I come to reflect on this situation, might I come to think either (a) it is my duty to help Pierre, or (b) wouldn't I look a fine fellow if I rescued Pierre, or (c) I'm damned if I'm getting my clothes wet – let him drown. The unreflective desire to help Pierre, i.e. the consciousness of Pierre-needing-to-be-helped, is clearly seen by Sartre as the 'authentic' one, while both the egoistic and altruistic variations are corrupt. I share this view, but I think his account of it is inadequate. 'Reflection poisons desire', he says; yet he also holds up the possibility of a kind of reflection that does not. Perhaps it is not reflection, but an atomist social ontology which poisons desire – think of Hobbes's excuse for being generous to a beggar. To clarify the nature of this atomism and its alternative, let us return to Marx.

Consider our nature as workers. I am not committing myself to the idea that this is our 'essence', as in Marx's early humanism. Nevertheless, we are so constituted that we must transform nature with and into artefacts in order to live. In so far as the nature of a species is given by its ecological niche, and our niche is a niche for workers (hence both our mobility between habitats and our dependence on artefacts), this is a fundamental ontological category. And a worker is not a worker without tools and raw materials – or, except exceptionally, fellow workers. His or her mental and physical constitution is not enough. Our bodies – if this means the physical beings that are essential to what we are – do not end with the epidermis. They include the means and objects of our labour. One might say, in a Heideggerian vein, our worlds are our bodies. Marx *did* say that nature is our inorganic body.

If this is so, it is not to be marvelled at that values, demands, etc., should spring up in our worlds, even at a distance from our bodies in the narrow sense. It is no more metaphorical to say that the quality of having to be caught exists in the bus than to say that the pain is in my foot (when a reductive neurophysiologist might want to locate it in my brain). I do not deny that my brain has to be in a certain state for either the bus to have to be caught or the foot to hurt. But in the world we inhabit, as opposed to speculative mechanistic reductions of it, the pain is in my foot, and the bus has to be caught. *A fortiori*, since our worlds are social worlds in which other people are essentially present, there should be nothing more puzzling about our being moved by the needs of others than about our being moved by the needs of our own limbs and organs.

Why is this notion so strange to us, and social atomism so familiar to common sense? I have already suggested that capitalism imposes the egoism/altruism dichotomy on us; it also imposes the underlying social atomism on our 'common sense'. For under capitalism, the worker is a proletarian, i.e. someone who is *not* a worker until they sell their labour power and thereby be allowed access to their exosomatic limbs and organs. So far as the 'labour market' is concerned, self-ownership does end at the skin, and what is left has to be sold in temporal chunks in order to recover the practical unity of one's being as a worker. Outside the 'labour market', though, we retain some of the non-atomistic awareness of ourselves as worlds, in the way we define ourselves in terms of our houses and familiar objects and haunts, as well as, most importantly, our 'significant others'. If my 'mind' is united to a 'body', that body includes my clothes, bicycle, habitat, and the people who are close to me, not just my brain, limbs, organs, etc. It may be said that, while I do not currently share my arm or kidney with other people, I do share the house I live in, the roads I travel on, etc. But the former point is not necessarily so; my body is not unconditionally mine and no one else's. If my little boy needs to be lifted down from a wall he has climbed, it is my arms that he uses; to a degree, they are his arms. Our worlds are our bodies, but they are in some measure shared worlds, shared bodies. And I take this to be the source of the so-called other-regarding part of ethics. It also, incidentally, founds certain obligations to beings other than human beings.

Now if I had the space I could easily fill in plausible details about the values and obligations arising out of our sharing of our worlds. But it would not get me much nearer my goal in this chapter. I would be talking about my obligations to my family and friends and neighbours and colleagues or, at most, my fellow townsfolk of Southampton. And my task is to show how universal obligations, which require us in the richer hemisphere to take sides against our own communities, economically speaking, can be founded naturalistically in our social being.

FROM THE SHARING OF THE WORLD TO UNIVERSAL OBLIGATION

If everyday ethics is founded in shared worlds, the ethics of universal obligation is founded in the (one) shared world – and not in the trivial sense that we all live on the third planet from the sun. In 1600, the peoples of, say, England and India had no obligations to each other beyond abstention from piracy, and hospitality to the occasional visitor. (And at that time, I am told, the Indian people's standard of living was a little higher than that of the English.) Today, however, we have become one world in two ways: economically, in that we are massively dependent on goods produced all over the world; and ecologically, in that we are *all* threatened by the ecological irresponsibility of *all*. The whole planet has become a shared world, even for those who never leave their village. Thus, a tie which is both real and universal has arrived; not yet in the form of a real collectivity embracing humankind, but of real relations of mutual dependence through the sharing of the world; and it is from just such relations, I have suggested, that values and obligations arise.

Marxist position

What does this mean in terms of the question what place Third World claims should have on workers' movements for self-emancipation in the industrialized countries? Emancipation for any group means its coming to have power over that on which it is dependent. Socialist politics aims to bring economic resources into the collective power of the workers. But such power *within any nation-state* leaves the workers in that state dependent on the rest of the world – a dependence which, in the absence of global planning, takes the form of subjection to the world market. It is well known how nation-states calling themselves socialist have behaved much like capitalist enterprises, for example, in their recklessness about environmental damage, under compulsion to compete in the world market. Emancipation from the world market can only be achieved by sharing in the collective power of humankind over planetary resources, and so passing from a universal tie which is only that of interdependence, to one that is also one of joint management of that interdependence, collective self-direction. This is made much the more urgent by the second, ecological aspect of the shared world; unless global resources are cared for by an enforceable global plan, we are done for.

In conclusion, I need to introduce a further clarification about what I am trying to do. While it is a commonplace of non-naturalistic ethics that it is one thing to show what ought to be done, another to get anyone to do it, naturalistic ethics might be thought to have merged these two tasks. For if you show what someone ought to do on the basis of what they are, not what they ought to be, will they not do it? In the prdsent c're, hf H bl'hl tn rhnv th't, in a shared world, some workers cannot be emancipated unless all are, am I not committed to the view that workers' movements *would in fact* pursue universal emancipation if only they were well enough informed, and is that not over-optimistic?

Well, if it is implausibly optimistic, that is for the following reason: the sort of global common ownership which I have said is a condition of workers' emancipation would inevitably lead to a massive flow of wealth from the richer to the poorer countries, and hence a reduction in the material consumption of western workers.[12] Hence their interest in emancipation and their interest in material consumption pull opposite ways. If some wish to sell their birthright for a mess of pottage, what can be said to them? Of course, if the mess of pottage means retaining the free market, something can be said, namely that this is a recipe for ecological disaster which will sooner or later – probably sooner – deprive us of birthright and pottage alike. But there is perhaps a third alternative: the collaboration of the rich countries in imposing *their* common plan – conceivably if improbably an ecologically sustainable one – on the poorer countries in a single, neo-imperialist world order. Western workers might occupy rungs somewhere in the middle of the ladder of oppression, and maintain their level of material consumption while acquiescing in a regime that would surely require frequent and bloody wars of global counter-insurgency, with all the consequent ill effects on the oppressor-nations. One can point out the unfree and unattractive features of this neo-imperialist alternative. But what can one say to someone who, with open eyes, chooses this option? My unsatisfying answer is: *nothing*, any more than Marxists have ever had anything to say to persuade millionaires to cross the barricades. So long as we remain within the limits of a historically situated naturalism,[13] which derives people's obligations from their historically specific social being, we have to forgo the idea of obligations incumbent upon all; what I have tried to incorporate in such an ethics is obligation *to* all, and incumbent on all proletarians *as proletarians*. Such obligations have no hold on the oppressors, and in so far as proletarians in the neo-imperialist countries occupy what have come to be called 'contradictory class locations', these obligations will have to compete for their hold on them too. We are left saying something like: in so far as you want your class to be emancipated, work for universal human emancipation through common ownership of the world.[14]

CONCLUDING REMARKS

To sum up: it has long been a byword among socialists that we cannot be free while others are in chains. But this is often said without any reason why, and may thus be taken as a pious platitude. I hope to have given some sort of non-mysterious account of it. But there are two difficulties that I would like to mention in conclusion.

A criticism sometimes levelled at the position I have defended is that by making certain obligations dependent upon class position, it lets the capitalists off the moral hook. I reply that morality does not have hooks. It is about how we should live, not whom we should blame. If the knowledge that capitalists act as they do because of their class position softens the personal hatred that we might otherwise feel for them, as a passage in the preface to *Capital* suggests,[15] I am a good enough Spinozist to say 'so much the better'. It certainly doesn't weaken the desire to dispossess them: 'we wrestle not against flesh and blood, but against principalities and powers'. If it is asked how I account for the occasional capitalist who *does* cross the barricade, I would say that my account of the possibility of non-corrupt individuals in a corrupt state applies here too. Capitalists are related to their fellow creatures in other ways as well as those attendant upon their being capitalists. These other ways may generate values other than capitalist ones.[16]

A more difficult point to answer concerns the appearance of 'all-or-nothingness' in my account of liberation. If I have only shown that some cannot be *totally* free unless all are free, I have not shown much, since total liberation is a mere Utopia, or at best a regulative idea. Real acts of liberation, however revolutionary, have always been partial and usually ambiguous: liberation in one respect may come with intensified oppression in others. There is no royal road to liberation. And I have not shown that the scrappy bits of partial liberation in which human emancipation consists (has always consisted) are intrinsically related in such a way that the liberatory interests of the workers of the two hemispheres are connected.

A brief indication of some such connections will have to suffice. Although the integrated neo-imperialist consolidation sketched above has not so far occurred, there is a lot of that sort of thing about. The Gulf War shows that. And every time an imperialist nation gets away with such things, the exploited within that nation are weakened in many ways: state repressive power is increased, persecution of ethnic minorities legitimated, dissent isolated, the exploited are divided and their resolve weakened by nationalist ideology, the workers are made to pay for costly imperialist adventures, and so on. These piecemeal oppressions are the stuff of which the neo-imperialist world order is being constructed; and every setback for that world order is a step towards liberation for the Third World and for the exploited of the capitalist nations alike.

One summary of the socialist project might be: where there had been relations of involuntary mutual dependence, let there be relations of co-operation towards a common plan. The political implication of the foregoing argument is a new internationalism embodied in concrete forms of co-operation between workers across the hemispheres. Multinational corporations necessitate multinational trade union solidarity; the struggle for the rain-forests unites, potentially, forest peoples with all whose concern for their planet is not outweighed by profits from tropical timber or fast food chains; since the end of the cold war, peace move-ments are inevitably directed mainly against imperialist inter-ventions in the Third World, and are therefore natural allies of Third World movements for liberation from imperialism. Liber-ation movements in the west need to become linked, not just by goodwill, but organically, with those in the Third World.

Third World liberation movements have often been victorious to the extent of forming governments, expropriating the exploiters and expelling imperialist armies. But economic block-ades, subversion and threats from imperialist powers, even when they do not succeed in overthrowing the new regimes, invariably deflect them from their programmes of self-emancipation, whether in the intended way, by imposing concessions, or by driving them into a permanent state of siege. In the absence of any allied states in the west, and even of the buffer against western imperialism which was previously provided by the Warsaw Pact countries (whose recent changes have been a mixed blessing for their citizens, but an unmitigated loss for the Third World), liberation movements in the Third World have a chance of success only to the extent that the imperialism of western powers is weakened from within. Global internationalism is, as never before, a necessary condition of furthering the socialist project of liberation anywhere.

NOTES

1 Karl Marx, *Early Writings*, Harmondsworth: Penguin, 1975, p. 361.
2 Lucio Colletti, *Marxism and Hegel*, London: New Left Books, 1973. It is worth noting in passing that Rousseau's account of Christianity, which Colletti accepts uncritically, is not defensible with regard to the early church. Its ties were far from otherworldly: they included community of goods within the local church (Acts 4.32), and equalization between rich and poor churches (2 Corinthians 8.14). Neither were the ties universal: they bound Christians, not human beings as such.
3 Milton Fisk, *Ethics and Society*, Brighton: Harvester Press 1980.
4 In my article 'Milton Fisk, Marxism and ethics', *Radical Philosophy*, 36, 1984, pp. 20–6.
5 F. H. Bradley, *Ethical Studies*, London: Oxford University Press, 1962, p. 199.
6 ibid., p. 204.
7 ibid., pp. 203–4.
8 Karl Marx and Frederick Engels, *Collected Works*, vol. 5., London: Lawrence & Wishart, 1976, p. 52.
9 Karl Marx, *Grundrisse*, Harmondsworth: Penguin, 1973, p. 265.
10 In my *Scientific Realism and Socialist Thought*, Hemel Hempstead: Harvester Press, 1989, and at greater length in my *Socialist Reasoning*, London: Pluto Press, 1990.
11 Jean-Paul Sartre, *The Transcendence of the Ego*, New York: Noonday, 1957.
12 In saying that material consumption would have to be reduced in the west, I am not saying that western workers would be, in general terms, worse off. In that case, one really would have to appeal to altruism of the sort I have called unnatural or else abandon hope of socialism in the west. I assume that socialism would bring western workers adequate housing and health care, healthier and more agreeable food, a more attractive environment, more free time and countless other goods which are of course 'material': I am certainly not contrasting material consumption with some 'immaterial' emancipation. But if 'material' has to be taken in a colloquial sense here, 'consumption' has to be taken in a strict one, referring, not to the enjoyment of any social product, but to the using up of scarce resources. The ecology movement has drawn attention to the fact that limited world resources preclude any 'levelling up' of world consumption to western standards. Socialism would give us in the west some things that we haven't got, but it would also deprive us of some things we have got.
13 My argument is elliptical in that I assume both ethical naturalism and

a certain substantive critique of the world market. I refer readers to chs 4 and 3 respectively of my book *Socialist Reasoning*, op. cit.

14 For those familiar with Kant's classification of imperatives: this 'in so far as' form might be called a defeasible assertoric imperative.

15 'I do not by any means depict the capitalist and the landowner in rosy colours. But individuals are dealt with here only in so far as they are the personifications of economic categories, the bearers of particular class-relations and interests. My standpoint, from which the development of the economic formation of society is viewed as a process of natural history, can less than any other make the individual responsible for relations whose creature he remains, socially speaking, however much he may subjectively raise himself above them' (Karl Marx, *Capital*, vol. 1, Harmondsworth: Penguin, 1976, p. 92).

16 Does this point open the door to a theory of universal obligation, such as I have declared impossible? It certainly concedes that capitalists may, as individuals, occupy contradictory moral positions, such that the sort of morality that motivater rncialists may speak to them too, even though its voice is likely to be drowned by voices closer to the capitalist ear. But there is no necessity that this should be so; it is quite possible that people exist for whom no relations but the cash nexus have any significance. They may even have a worked out moral code on this basis – perhaps along Nozickian lines – and may lead moral lives in accordance with that code. But there is nothing in their condition to which an ethic of solidarity and emancipation could speak. That is what I meant by referring to them earlier, speaking from the standpoint of the latter ethic, as evil.

Chapter 5

Sustainability and the right to development

Nigel Dower

In recent years two ideas have gained prominence in international thinking about development – that of 'sustainable development' and that of the 'right to development'. The former has become particularly fashionable since the use of it in the Brundtland Report (1987), and the latter received its formal launch, after some years of gestation, in the United Nations *Declaration on the Right to Development* in December 1986. In this chapter I explore a number of philosophical problems to do with these two ideas and their juxtaposition, and conclude with a highly qualified endorsement of a 'right to sustainable development'.

SUSTAINABLE DEVELOPMENT

Although the phrase 'sustainable development' makes no explicit reference to the environment, it is quite clear that the context in which the idea has gained prominence is that of environmental problems, both to do with the using up of resources and the problems of future shortages, and to do with the general effects of human activity, particularly industrial activity, on the natural environment – in terms of pollution, land degradation, alteration of the atmosphere, and so on.

Maybe in the abstract sustainable development is as much about sustaining the social, political and economic basis of development as about anything else. But the core idea of sustainable development in the modern context is that of a kind of development (i.e. socio-economic process), whether in poorer countries or in richer countries, which so treats the natural environment that the process of development, or at least the products or benefits of that process, can continue into the future in a sustainable way, both for

ourselves and our children, and for future generations. As the
Brundtland Report puts it: 'Humanity has the ability to make
development sustainable – to ensure that it meets the needs of the
present without compromising the ability of future generations to
meet their own needs.'[1]

Given then the value assumption, based on sheer collective
enlightened interests if not on moral concerns for the future, that
development ought to be sustainable, the key practical challenge
has become that of working out strategies for development that
satisfy this condition of sustainability. It is fair to say that the
Brundtland Report, the Pearce Report (advocating sustainable
development for the UK)[2] and most political parties which have
adopted a 'green' agenda assume that such policies are about
economic growth, i.e. a new kind of economic growth which is
environmentally friendly. As we shall see later, this assumption
that sustainability is combinable with economic growth may turn
out to be highly suspect.

THE RIGHT TO DEVELOPMENT

The *Declaration on the Right to Development* asserts that all human
beings have an inalienable human right to development, which it
characterizes as follows:

> Development is a comprehensive economic, social, cultural and
> political process, which aims at the constant improvement of
> the well-being of the entire population and of all its individuals
> on the basis of their active, free and meaningful participation
> in development and in the fair distribution of benefits resulting
> therefrom.[3]

What is interesting is that it clearly grounds the 'right to development' in the idea of human rights as expressed in earlier UN
declarations and covenants. It is because development is a process
in which human rights are progressively realized that people have
a right to it. The right to development so to speak makes explicit
what has been implicit in earlier human rights assertions, namely
that if people have rights they have rights to the conditions
necessary for the realization of those rights. What the word 'development' indicates is that, if those necessary conditions cannot
now be met, at least a process of moving towards them and thus
progressively realizing them is something which people have a

right to. This is especially evident with regard to a whole range of rights such as economic rights and rights to subsistence, which require economic resources and institutional infrastructures, which simply may not be available in many poorer countries.

Second, the operational context of this declaration is that nation-states have a right to development, and that governments have special obligations to realize the right to development, both nationally and internationally. Indeed, subsequent work in the UN Commission on Human Rights is precisely concerned with finding ways of implementing such rights and obligations in international law. The whole UN process of declaring and implementing a right to development can thus also be seen as a way of making explicit (and effective) the idea that human rights generate moral obligations which are international or global in scope, not just national.[4]

A RIGHT TO SUSTAINABLE DEVELOPMENT?

Why cannot the two ideas briefly sketched above be fused together? After all, if what the idea of 'sustainable development' really brings out is the fact that the forms of development that should be pursued are sustainable forms, and the idea of a right to development simply stresses that development is based on human rights and on duties, national and international, to promote it, surely we can acknowledge that people have a right to sustainable development. This would be then a right to the kinds of social, political and economic changes which both improve the well-being of people now and preserve the conditions (environmental, institutional, etc.) so that people in the future can achieve well-being as well.

Now such a synthesis does seem to make intuitive sense. Indeed, if one accepts that there are human rights and that sustainability is a necessary element to a satisfactory definition of development, and that a right to development is grounded derivatively in the realization of human rights, then intellectually there seems no alternative. And this broadly is the conclusion I reach at the end of the chapter. What on the face of it is problematic about fusing the two ideas of sustainability and rights together in this way is this:

(a) Whatever the merits of the attempts to bring together the concerns of the environmentalist with the concerns of the developmentalist under the umbrella of one phrase, there remain deep divisions between them. The former are concerned to contain or even question development as growth, for the sake of their concerns for future well-being or their concerns for the natural environment or biosphere in its own right. The latter are concerned with the current economic well-being of people, and, in the case of poorer countries, with strong international commitment to further such development. The phrase 'sustainable development' already contains this tension, but the phrase 'right to sustainable development' only accentuates it.

(b) The agenda behind 'rights' discourse is essentially that even if all basic human rights are not now realizable in the world (because of economic limitations) then at least they will be realizable once sufficient economic and institutional changes in the world have taken place. (Development generally is premised upon the real possibility – though not inevitability – of progress.) This simply comes up against a very different worldview of many who are impressed by the seriousness of our environmental predicament – the idea that universal growth is not possible and that the extensive failure to meet basic human needs will remain part of and indeed will become a larger part of the human predicament.

These problems are I think genuine problems for anyone wishing to assert a right to sustainable development. But they can I think be met, once our ideas of sustainability and development and the right to development are more fully developed. To say they can be met does depend upon certain broad empirical assumptions in addition to certain lines of philosophical argument and analysis, and as a philosopher I cannot authoritatively assess those assumptions. The chapter is premised upon a broad 'middle ground' set of assumptions about the developmental and environmental possibilities before us and the fact that they present us with real choices which require careful moral thought. The relevance of these reflections would be much reduced if one adopted a wholly optimistic scenario which renders the philosophical 'problem' otiose, or a wholly pessimistic scenario which renders it academic and irresolvable.

DEVELOPMENT

Central to the discussion is the question: what is development? One common view has been that development is essentially economic growth, and that the way to achieve economic growth is through modernization, i.e. the general introduction of and increase in industrialization, advanced technology and modern bureaucratic and economic mechanisms. What developing countries need to do is to catch up with and essentially imitate developed countries, which, even if they haven't achieved full development, are well on the way to doing so, and provide the model which poorer countries are to copy.

It is well recognized by many that development cannot simply be about economic growth. For we can imagine countries in which economic growth occurs and the GNP goes up, but certain other things do not occur, like improvements for the very poor who are left out, or maintenance of civil liberties and democratic freedoms. Concern for the position of the poor, the improvement of which was not seen as occurring as a result of a 'trickle-down' effect of general prosperity, led to ideas of development like 'development with equity', i.e. economic growth coupled with appropriate distribution of wealth so that the poor had a fair share, not to say a priority in the general increment of economic benefits. Consider, for instance, the 'basic needs' approach to development as a way of giving expression to this concern.[5]

What this suggests is that at root the idea of development is about a process of change which occurs in a society in which the well-being of people is increased. This begins to look like the UN definition given above, for the UN definition talks of a comprehensive process aiming at the constant improvement of the well-being of the entire population and of all individuals. The UN definition in fact makes reference to well-being in two rather different ways: first, it talks of well-being in terms of a number of dimensions, social, cultural, political, as well as economic well-being. Second, it refers to certain characteristics of social life such as free participation and fairness in the distribution of benefits, i.e. to certain moral characteristics of a society, such as justice and liberty.

Now we might want to argue about the details of the values indicated here, but the essential point to make about this UN definition is that it makes it very clear that 'development' as a goal of human endeavour is essentially the label we use for the processes of change which are seen as good, or even seen as what ought to occur. Indeed, this reflects the fact that much discussion about the nature of development is about the values which we believe in. Disagreement about what development is turns out often to be disagreement about what values we think ought to be instantiated in the process of change which we advocate.[6]

In one respect, however, I do want to comment critically at this stage on the UN definition, namely for its omission of any direct reference to the priority of alleviating extreme poverty within development. Is this accidental? After all, it talks of improvements for all individuals and also of fairness of distribution, so one might think that commitment to the reduction of poverty was clearly implied by these ideas. This would be a generous interpretation, I think, since the general tenor of the document is on development for all countries, and on the more rapid development of poorer countries as such.[7]

It is important to make explicit the difference between the right to development and the right of poor people to such development as will enable them to escape from extreme poverty. Any doubts which may be raised about the general right to development should not be seen as raising doubts about the rights of poor people to the basic necessities of life, and thus to a right to the kind of development which is essential to this.

DIFFERENT KINDS OF OBJECTIONS TO THE RIGHT TO DEVELOPMENT

(a) There might be a general objection to the whole idea of human rights. If the right to development is seen as an expression of the conditions necessary to human rights, and there are no human rights, then the argument has lost its basis.

(b) There might be a slightly less general but still broad objection based on doubts not on human rights in general but on certain kinds of human rights in particular, such as the sorts of socio-economic rights which are seen as 'recipience' rights. Since the right to development is primarily based on economic progress, it might be seen as logically underpinned by certain kinds of rights which are denied.

(c) While it may be granted that human rights do exist, the

right to development goes well beyond the assertion of human rights in ways which are problematic. For instance:

(i) It asserts the existence of international obligations and/or global obligations, i.e. obligations on the part of other countries to further development and/or obligations on the part of other people in the world to help further development.
(ii) In stressing general improvements in well-being in a country it goes well beyond what it is appropriate for any community to impose on itself or its government (let alone other countries or peoples). Protecting and promoting rights are one thing, improving general well-being (economic or otherwise) is another.

(d) In so far as the right to development is actually asserted in the present international system, it raises problems:

(i) about the extent to which countries have a right to define development in their own ways (the autonomy condition) and at the same time impose obligations on other countries;
(ii) about why nation-states, as opposed to smaller subnational units or larger supranational units, or as opposed to other institutional arrangements for managing world affairs, should be seen as the obvious units of development anyway.

(e) Disagreements about how to define development make it inappropriate to assert a right to development.

OBJECTIONS TO HUMAN RIGHTS

It is of course clear that a central prop to talking of the right to development would be taken away if one took away the commitment to human rights. There is much debate in the philosophical literature, which I will do no more than touch on, as to whether human rights exist and in what sense they do. Whatever else may be a matter of dispute it would generally be accepted that a human right is a right asserted to belong to all human beings as such anywhere and that the assertion of it is the expression of some moral claim – and that its existence does not depend upon positive social morality or established law.[8] Thus it is clear that the assertion of human rights is in some sense the assertion of a universal or global moral standard – and the Universal Declaration of Human Rights (1948) is often taken to be an embodiment of such a global moral perspective. The chief objection to this comes from ethical relativism which denies that there is an extra-cultural perspective from which to assert universal rights *qua* human or indeed any other universal values.

If, however, one is prepared to assert that human beings have rights, there is no good reason to restrict those rights to the so-called 'negative' rights such as liberty, and not extend them to subsistence rights. Indeed, as Henry Shue has well shown, the positive/negative distinction is unhelpful since all types of rights have positive and negative aspects to them. It is as true of liberty rights as it is of security rights and subsistence rights, the human rights that Shue has defended as basic, that the duties correlating to them are of three kinds: duties not to deprive (of that to which someone has a right), duties to prevent from being deprived and duties to aid the deprived.[9] On Shue's argument, the right to subsistence and security is basic in the sense that if it is not realized all other rights are meaningless.

Assuming then that human rights exist, it seems plausible to include social and economic rights with their heavy emphasis upon the duty to protect from economic deprivation and aid the economically deprived. Since much of development is about precisely that, a right to development can be seen as based on this, if not other considerations.

INTERNATIONAL/GLOBAL OBLIGATION

One of the key questions which now arises, though, is the question of whose duty it is, if people have rights, e.g. to liberty, security and subsistence, to realize those rights? It is commonly recognized that within an organized community (or more generally a country under one legal system) all people have a duty to refrain from depriving individuals of what they have a right to, but that governments have a special duty to protect people from deprivations, by enforcing law and by providing social security, a free health service, etc., and to aid the deprived in similar ways. However, in circumstances where governments and institutional agencies cannot for lack of resources realize basic human rights (the typical situation of poorer countries), or do not from indifference or connivance, or actually thwart their realization, fellow citizens have not merely duties not to deprive, but also duties to protect and aid as well.

What, however, of the wider context, internationally or globally? The *Declaration on the Right to Development* is certainly seen as entailing obligations in the international community and in other states to help promote development. What is the source of these obligations? Do the human rights, which the right to development expresses, themselves generate international obligations? The following argument, which I call the Cosmopolitan Model, is promising:

(a) Global obligation

Human rights are asserted as part of the commitment to a global moral community, i.e. to one moral domain of relations, responsibilities and obligations. We are all responsible in principle for the realization of human rights anywhere.

(b) International obligation as the expression of global obligation

Governments, whether acting on their own or multilaterally, ought to reflect, as far as is possible, the moral imperatives and priorities of the global moral community.

(c) Conclusion

Governments therefore have duties to other governments to support efforts to realize global values, e.g. the realization of basic human rights.

COSMOPOLITANISM AND GLOBAL ETHICS

Do human rights generate international obligations via global obligations? The answer to this depends upon whether one accepts the two crucial premises above.

First, it has to be recognized that the claim that human rights are universal, i.e. applicable to all human beings everywhere, does not entail that the correlative obligations extend in principle to all people in the world. It may be insisted (mistakenly) that human rights, though universal in character, essentially generate only local obligations, local in the sense that the obligations which arise arise in the context of an ongoing community, and in the sense that a government of a country stands in a special relation of protection and aid *vis-à-vis* the rights of its citizens (for contractarian reasons or whatever).

Certainly ethical universalism is not the same thing as cosmopolitanism. The latter idea is, as I understand it, the idea that we all belong morally to one community in which responsibility and obligations for one another in principle extend across the globe. (Cosmopolitanism is in fact consistent with acknowledging a degree of diversity in values in different societies.)

The idea of a 'global ethic' is no doubt normally intended to cover both universalism and cosmopolitanism, but we have to acknowledge that they are distinct strands. (The distinction is valid whether the universal values in question are about rights, duties or well-being.)

If human rights are to function as the direct generator of international obligations then they must at least be seen as asserting in principle obligations on the part of people anywhere in the world to do something about them. David Luban makes use of an intriguing claim made by Shue that socially basic human rights are 'everyone's minimum reasonable demands upon the rest of humanity'.[10] He reads this (which seems to me to be right anyway) as asserting that any human being anywhere may in principle have obligations to realize human rights.

Thus, although it has to be granted that the idea of a human right on its own without a wider theory behind it does not strictly entail cosmopolitan responsibility, it is difficult to see what the function of human rights discourse is, if it is not to assert the oneness of humanity and the idea of global solidarity and moral community. It is likely that the kinds of reasons advanced for defending human rights will be the kinds of reasons for seeing the scope of morality in global terms. At any rate the assertion of subsistence rights seems as good a way as any for showing why those who are well off in richer countries have duties to help alleviate suffering in other parts of the world.

The second crucial premise is that international obligations, i.e. the obligations which governments or nation-states have towards one another, are derivative of this cosmopolitan/global perspective. But this can be denied, and, if it is denied, then human rights play no special role is underpinning international obligation.

THE INTERNATIONALIST TRADITION

This takes us into the heartland of normative international relations theory. The idea that there is a morality of states, as Beitz calls it, which is distinct, both in content and in rationale, from ordinary moral norms, has been popular in the so-called 'internationalist' tradition – and in many ways is to be welcomed as an alternative to harsher forms of realism, i.e. to the idea that moral norms have no relevance or application in international relations at all. Its characteristics have been an emphasis on the importance of principles of sovereignty, non-intervention, honouring international pacts and agreements, rules of war, and so on. This is very much what has been called the 'international analogue of nineteenth-century liberalism', for within the framework of moral restraint lies the idea that each nation-state has the right to pursue its interests, including its economic interests, as best it can.[11]

Now one might say that this chimed well with the idea of a right to development. For is not a right to pursue the national interests and in particular the economic interest of a country another way of saying that each country has a right to development?

The answer is that it is not; for the essential import of asserting a right to development is not just to say that there is nothing wrong in a country's pursuing its own development, and that if it fails to do so because of competition from other countries bent on the same, there is nothing wrong about that either. It is rather that countries have a right to certain forms of co-operative behaviour on the part of other countries, which will permit if not actively promote their development. That is, the right to development asserts a duty in other countries in the international community not to hinder – and in the case of the right to development of poorer countries, actively to assist in – their development.

Now it has to be granted, even stressed, that within the framework of the international tradition, there is room for the development of co-operative norms – and one of these areas has been that of environmental protection in recent years. Likewise one can see the commitment of the richer countries in the early 1970s to give 0.7 per cent of GNP as aid and the more recent *Declaration on the Right to Development* as helping to establish a duty to further development in poorer countries (by appropriate aid, favourable international trade regimes, etc.).

But we should note, on the one hand, that the traditional right of countries to pursue their interests including development had nothing particularly to do with human rights. The relevance of social and economic rights (with their emphasis on recipience) was often not acknowledged and the civil and political rights of citizens were seen as an alien intrusion into the smooth running of international relations. As Hedley Bull noted, international order was seen as inimical to the demands of human justice.[12] (By 'human justice' he meant appeal to human rights.)

On the other hand, what I think has to be acknowledged is that the extent to which co-operation in order to further development in poorer countries has become accepted as a norm of international relations is a reflection of the extent to which the norms of international relations have become influenced by wider moral norms of a cosmopolitan kind. This could be presented as the Internationalist Model alternative to the Cosmopolitan Model given earlier:

(a) Autonomy of international morality

The moral rules which ought to govern the relations of states are those which by and large have evolved in the 'society of states' to suit the mutual interest of states in their external relations.

(b) Indirect influence of global values via international actors

Global ethical values such as human rights have an influence on the morality of states in proportion to the extent that past and present consideration of them by international actors informs the formation of international law, customary rules and particular policy decisions.

(c) Conclusion

Governments therefore have obligations to support development, including development directed to the realization of basic human rights, to the extent that the international morality of states has endorsed it.

This is arguably an unsatisfactory way of grounding an international obligation, precisely because it relies on the moral views of international actors themselves and conservatively upon the state of established international norms, whereas the cosmopolitan approach appeals directly to basic moral norms that are rationally defensible – norms which reflect the fact that human beings are morally primary (in relation to states), that we live in one moral community and thus that the norms of international relations between states ought to, even if they do not, reflect these more basic norms of a global ethic. Human rights contribute an important part of that wider moral framework which should be used to evaluate and criticize the behaviour of states and the norms they have come to accept.[13]

GENERAL WELL-BEING

If development is seen as a process in which there is a steady increase in well-being for all the population, the question might be asked: is there a right to this? There is a difference between saying that people have a right to seek a further increase in their well-being, and saying they have a right to get it, in the sense that others should not hinder them or should aid them in so doing.

It seems odd to say that a person who is already well off has a right to a further increase in his or her standard of living, or that someone who is well educated has a right to further learning, or that someone who has an adequate social life has a right to an even richer one.

A definition of 'development' as general improvements does not really discriminate between the improvements (in income, learning, social life) for people who are economically, educationally or socially deprived or disadvantaged and the improvements for those who are not. The point is not just that the rights of the former are more important than the rights of the latter. It is that it makes less or little sense to talk of the rights of the latter group – at least in the same sense of requiring action of others. The trouble with a blanket definition of development as general improvement, although it may capture something of what development means, is that it somehow creates an overstatement when coupled with the assertion of a right to it.

We should remember that the right to development is asserted not just as a right of poorer countries but also of richer countries. Once we attend to what a right to continued improvement in economic well-being means as applied to rich countries, we can see what a strange idea it is. Indeed, it seems clear that a richer country may not even have a right to development in the weaker sense that there is nothing wrong in its seeking further development – especially if that is linked to continued economic growth within environmental constraints, as discussed below.

What, however, about poorer countries? It certainly seems clear, if there is anything in the line of thought being developed here, that people have rights to a reasonable standard of living, and so, given the fact that hundreds of millions of people in poorer countries live clearly below that level, their rights require urgent action. In so far as development programmes are either targeted towards the improvement of their situation or are such as clearly to have such improvement as a significant part of the process, development in poorer countries can be seen, instrumentally or derivatively, as a process in which these rights are increasingly realized. So the right to development is generated by these rights and in turn transmits obligations to people and governments generally.

But are the goals of development in poorer countries necessarily of this kind – i.e. targeted wholly or significantly on poverty eradication? The answer is: never wholly, and sadly sometimes not significantly. My point is not here to criticize the policies of Third World governments; rather it is to point to the fact that their development policies have quite legitimately other goals as well, including economic growth and general improvements in many other areas. The question nevertheless remains: in so far as these development goals lie beyond the meeting of basic rights and aim at general improvements, do these countries have a right to development against the international community? The 'right to development', unless otherwise qualified, explicitly does not discriminate between different development goals. While all these goals might well be legitimate goals for a country to pursue, it does not follow that all these goals are such that that country has a right that other countries help it achieve them.

This argument may seem a bizarre one, given the evident fact that most poorer countries in the world are so much poorer than rich countries. Surely it is self-evident that poorer countries have a right to development precisely in the sense that economic development, indeed rapid economic development, is something the international community has a duty to help further (and is in fact doing little about) in poorer countries. And it may also seem self-evident that this is not just because basic rights are not currently being met on a large scale, it is also because there is an immense gap between rich countries and poor countries which is morally unacceptable.

Now the gap between rich and poor countries is indeed a matter of grave moral concern, but we have to ask ourselves what the basis of this is. Is it simply because there are significant inequalities between countries' wealth or their levels of economic development? Is it the fact that economic exploitation, past and present, has created and sustains the great gap between countries? Is it the fact that the level of economic well-being of poor countries is simply too low for them to meet the basic needs of their people?

The first argument has to be handled with care. There do not seem to be any good reasons for claiming that all countries should have the same *per capita* wealth any more than there are for saying that all individuals in a society (or the world) should have the same level of wealth. Indeed, the argument is less plausible since one can readily imagine a world in which the average *per capita* wealth of all countries was the same but there were still unacceptably wide ranges of income/wealth distribution within countries. Though inequality as such may not be wrong, great inequalities generally ought to be reduced, but this is usually for the other reasons mentioned.

What makes inequalities of wealth unacceptable to the extent that they are is arguably (i) the fact that those inequalities reflect exploitative or unjust economic relations (e.g. where workers because of their weakness do not get a fair wage, or where discrimination such as racism or sexism operates) and (ii) the fact that the outcome of such inequalities is that some people live in unacceptable poverty, i.e. are denied their basic rights. This applies as much to relations between countries as to relations within countries. The unacceptability of these inequalities thus underpins a right to development of a country as a means of rectifying a situation in which the rights of its people are denied by these inequalities.

Poorer countries, then, do have a right to development and one that generates international obligations to assist them in realizing it. It turns out to be a right to general improvements in economic well-being, not because they have a right to catch up fully with the level of economic well-being in richer countries, but just because this would be a consequence of a fairer, less exploitative global economy and because it is required for the meeting of basic needs. (Since it is justified in terms of justice and rights, it must in consistency be development directed to goals justified by moral argument.)

RIGHTS OF GOVERNMENTS

I noted earlier that in operational terms, i.e. in terms of what it means in practice in the world, the right to development is very much understood to mean the rights and duties of governments. Now if we think of governments as having a duty to promote the development of their country, there is an implication here (i) that the process of development is the process of change in the whole country, i.e. that the unit of development is at the level of a country; (ii) that governments are in control of that process; and (iii) that governments are as it were entitled to define what the development process is for their countries. There is also the implication (iv) that governments can make demands on other governments in the framework of international agreement and law to further development.

The present reality of the world is of course that governments play a large part in defining both the content of and units of development. Development is often assumed to be national development – understandably inasmuch as national governments have, if any institutional actors have, the power to influence the way things go in areas of the world. But it is clear that this need not be the only level of description for development. All sorts of entities can be the object of planning, from small communities, farms, cities, regions, to supranational areas such as the EC or even, from the perspective of UN agencies or thinkers who take as their concern 'world development', the world as a whole as a developing system.

The amount of interest we focus on these different levels is in part a function of how much power actors have to influence or control change at these different levels; and in part a function of how much power and influence we think ought to exist at these different levels. There is nothing inevitable about the current concentration of planning power at the level of national governments. Greater devolved decision-making to communities and regions is perfectly possible, as is the transfer of decision-making to larger bodies (thereby chipping away at the sacred cow of absolute sovereignty), or a combination of the two.

If governments do have *de facto* great control over the development processes that occur within their borders, then of course if people have a right to those development processes, governments, as representing those interests, both have duties to further them and rights (up to a point) against the international community not to hinder them. But governments only have those rights on the assumption that they do further the genuine development needs of their people. A government cannot legitimately define its own development goals without taking into account the genuine development needs of its people. If it fails to do so, morally the basis for a claim against other countries simply lapses.

DEFINING DEVELOPMENT

The preceding discussion leads us to look more generally at a difficulty with defining development. The problem philosophically with saying that someone has a right to development, where it is left open what development is, is that a right surely needs a content which seems to be missing. If one has correlative obligations to support it, it would be like signing a blank cheque. Politically it is also problematic granting other countries a right to development, especially if one's country is seen as having an obligation to support their development, if it is possible that the country may define its own development in ways which are judged to be (say) inappropriate, contrary to the ideal of development one's own country has itself, or even contrary to one's own country's development interests.

On the other hand, 'development' is like certain other concepts such as liberty, self-determination, autonomy, participation and empowerment. The ways these ideas are interpreted and expressed vary considerably from individual to individual and are expected to do so. That, one might say, is the point about these important social concepts. Yet we accept that people have rights to these – not just in the sense that there is nothing wrong in their exercising these rights, but in the sense that others have an obligation not to hinder such exercise and indeed to help such exercise where circumstances thwart it. Indeed, these concepts are not merely parallel to the idea of development; they are for many thinkers part and parcel of the idea of development itself.

Thus it must be granted, indeed stressed, that countries, communities, and rn nn, h'vd a rhfht tn detdrmhnd thdhr nwn ddvelnpment; this does not just mean that they are in control of what they are doing, but also that in exercising that control they also exercise choices of policies, programmes and general orientations in development which may be different from those of others. Other countries may have duties to assist if external assistance is needed. But there are limits to the extent that countries are free to determine their own development – limits which may apply to rich countries whose policies may not be fair in relation to the rest of the world, as much as to poorer countries whose policies it would be unfair to expect donor countries to support.

This political limitation is paralleled by the philosophical point that, granted that development is that process of socio-economic change which ought to happen, it will not do to translate this as: any process that those involved think ought to happen. For instance, an environmentalist is unlikely to accept a growth paradigm just because most people think it desirable. From the point of view of any thinker a right to development must be constrained by the thinker's own view of what genuine development is (including the degree of self-determination which he or she endorses).

The general thrust of my argument has been that poorer countries have a right to development as a condition of reducing extreme poverty and as a consequence of removing global economic injustice. But I have raised a doubt about defining development as general economic growth (for rich or poor countries alike), at least in the sense that this implies a right to it, either in the strong sense (as implying a duty in others to aid or not to hinder) or in the weaker sense (as implying that it is not wrong to seek/pursue it). These doubts are confirmed if we turn to the environmental constraints of sustainability.

SUSTAINABILITY

The idea of sustainability seems fairly clear: an activity, state of affairs or process is sustainable if it is capable of being sustained, that is, capable of continuing in the future without change. A pattern of agriculture on a given area of land is sustainable if it can be maintained indefinitely; i.e. the same pattern of agriculture could occur in ten years' time, fifty years' time, etc. A pattern of agriculture, for instance one reliant on high inputs of chemicals, or a monoculture, might not be sustainable if it turned out that after some years the soils had become ruined. An industrial practice would be sustainable if there were an indefinite supply of the materials needed to run it and if the effects it had on the local environment were not such as eventually to damage it so as to undermine the industrial practice.

What I have just said illustrates the idea of sustainable development, since agriculture policy and industrial activity are two key ingredients of development. What makes development sustainable has a lot to do with the levels and kinds of agricultural and industrial activity which are generally involved.

However, the above account of development simply in terms of what is capable of being sustained is not in fact adequate for several reasons. It is not sufficient that an activity be capable of being sustained. There must also be a will/commitment to sustain it. The future is not just foreseen; it is also planned for. Furthermore one key assumption of even greater significance needs to be brought out into the open. It is assumed that sustainable agriculture, industry and development generally ought to be pursued; that it would be wrong to pursue policies which were not sustainable. Why is this? The assumption must be that if certain kinds of agriculture or economic activity are good now, they will be good in the future, whether that is the future of ourselves, of our children or of future generations unknown to us. This evaluative component to the idea of sustainable development points up the weakness already noted in thinking of sustainable development (or anything else that may be the object of commitment or planning) as merely that which is capable of being sustained. For there are many kinds of activity which can be sustained in themselves but only at great costs. Indeed, to apply a point which G. E. Moore used in connection with J. S. Mill's use of the word 'desirable',[14] what is perhaps significant about sustainability is that it is about what 'ought to be' sustained rather than what merely 'can be' sustained. This is already implicit in the point made above that a practice which is unsustainable ought not to be carried out. But this gives merely a negative reason to do with the need to continue the value of the activity itself. The wider point is that there may a number of different respects in which sustainable development should be evaluated as what ought to be pursued or what is worth pursuing.[15]

A form of development worth sustaining will at the very least not only protect the future, but also be:

(a) just in terms of the present social structures and practices of the society;
(b) non-damaging to the natural environment;
(c) non-damaging to people in other countries; and
(d) fair in relation to the like aspirations of other countries.

(Not everyone will of course accept these evaluative positions. What is important, analytically, is that any form of sustainable development which someone is prepared to endorse will be a form which satisfies the range of moral criteria which that person accepts, whatever those may be.)

What I mean by this check-list is that if a country was pursuing a form of development which could be sustained into the future but which either (a) was manifestly repressive or indifferent to its own poor now, or (b) destroyed either within its own borders or in other countries the natural environment, or (c) involved economic policies, perhaps because of the country's economic power, which actually damaged other economies or helped to cause or perpetuate poverty elsewhere, or helped to create unsustainable situations in other countries, or (d) manifestly involved policies which, if generally practised, even just by those countries with the resources to do likewise, would create unsustainable conditions in the world – then, if any of these consequences were the case, we would not want to endorse that model of sustainable development.

An example of (d) would be this: it might well be the case that if one industrial country were to continue emitting carbon dioxide (CO_2) at present rates and all other countries stopped altogether, the effects on the atmosphere would not be significantly bad. But the fact is that many other countries are emitting at similar levels and yet more countries would like to do so and are moving into a position to do so. Here the test 'what if other countries do what you are doing?', given that other countries have as much reason or interest in selfishly doing so, becomes a critical test.

But this 'generalization' test is ambiguous. Is the test merely 'what if all other countries who want to and are in a position to do so, do so' or is it really 'what if all countries everywhere were to do so'? Either way, it can be argued, major changes in the levels of western economic practice are called for; but the latter test has much more radical consequences.

Take, for instance, the general standard of living and general level of economic activity in rich countries. Suppose that all countries were like that. Imagine a world in which all countries have our average level of economic well-being. Many would accept that we are imagining an impossibility. It has, for instance, been estimated that if all the world had achieved the typical energy consumption of rich countries, energy consumption globally would be (in 2025 AD) over five times, or 55 terawatt years (Twy), what it was in 1980 (10 Twy).[16] It seems reasonable to suppose that we would have created a total environmental catastrophe from CO_2-induced global warming, general pollution, increased radiation problems from increased reliance on nuclear energy, etc.

Suppose then we are imagining an impossibility. Does it follow from this that because we cannot generalize western levels of economic activity (either literally or because the effects would be too bad), that we in the west ought to reduce our levels of economic activity (energy consumption, etc.) to that level which could be generalized on a sustainable basis for all countries in the world? While there are good reasons for saying that the west ought to cut back somewhat, it is not clear that the simple generalization argument provides the right basis or the right prescription. If there is nothing intrinsically wrong in differences of wealth between countries (as noted earlier), then the fact that the levels of wealth and economic activity of rich countries cannot be universalized in itself does not make it wrong.

There are, however, plenty of other reasons why a commitment to continued growth might be questioned. Briefly, and in the absence of space to argue the points properly, these are that the actual practices of industrialized countries, taken together (the limited generalization argument above), if not taken individually, are (a) damaging the global environment – i.e. the environment for Third World countries (and non-human life) as well as for future generations – and, (b) controlling the global economy in ways that are economically either damaging to countries in the South or failing to further their development, including the reduction of extreme poverty. There is therefore ample reason for richer countries (a) to share their wealth through better aid and more general trade arrangements and, (b) to reduce their contribution to the unsustainable levels of resource use, pollution, CO_2 emissions, and so on.

If, for instance, it is the case that continued economic growth by rich countries is sustainable if poorer countries do not catch up at all (and continue to be economically exploited), but that it is not sustainable if poorer countries make significant improvements essential to their escaping the problems of extreme poverty (and get a fairer deal from the international economy), then poorer countries would have every right to feel that the maintaining of that growth was unjustified.

What I am really suggesting is this: the only real way to get a handle on the problem of whether a form of sustainable development for a country is justifiable (assuming it is sustainable for that country itself) is to consider it from a global perspective, i.e. from the perspective of world development. That is, to consider the situation of all countries in the world, and to ask what levels and kinds of economic activity, i.e. what kinds of development, could consistently be put together into a sustainable global package. If talk of the 'new world order', popular since the ending of the cold war and the Gulf crisis, is to mean anything it will have to do with the willingness to subsume national interests, which as I have noted include development objectives, under broader considerations.

A QUALIFIED RIGHT TO SUSTAINABLE DEVELOPMENT

There are therefore a variety of reasons for arguing that if sustainable development is to be taken to be sustainable economic development or growth, the idea, though internally coherent, is not realizable in the real world – certainly for rich countries. On the other hand, real economic growth for poor countries would be realizable in the real world, if only richer countries changed their ways to allow it. Indeed, economic growth for poorer countries, especially that was targeted on the very poor, would actually be beneficial to the environment since extreme poverty is often a cause of environmental degradation.

If, then, one recognizes that development need not, and should not, be defined in terms of general economic growth for all but

as a process of improving well-being (broadly defined) in conditions of justice and freedom, and with commitment to such
real economic growth as is necessary for the sake of the poor,
then the idea of a world in which development can occur for all
peoples seems wholly realistic.

Although I have expressed reservations about the right to development partly because of the difficulty of saying that countries
or peoples could be said to have a right to continued general
improvements in well-being, the reality of the world is one in
which the pressing need to ensure that all people achieve a reasonable life to which they have a right exists almost everywhere, in
poor countries to a great extent as well as in rich countries to
some extent. Our environmental predicament, and the concern
to sustain what we have achieved into the future, will only make
the problems of development in the present that much more
urgent. Therefore in practice the right to development, where
development is suitably qualified in the ways I have indicated and
puts emphasis upon what is needed to enable people to realize
their basic rights, is worth articulating and defending.

Is it a right to sustainable development? Well, if sustainability
is one of the attributes that an adequate definition of development
must contain, it follows that if there is a right to development
there is a right to sustainable development. If we assume the
point of view of an agent whose interest is in their life and the
lives of those around them we might be better to say: it is a right
to development which is at the same time sustainable. If, on the
other hand, we assume the point of view of an agent who sees
it as part of their own objectives in life that their life harmonizes
with that of their neighbours distant in both space and time, then
the very sustainability of development, far from being a constraint, is precisely part of what we each have a right to, and can
demand of our governments and of ourselves to be realized.[17]

NOTES

1 World Commission on Environment and Development, *Our Common
  Future* (the Brundtland Report), Oxford: Oxford University Press,
  1987, p. 8.
2 D. Pearce, A. Markandya, E. Barbier, *Blueprint for a Green Economy*
  (the Pearce Report), London: Earthscan, 1989.
3 *Declaration on the Right to Development*, United Nations, December
  1986, 41/128, preamble para 2.

4 See e.g. F. Stewart, 'Basic needs strategies, human rights, and the right to development', *Human Rights Quarterly*, 11, 1989, pp. 347–74, for a detailed exploration of the issues on the implementation of this approach.
5 See e.g. P. Streeten *et al.*, *First Things First: Meeting Basic Needs in Developing Countries*, Oxford: Oxford University Press, 1981.
6 See e.g. N. Dower, 'What is development? A philosopher's answer', Glasgow University Centre for Development Studies Occasional Paper Series no. 3, Glasgow: Glasgow University, 1989, for the evaluative character of defining development. Note that 'definition' in this chapter is not the philosopher's cherished neutral 'common denominator' (or 'concept') but the central account or conception used (about which agreement is not expected).
7 See e.g. article 4.2 of the *Declaration*, op. cit.
8 See e.g. J. Feinberg, *Social Philosophy*, Englewood Cliffs, NJ: Prentice-Hall, 1973, ch. 6; R. J. Vincent, *Human Rights and International Relations*, Cambridge: Cambridge University Press, 1986, also provides a useful general discussion of different views on human rights.
9 H. Shue, *Basic Rights: Subsistence, Affluence and US Foreign Policy*, Princeton, NJ: Princeton University Press, 1980, pp. 52–3.
10 D. Luban, 'The just war and human rights', *Philosophy and Public Affairs*, 9, 2, 1980, pp. 160–81, quoting Shue, op. cit., in which he seeks to show how serious violations of human rights in one country may provide a 'just cause' for intervention by another country.
11 C. R. Beitz, *Political Theory and International Relations*, Princeton, NJ: Princeton University Press, 1979, p. 66. This book provides a useful critique both of sceptical realism and of the internationalist 'morality of states'. Beitz also provides a strong form of cosmopolitanism, based on globalized Rawlsian theory, rather than on rights.
12 H. Bull, *The Anarchical Society*, London: Macmillan, 1977, p. 88, and the chapter 'Order vs justice in world politics' generally.
13 See Vincent, op. cit., pt III, for a useful exploration of the implications of human rights for international relations. (He rather combines cosmopolitan and internationalist considerations.)
14 G. E. Moore, *Principia Ethica*, Cambridge: Cambridge University Press, 1903, p. 67, criticizing J. S. Mill, *Utilitarianism*, 1861, for failing to note the sense of ' –able' in his famous proof of the principle of utility.
15 See N. Dower, 'Philosophy, the environment and sustainable development', *Revista de Filosofia*, Autonomous University of Yucatan, February 1990, pp. 46–57, for further discussion of sustainability and the general conflict between development goals and environmental goals.
16 World Commission on Environment and Development, op. cit., ch. 7 'Energy: choices for environment and development', pp. 169–70.
17 A longer version of this chapter is available on request. For the more general arguments for aid see N. Dower, *World Poverty: Challenge and Response*, York: Ebor Press, 1983.

Chapter 6

Is there a conflict between environmental protection and the development of the Third World?

Geoffrey Hunt

The development of the Third World countries and the global state of the environment present humanity with two of the most urgent and intractable problems of the late twentieth century. Only in the last decade or so have attempts been made to relate theoretically these two sets of problems. The debate is still unsystematic and confusing and the different positions adopted are often in conflict with one another. A contributor to the discussion states frankly in a recent book: 'Despite the continuing efforts of international organizations to promote environmental issues, no generally recognized model of the relationships between environment and development is available.'[1] However, this commentator, like others in the new 'ecodevelopment school', regards the question as a technical one which can be resolved in a theoretical vacuum. What is needed, and what I try to achieve here in a preliminary way, is a survey and conceptual clarification of the whole *theoretical* field. I take this to be an exercise in the philosophy of political economy.

One significant form of the debate, which will provide a fulcrum for my analysis, is the question of resolving an apparent *conflict* between concern for the environment and the urgent development needs of the Third World.[2] On the one hand, it has been claimed that environmental protection must be given priority over economic development programmes because further neglect of the environment threatens all human life including that in the Third World; and, on the other hand, it has been said that in the Third World human life is already threatened, in fact being extinguished, so that rapid development must have priority over environmental protection.

For example, environmentalists have often expressed alarm at the environmental costs of the increasing use of pesticides in the Third World, while developmentalists have emphasized the enormous benefits of pesticides in increasing food production. Thus, while a 1970 Massachusetts Institute of Technology report advocates the phasing out of chemical pesticides, Susan George has asserted that worry about pesticides may be appropriate in the developed countries but is quite inappropriate in the Third World which could feed itself if it had the crop protection which the developed world has.[3]

Again, developmentalists have often stressed the importance of industrialization for the self-reliant development of the Third World nations, while many environmentalists, especially those in the European Green parties, have urged the abandonment of industrialization in the developing countries and the running down of large-scale industry in the developed world. While the Greens argue that global environmental damage is rapidly becoming critical so that economic growth must be slowed down and even halted, most developmentalists see continuing economic growth as necessary for development as well as for the resolution of environmental problems. Many still adhere to the now classical critique of environmentalism put forward by Wilfred Beckerman. He stated that

> poor countries, in which a large proportion of the population may be constantly preoccupied with the problem of obtaining enough to eat for the next twenty-four hours, would be foolish to make heavy sacrifices of economic progress in the interests even of their own environment, let alone that of the world in general.[4]

Of course, the characterization of the conflict involves very complex empirical and theoretical issues. On some economic interpretations it seems that there would be no general conflict at all; and regarding some particular and specific environmental and developmental issues perhaps everyone would agree that there need be no conflict.[5] Still, no one can deny that there are confusing disagreements, often rather implicit, about a conflict or conflicts between environmental protection and Third World development, and I believe the foundation of this confusion is the cross-application of quite different methodologies, most especially a broadly 'liberal' paradigm and a broadly 'Marxist' one.[6]

I offer here a rather schematic survey and analysis of five models of development in its relation to environmental problems. These are, in the liberal mould, the Market Model, the Regulation Model and the Green Model; and in the Marxist mould, the Statist Model and the Participatory Model. I give more attention to the Green and the Participatory models and provide grounds for considering the latter to be the most adequate of the five despite its defects. What I have in mind when I speak of environmental crisis and ecological imbalance are such processes as soil degradation, deforestation and desertification, and pollution of water and air.[7]

Future generations may well wonder at the dire paucity of philosophical discussion in the late twentieth century about the plight of half of humanity while journal articles about the liar's paradox or the prisoner's dilemma continue to proliferate. While many, perhaps most, philosophers are disturbed and even appalled by the condition of so many in Africa, Asia and Latin America, it seems that immediately they wish to discuss the matter, and go beyond expressions of dismay, they find that there is hardly the barest consensus about causes and remedies. It is also understandable that the attempt to comprehend and debate should be shrugged off with a donation to Oxfam or Greenpeace (valuable as that may be) and a crude assumption that greed or ignorance is behind it all. It is also widely thought that the problems of development and environment are technical matters best left to the economic experts. The philosophical value of an enterprise such as mine lies, I think, in the need among philosophers for a very general understanding of theoretical frameworks by which the 'problem of development' is variously conceived. No one can do this without adopting a perspective akin to one or other of these frameworks, and those who pretend to impartiality almost always have a tacit and unexamined allegiance to a model in the liberal mould, most often some variant of the Regulation Model. I make my own allegiances perfectly clear.

PART I: LIBERAL MODELS
Market Model

This model rests on neo-classical economic theory and conservative (*laissez-faire*) political views. The writings of P. T. Bauer are representative.[8]

The cause of underdevelopment is regarded as the initial failure to seize opportunities presented by world trade and commerce, a failure itself due to human inequalities in abilities, motivations, beliefs and skills. This is exacerbated by the intervention of states and international organizations which, in attempting to ameliorate the inequality, take away the possibility of challenge and initiative in responding to market signals. In fact, it is claimed, international aid has created the 'Third World' as we know it, diverting scarce resources from optimal allocation for economic growth by politicizing the underdeveloped country in creating a diversionary struggle for control of government organs and revenues. In this model the wealth of the developed countries is 'earned' and is in no way connected with the poverty of the Third World.

The remedy for underdevelopment is to generate economic growth by stimulating innovation, enterprise and efficiency through the free play of the world market unfettered by any controls. The benefits, it is said, will trickle down. Minimal government will ensure law and order and may assist in improving communications and diffusing the values of achievement and discipline. Aid should be limited to non-tied cash grants. An 'open door' economic policy in the underdeveloped country will stimulate high consumption and competitiveness in production to pay for imports.[9]

Environmental problems are given very little attention in the Market Model. Bauer is not untypical in suggesting that environmentalism is a mere ideological ploy of critics of the free market system.[10] The assumption is that environmental problems can gradually be resolved through the price mechanism, and public policy should ensure that this is allowed to happen. For example, pollution will change consumer demands and generate an industry for anti-pollution devices and 'clean' products.

Food shortage, famine and the associated soil degradation and erosion are, in this model, the result neither of population pressure nor of economic exploitation but ultimately a consequence of institutional interference in the market with subsidies, tariffs and restrictions, and market imperfections such as poor communications, inadequate storage facilities and outdated land tenure systems.

A major criticism of this model, which comes from adherents of the Regulation Model, is that the price mechanism cannot adequately work for externalities such as pollution, and in general cannot cope with the degradation of the 'global commons' such as the oceans, atmosphere, ozone layer and rain. A more fundamental criticism, which comes from adherents of the Marxist models, is that the market has never worked, and cannot work, as envisaged, because it is only the surface which conceals the underlying structural economic and political inequalities on a global scale, the very inequalities which generate both poverty and ecological imbalance. As we shall see, on these models free market policies must worsen the problems.

Regulation Model

This rests on Keynesian economics and the social–democratic (not Social Democratic) political outlook. The two Brandt Commission reports are representative.[11] A fairly wide diversity of views may be subsumed under this model, but the major features can be picked out.

The cause of underdevelopment is discontinuity in the expanding cycle of income, savings and investment which is necessary for economic growth. Incomes are too low and dispersed (largely because population growth is too high) for the necessary accumulation of savings, and even when saving is possible other blockages such as poor banking facilities and unskilled manpower prevent it being used for investment. Thus there is a vicious circle in which 'economic take-off' is impossible. External trade in free market conditions is insufficient for development and worsens underdevelopment through the wasting of income on imports which are unproductive or with which local industry cannot compete. However, in the Regulation Model the poverty of the Third World is not structurally (i.e. intrinsically) connected with the wealth of the developed world, but it is said that there have been, and still are, unfair practices and inequalities which can and should be rectified.

The remedy for national underdevelopment is state regulation of trade through tariffs and subsidies, state intervention in the economy to provide basic infrastructures and indirect support for industry and agriculture, and the promotion of institutions of international stabilization and global redistribution policies. Foreign aid is vital to provide some of the capital necessary to break the vicious circle. The earlier view was that this could be done by creating import-substitution industries, but now more emphasis is placed on the creation of export-oriented industries. The private sector, it is said, must not be stifled but state-supported, so a mixed economy is best.

A tension exists in this model between the demands of *national* regulation and *international* regulation. Most significantly, national fiscal policies often require protection to indigenize demand, which is seen as especially important in the developing countries, while policies for the international promotion and stabilization of trade rule out protectionism as an obstacle to global growth.[12] The Brandt reports do stretch the traditional Regulation Model to its limits, putting the emphasis on international rather than national regulatory policies with their call for reform of the International Monetary Fund (IMF), the World Bank and the General Agreement on Tariffs and Trade (GATT), a new World Development Fund and a system of international taxation to facilitate Third World access to markets and financial resources. This is meant to provide a framework within which a Third World industrialization deeper than mere import substitution could take off, thereby providing an 'engine of growth' for the world economy.

In the Regulation Model environmental problems are regarded as a result of the misallocation of resources. While the Market Model presents this misallocation as flowing from imperfections or interference in the market, this model presents it as flowing from a lack of proper regulation of the market. Both models rule out the idea that the environmental crisis results from economic growth. Quite typically Beckerman says that it results from a misallocation characteristic of enterprises in an 'unregulated economy because of their associated external diseconomies' and that a failure to correct for these diseconomies 'does not necessarily mean that the growth rate is wrong'. Slow or zero growth would not prevent misallocation, and in fact they would make environmental protection more difficult.[13]

The Third World's environmental problems were, up to the early 1970s, interpreted in this model as primarily those of poor sanitation and water supplies, bad housing, disease, etc., to which economic growth is the *answer*. Beckerman says of the Third World: 'in these countries there is no conflict between growth and the "quality of life"; growth is essential in order to preserve life and to remedy some of the worst features of the environment from which these countries suffer.'[14]

The general remedy for environmental degradation is piecemeal reform and regulation through government legislation: 'The market mechanism cannot be expected to supply the socially optimum amount of such [environmental] services, so that the state has to fill the gaps.'[15] Most importantly, firms should be made to contribute to the *social* costs of their activities, for example, through the 'polluter pays' principle.

The Brandt reports extend the definition of the 'environment' and do show concern for problems such as soil degradation and deforestation, recognizing 'the prospects of cumulative and irreversible degradation of the Biosphere on which human life depends'.[16] In fact they present this as an independent ground for adopting their economic proposals for reformed institutions of international stabilization.[17] The argument is that without this global stabilization effort the Third World will sink deeper into poverty, and poverty entails environmental damage as hungry people overwork the soil and cut down forests for land and fuel.

Brandt sees massive aid and other financial transfers as a priority for a form of agricultural development which will *both* increase food production for domestic consumption and protect the environment.

The reports, and the Regulation Model in general, leave unanswered the question of whether the general programme for boosting economic growth is actually compatible with environmental conservation. Adherents of the Green and Participatory models would say it is not compatible.[18] There appears to be a tension, for example, in Brandt's agricultural programme as it relates to environment. It calls for massive investment in Green Revolution-style food production involving irrigation, pesticides and fertilizers while at the same time elsewhere expressing reservations about mechanization and the 'incautious use of chemicals and fertilizers'.[19] Its mention of a need for 'environmental impact assessments' of development programmes may appear rather timid. Thus the manifesto of the British Green Party asserts:

> More development, more trade, more aid; that's the usual recipe for Third World 'progress' . . . The Brandt Report identified some of the problems but came to the wrong conclusions. It endorsed many of those policies which have already done such harm.[20]

Green Model

While the other four models in this survey derive environmental conceptions and policies from an economic analysis and policy, the Green Model is unique in trying to derive economic analyses and policies from its environmental conceptions and policies. The writings of Rudolf Bahro (formerly German Greens) and Jonathon Porritt (British Greens) may be taken as representative.[21] The conception of 'ecodevelopment', associated especially with United Nations Environment Programme discourse, is in some ways quite close to the Green Model, but I do not discuss its distinctive features here.[22]

Environmental problems are said to be due to *industrialism*, a system of large-scale production which pursues economic growth as its main objective, using ecologically damaging technology in this pursuit. This system is supported by a consumerist and competitive culture and politics. Industrialism is undermining our life-support systems and must be abolished soon – what Rudolf Bahro calls 'industrial disarmament'.[23] This will be accompanied by a non-violent transition to small-scale self-sufficient ecologically benign co-operative and communalistic production.[24] Neither the political right nor the political left can undertake this because they are both committed to economic growth. An understanding of society in terms of 'class' and 'class struggle' is now outdated and irrelevant, because trade unionists and socialists only want more economic growth and a bigger share of it.

The concept of 'industrialism' is meant to transcend the idea that it is the political form of industrial production (market capitalism, state capitalism, socialism) which is the basis of the environmental crisis. The suggestion is that, as Bahro put it, 'every known kind of industrialization . . . gobbles up the end, which was to have been freedom, love, happiness for all', and 'we certainly deceived ourselves in seeing the ultimate cause of . . . alienation in the capitalist *form* of industrial progress'.[25] The powerful technical forces and vast scale of modern industrial production are in themselves the principal cause of oppression and destruction, using up resources without regard for their finiteness, polluting the environment and tending to damage ecological balance beyond recuperation.[26]

Most Greens speak as though industrialism is the means we have created, and had to create, given our *choice* of objective, namely, constantly to increase production of material goods. The means have an 'exterminist and self-destructive tendency',[27] therefore we must change our minds about the objective. For some in the Green movement this requires bringing growth to a standstill, for others it means slowing it down, and for yet others it means changing its character in some way. It would be fair to say that there is a good deal of vagueness and confusion in the Green Model about what growth is, why it is bad, how to curtail it and what the consequences of this would be – but more of this later.[28]

All Greens tend to identify and explain the characteristics and consequences of 'industrialism' in terms of the motive to *consume* material goods. The more right-leaning Greens such as Porritt tend, rather incoherently I think, to present consumerism (as a set of beliefs and values) as the root cause of the crises of 'industrial civilization'; thus industrialism is the historical outcome of the widespread *belief* that material goods bring happiness, that economic growth creates wealth for all, beliefs engendered or supported by the Newtonian mechanistic revolution in thought, and so on.[29] The more left-leaning Greens such as Bahro, more convincingly, I think, put greater emphasis on the industrial system itself as the creator of certain values and beliefs, beliefs which then serve to sustain the system. Bahro speaks of 'compensatory needs', which are 'materialistic' substitutes for the truly human needs of love and co-operation in the family and community.[30] Consequently all Greens tend to conceive social transformation as primarily, or largely, a question of culture or life-style, of the individual's moral choice to consume less, to live simply, even a question of religious conversion.[31] I shall say more about this later.

Taking as its starting point an environmental crisis which threatens the entire human race the Green Model implies that the Marxist conception of resolving the class struggle is of secondary import or entirely outdated. It has been superseded by a general struggle between 'human life' and 'nature' and a political struggle between industrialism and the Green movement. Says Porritt: 'I would claim that the divide between Greens and industrialists, with their opposing world views, is of far greater significance than the notional class distinctions by which most politicians are still obsessed.'[32]

The notion of the redundancy of class is not confined to the right wing of the Green movement. Thus Bahro, who once considered himself a Marxist, has also jettisoned the idea of a class struggle and produced a Green version of the Eurocommunist concept of 'historic compromise'.[33] He regards the working class of the developed countries as implicated in 'industrialism', as 'a second industrial class alongside the bourgeoisie', and the trade unions as generally exploitative and reactionary.[34]

It is not surprising if Green politics vacillates between Utopian communalism and social–democratic *realpolitik*.[35] I say this because of the confusion in Green writings about the question of private property in the means of production, although it is clear enough that the dominant position uncritically accepts this central institution of capitalism. Porritt says growth is bad, 'irrespective of who owns the means of production', and that 'socialization of the means of production makes little difference'. The British Green Party suggests that private ownership of the land should be done away with in Britain, but is silent about the immense and pervasive power of British corporations, banks and financial institutions. At the same time the party promotes the idea of small-scale self-financing private enterprises – a kind of interstitial capitalism. The programme of the German Green Party says nothing about the question, although another document of the party vaguely suggests that private property in the means of production is acceptable but its 'current conditions' need further control. Jo Müller of the German Greens also states that 'ownership of the means of production is no longer the decisive question' but also goes on to call for 'control'. Greens appear to be unanimous in rejecting nationalization because it brings large-scale and centralized enterprise.[36]

In the Green Model the cause of underdevelopment is again industrialism and the pursuit of growth. This pursuit, it is said, has generated a high-consumption, wasteful society in the developed world by impoverishing the Third World – depleting its resources, redirecting its land use to serve the developed world's consumption, encouraging it to squander resources on importing often useless or dangerous consumer goods and forcing it into debt through loans for trade and through unfair prices. The overconsumption thesis is particularly evident in the right-leaning version. Thus Porritt says:

> The basic, unmet needs of the poor can be met only by a reduction in the consumption of the developed world. . . . And

above all, should we not recognize *for ourselves* that helping the Third World is not just a question of giving more, but of taking less? Which brings us right back to the voters of Croydon and the need to promote a simpler, less materialistic way of life. We could all aim to eat more simply, travel more cheaply, live less wastefully and cut out the horrors of conspicuous consumption.[37]

Bahro too, despite a generally deeper analysis, tends to fall back on this overconsumption explanation of underdevelopment: 'Anyone who views abandoning this standard of living and sharing resources simply as a loss, or alternatively simply as a capitalist solution, still has a great deal to relearn.'[38]

Environmental problems such as soil degradation and deforestation are basically due to overconsumption in the developed world, in the Green Model. Thus to try to increase Third World food production with fertilizers, pesticides and mechanization is regarded as basically misconceived.

The remedy for underdevelopment is as follows. The developed world's consumption will have to drop, and although some economic growth will have to continue for a while in some regions eventually it will have to be curtailed and, some Greens say, halted. Non-tied aid from the developed world may be useful for a time, but eventually the Third World must 'delink' (i.e. withdraw) from world trade and the industrial system, and must avoid industrialization, instead developing self-sufficient communalistic production. Greens appear to be unanimous about this. Porritt declares: 'Essentially, they [Third World leaders] must find ways of gradually delinking their economies from those of the developed world, and building up more sustainable patterns of trade between themselves.' Developed countries like Britain too should 'withdraw from international markets'.[39] The British Green Party manifesto speaks of the 'need for tariffs to *restrict* world trade', and adds that 'Trade over long distances is wasteful of resources, encourages the exploitation of less developed countries and discourages self-reliance.'[40] The German programme also demands the 'creation of opportunities for Third World countries to disconnect themselves from the world market, which has proved to be more of a hindrance than a help'.[41]

Bahro has perhaps been the most strident about delinking. In 1981 in Caracas he said:

On a world scale industrialization *cannot* be achieved any longer, for the earth will not yield the material consumption of the North American middle class for the 10 or 15 billion people of the next century. And at the national level industrialization can no longer solve any problems of *general* interest. As has been shown in the last decade – the so-called decade of development – industrialization will only increase the sum of absolute impoverishment. The conclusion is to disengage, not for a better industrialization but for a different type of civilization, not for a later return to the world market but as an option for self-reliance, given that the world market itself must be forced into an involution.[42]

When an interviewer suggested in 1983 that 'For the underdeveloped countries the only way out of poverty is more trade with the richer nations, more industry', Bahro replied that this model would 'send the peoples of the Third World into a tunnel without an exit, because the living standard they are aiming for is no longer achievable'.[43]

For the Greens, then, delinking is certainly not part of a strategy to allow the Third World to develop an independent industrial base, but is seen as a necessary consequence of the undesirability (and ultimate impossibility) of its industrializing at all.[44] The marginalized masses of the Third World must return to the 'countryside' and organize self-reliant communities.[45] Porritt too is quite emphatic that 'the industrialization of the Third World' is among the things that 'now threaten our very survival'.[46] It seems unlikely that he would find many supporters for that thesis in the Third World itself.

The Green Model entails a rejection of all four alternative models on the grounds that they assume the necessity of economic growth and industrialization, an assumption which dangerously fails to recognize environmental limits. The other liberal models would object that even if the environment does present certain obstacles these are not absolute and can be overcome within the bounds of economic growth.

What we now need is a deeper understanding of the concept of 'growth', which I believe the Marxist models provide. My critique of the Green Model will emerge from the exposition of the Participatory Model in Part II.

PART II: MARXIST MODELS

Statist Model

This model rests on vulgar Marxism and the theory of centralized economic planning and is associated with bureaucratic and authoritarian politics.[47] So-called 'Big Push' theory is a technical version which dispenses with the vulgar Marxist form of discourse.[48]

Although the entire eastern bloc is presently introducing market mechanisms into its economies, it would be a mistake to think that the Statist Model is now irrelevant. First, it is still not clear how far the former communist economies will go in dismantling bureaucratic central planning. Second, many countries (especially in the Third World) have a large degree of such planning and intervention even though they have never been thought of as 'communist', e.g. Japan. Third, it seems probable that neither meaningful development nor environmental protection can be served without some degree and kind of central planning. It is still very worthwhile considering what is involved in the Statist Model.

In this model, underdevelopment is said to be due to the absence of an independent and concentrated base of capital and this entails a lack of the independent industrial and financial means essential for development. Small private investors cannot, in the conditions of poor infrastructures and fierce international competition, concentrate and productively invest their scarce capital for national progress. Piecemeal regulation and policies like import substitution are too weak to generate the economic growth necessary for take-off.

Both the Statist and the Participatory models present underdevelopment as a condition of neo-colonial exploitation. Assuming the labour theory of value the Marxist models present exploitation as the appropriation of the surplus-value created by labour. This exploitation has two dimensions. First, a phenomenal 'face' in the *exchange* of labour-power for wages. In terms of exchange-value the wage is a fair and equal exchange. Second, an essential core in a *production* process involving the encounter between labourers having no control over means of production, i.e. over the means to sustain themselves, and owners who control these means and require the labour-power to set them in motion. Thus the production process involves an unequal and coercive relation (a class relation), but this is veiled by the equality and consent of the exchange of commodities (labour-power being included among these).

The profit made by the owners is essentially surplus-value, that is, the difference between the value created by labour and the value embodied in the wages exchanged for labour-power. In the long term the rate of profit tends to decline,[49] and to overcome this capitalists export capital overseas in the pursuit of cheaper labour. This, in the standard Marxist account, is how imperialism arises.[50] The colonial period of coercive appropriation is followed by a neo-colonial period in which exploitation operates through a structural inequality of exchange on a global scale.

How does this neo-colonial appropriation work, according to the model? Different quantities of materialized labour in commodities (due to different productivities of labour, associated with the level of technology) are exchanged on the basis of their *equivalence* on the market. On this basis the Market Model is rejected as superficial and an apology for capitalism; and the Regulation Model is rejected as ambivalent because while it recognizes so-called 'deteriorating terms of trade' for the Third World, it rejects the labour theory of value which provides the only adequate theoretical explanation for this deterioration. So the basic problem of the Third World lies in the sphere of production, not in that of circulation and exchange as the previous three models suggest.[51] The Green and Regulation notion of 'unfair prices' in the international market and the Green notion of overconsumption in the developed countries are not completely false, but are shallow and misleading in the light of the Marxist models.

The Statist Model has one paradigmatic feature in common with the liberal models, and that is a linear evolutionism. It conceives underdevelopment as a pre-capitalist or semi-capitalist *stage*, as though developing countries are still at various stages that developed countries were once in. For the Participatory Model this is quite wrong, as we shall see.

In the Statist Model the remedy for underdevelopment is to create heavy industry with all the necessary linkages in one integrated and long-range plan using surplus generated by collectivized agriculture or primary exports. Heavy industrialization means creating the means to produce and sustain independently the fundamental means of production, such as iron and steel works and chemical plants. This industrialization must incorporate modern technology, because only by reducing the value embodied in the unit product (raising the productivity of labour) can a Third World country overcome the structural inequality of exchange characteristic of neo-colonialism. Modern capital-intensive technology also allows the developing country to leap over entire stages of development by accelerating the rate of accumulation of economic surplus,[52] and revolutionizing the entire political and cultural life of the society.

Proponents of the Statist Model claim that only the state has the power to appropriate, concentrate, productively invest and direct the national surplus. Only the state can ensure the necessary sacrifice of current consumption, comprehensively mobilize and train labour, ensure complementarity of industries, reduce externalities, create the necessary economies of scale and cope adequately with the required social overheads. For national independence and development in poor countries the economy must be commanded, the private sector strictly limited and controlled, and the strategic elements of the economy nationalized to free them from foreign control and interference.

Only state control and planning can destroy outmoded systems of production, such as small-scale artisanal production, which are seen as economic, political and cultural obstacles to rapid accumulation and the high standards of living which it will eventually bring. Thus the Soviet theorist V. G. Solodnikov says: 'We are firmly convinced that the African community has outlived itself and is no longer in keeping with the modern level of social organization of production.'[53]

In this model environmental problems are again defined as poor sanitation and water supplies, bad housing, disease, etc., and rapid growth through forced industrialization is seen as a quick solution to these problems. The Soviet Union's Baikal paper and pulp industry, which has been ecologically disastrous for Lake Baikal, was justified on the grounds that the 'backward' province of Buryatia would by its means be brought into twentieth-century industrial society with all its benefits.[54] Some theorists employing this model now reluctantly admit that forced industrialization brings its own environmental problems such as pollution, deforestation, the death of lakes and soil erosion. In his well-known book *The Destruction of Nature in the Soviet Union*, Boris Komarov, a Soviet ministry official, brought substantial evidence to show that pollution in the Soviet Union is at least as bad as, and in some respects probably worse than, that in the west. However, it has been claimed that these problems are created only by the rapid *pace* of industrialization and that they may now be more adequately managed in a comprehensive and integrated way by state planning than either the market or piecemeal regulation approaches would permit.

State farms and collectives certainly boost food production. Although the associated mechanization and large inputs of fertilizers and pesticides bring their ecological difficulties it does seem true that infrastructures such as irrigation and drainage can, in this system, be both ecologically sensitive and economically productive because they are a collective, as opposed to individualized, responsibility.

A principal criticism of this model is that not only the pace but the necessarily authoritarian political form of this kind of industrialization does entail ecological imbalance, just as, intimately connected with this, it entails human oppression. This is because a centralized decision-making body, with its characteristic lack of accountability and participation, is typically insensitive to the diversity of conditions and experiences, and to grass-roots concerns, viewpoints and problems. Furthermore, feedback from the consequences of its decisions is slow and often concealed or distorted by the imperatives of bureaucratic power-relations, as the events surrounding the Chernobyl disaster would seem to confirm.

Komarov suggests that only a democratic, participatory political system, in which environmental and ecological knowledge is public, can ensure both a socially harmonious and just economic development and ecological balance.[55] But, as he recognizes, decentralized and democratic forms of production do not square with the established Soviet model of rapid capital accumulation.[56] He further suggests that a bureaucratic and privileged elite, which obstructs the public flow of information, is likely to become even more authoritarian, defensive and unaccountable as environmental constraints make themselves felt: 'The entire life of society will be regulated,' he says.[57]

Of course, the Statist Model of development for the Third World entails precisely this bureaucratic and authoritarian political system. Rejections of the Statist Model come, in different theoretical terms, not only from the perspectives of the Market Model and Regulation Model but also from the Green and Participatory models. For example, Rudolf Bahro said in his talk in Caracas that the Third World nations must avoid 'the Soviet road', however attractive it may appear to them – but his grounds for this is that a globally destabilized environment cannot tolerate further industrialization.[58]

Participatory Model

This model rests on the essential elements of Marx's economic theory and on participatory-democratic politics. Some adherents of this model have been called 'neo-Marxist'. These include Samir Amin, Immanuel Wallerstein, André Gunder Frank and Ernesto Laclau. With the notable exception of André Gorz, Participation theorists have not had a great deal to say about the environmental crisis. My task here is to sketch the elements of a Participatory Model which relates environment to Third World development, in the hope that a philosophical discussion may be opened which moves beyond the assumption made by many critics of 'Marxism' that the Statist Model is its only and proper target of criticism.[59] In my view, Participation theorists have a critique of Statist Marxism which is far more consistent and cogent than anything liberal theorists have produced.

Underdevelopment and ecological crisis are here seen as the results of a global economic system, in which developing and developed countries are structurally linked. The essential economic features of this system must be grasped before these results can be fully understood. As in the Statist Model, economic analysis is not limited to the quantitative dimensions of production, exchange and distribution but theoretically broadened to include structural social relations.

In the terms of this model the previous models repeat the history of ideology, a distorted reflection of social relations.[60] The Market Model embodies the ideology which reflects the conditions of nineteenth-century *laissez-faire* capitalism, a conception of society based on (and thus unable to penetrate the domination of) commodity exchange relations; the Regulation Model embodies the ideology reflecting the general crisis of imperialism in the first half of the twentieth century when some planned redistribution and regulation of surplus-value was necessary for the continuation of accumulation; the Green Model is an ideologically eclectic response to the environmental crisis which must in practice fall back on the Regulation Model and its policies; the Statist Model is a refinement of the ideology which reflects the conditions of a *late*, and therefore distinctive kind of, capitalist revolution against feudalism, having to present itself as a revolution against capitalism. The superiority of the Participatory Model, I would claim, is revealed in its capacity to embrace and explain the other models as shallow, but historically rational, representations of social reality. (Marx employed this capacity in his *Theories of Surplus Value*.)

I shall speak of 'collective human good' in explicating this model. I do not pretend that this is a philosophically uncontroversial concept. After all, it will be said, are there not different conceptions of this good? I certainly do not wish to defend some metaphysical notion of 'human good' based on abstract concepts such as 'needs', 'rights' or 'interests', although this might be expected from a philosopher. They all share the same problem: either they are too general to do any theoretical work or they are defined in terms of some specific content which is contestable and thus philosophically inadequate. I take an entirely non-metaphysical approach. I submit that, while there may be no coherence in a transhistorical conception of 'human good', capitalism itself has generated such a conception over almost the whole planet. Before a worldwide capitalist market arose, the secular idea of a worldwide and collective human good could occur to no one.

Thus rather than found my thinking on metaphysics I found it on what I and most other people already believe as a result of living in the kind of society we have in the 1990s. The contemporary United Nations concepts of 'human rights' and 'basic needs' (which include food, shelter, clothing, access to water, hygiene, health, education, basic human rights) bear witness to this. These rights and needs are no longer so controversial, although it has to be said that it is precisely when they slip into metaphysical generality that they run the danger of being employed as a screen to cover exploitative intervention in the Third World.

I take three features of the capitalist system to be fundamental in grasping the environment–development relation: double separation, autonomous appropriation, and concentration and centralization of capital. The vulgar Marxism of the Statist Model would embrace these features, but would give them a somewhat different emphasis and interpretation.

Double separation

The emergence of private property in the means of production (initially land) entailed a double separation. The human producer is separated from nature (the natural conditions of production) *at the same moment* that they are separated from other human beings, namely from those who own rather than produce. This double separation is a necessary condition for the neglect and abuse of collective human good[61] and of ecological balance. As Marx put it: 'Capitalist production, therefore, develops technology, and the combination together of various processes into a social whole, only by sapping the original sources of all wealth – the soil and the labourer.'[62] Both human labour and nature (soil, etc.) are turned into *means* to serve a sectional (class) interest, namely the maintenance and expansion of that power which can command human powers and the powers of nature. I think we hear an echo of this point in the Green emphasis on a general struggle between 'human life' and 'nature'.

The Market Model promotes private property in the means of production; the Regulation Model mitigates the effects of the double separation but does not challenge it; the Green Model inconsistently defends private property in the means of production and bemoans its consequences for humanity; the Statist Model replaces private property with bureaucratic control and thus still presupposes, now in political rather than economic form, the same double separation.

Autonomous appropriation

A divorce arises between collective human good and the ends of production when the social product is compelled to feed increased production *as its end*, i.e. when accumulation becomes an end in itself, a *self*-expanding process. This process, which is an autonomous appropriation of the product of human creativity *at the same time* that it is an autonomous appropriation of nature, arises not as a conscious social abandonment of control over production but as the result of a structural constraint on the now atomized units of production. This constraint is competition. In competition owners of capital are *compelled*, if they are to remain competitors at all, to maximize profits and this becomes for each an end in itself which when aggregated emerges as so-called 'economic growth'. This aggregate *may* overlap with the satisfaction of collective human good but need not, for human good is only one profit-satisfying *means* among others. What is indifferent, evil or even self-destructive in the long term may be more profitable.

The Market Model allows, even encourages, this autonomous appropriation to proceed unabated; the Regulation Model partially brings it under conscious control; the Statist Model brings it under the conscious control of an authoritarian bureaucracy which must still fail to unify collective human good and human production. Failing to recognize in economic growth the self-expansion of capital the Green Model inconsistently opposes 'growth' while defending the general conditions of its existence.

The Statist mode of production of the former eastern bloc is regarded in the Participatory Model as providing a special case of double separation and autonomous appropriation. The double separation, as I have mentioned, is effected *politically*, rather than economically through the commodification of labour and legally through the institution of private property as in the monopoly capitalism of the west. Appropriation is largely under bureaucratic control but at the same time it is under the strong influence of the autonomous appropriation of the western capitalist metropolises, e.g. through the arms race and commodity markets. This means for thinkers such as Wallerstein and Gunder Frank that the former eastern bloc is as much an integral element of a world capitalist system as the Third World is, but in its own distinctive way.[63]

Concentration of capital

In conditions of competition the process of autonomous appropriation culminates in the concentration of economic and political power in two alien forms, namely, transnational industrial and financial corporations and the public corporations of the national state (and a still-inchoate transnational state represented by institutions such as the World Bank). The former serve only profit; the latter are ambivalent, serving profit and mitigating its consequences especially when its consequences are detrimental to profit itself.

These two political forms of the product of human labour stand against collective human good and ecological balance whenever ends other than these more effectively serve the further accumulation of the social product.

This process of concentration and centralization of capital has changed the face of contemporary capitalism, creating what Osvaldo Sunkel calls a 'transnational corporate system' in which international *production* (i.e. production in host countries by transnational corporations – TNCs) has overtaken international *trade* as the medium of world economic exchange.[64] This makes the perspective of the Regulation Model, with its emphasis on the regulation of trade and finance between *nations*, very limited and even diversionary.

On this account the Green concept of 'industrialism' is unduly vague and has quite serious deficiencies. For example, while it implies that modern technology needs to be scrapped in favour of small-scale artisan manufacture (not endorsed by all Greens, admittedly) what needs scrapping is the compulsive employment of scientific understanding serving autonomous appropriation instead of collective human good. Only a technology which is *both* highly developed and under democratically collective human control can liberate humanity from the narrowest constraints of nature at the same time that it regulates a *balanced* relation between humanity and nature.

Underdevelopment

Now to the Participatory account of underdevelopment in particular. Despite certain shared features already described, this model departs from the Statist Model in respect of its greater openness, innovativeness, subtlety and sensitivity to the diversity, and ongoing changes, in the Third World. There is a crucial methodological difference between this model and the previous one.[65] The naturalistic idea of an independent evolutionary historical process in which 'the party' can intervene 'from above' is replaced with the idea of 'praxis', the idea of history as a process with *inseparable* conscious and unconscious dimensions. Politically this entails a difference between bureaucratic authoritarianism and participatory democracy.[66]

Earlier I pointed out the way in which the Green Model emphasizes the moral choice of individuals, e.g. to consume particular commodities or not. Standing in marked contrast to this approach, the Statist Model, with its deterministic Marxism, emphasizes impersonal socio-economic structures. While the orthodox Marxist accounts provide us with powerful historical and economic *explanations* they fail to impress upon us our individual moral responsibilities in the way in which the Green Model does. Indeed, it seems that any explanatory mode of approaching human issues carries with it a certain attitude – the tendency to assume that somehow human events work out according to some logic of their own. On that basis it would appear that we have only to sit back and wait for 'it' (what?) to work out. With varying degrees of success the Participation theorists have recognized this as a moral and conceptual issue. In general they take the view that moral outrage and an emphasis on individual responsibility often carry with them quite a different attitude – one which is uninformed by what is necessary and what is possible under concrete economic and political circumstances. Participation theorists, however, in their different ways, have tried to avoid both economic and moral reductionism and assumed a position of moral responsibility informed by economic and political context.

Tied up with this, in place of the 'Soviet' paradigm of linear stages of development this model conceives both underdevelopment and ecological imbalance as necessary dimensions of an integral world system. Indeed, an outstanding difference between the vulgar Marxist Statist Model and the Participatory Model *vis-à-vis* development is that, while for the former (as I mentioned earlier) the Third World countries are trapped by imperialism in a pre-capitalist or semi-capitalist stage (and only the intervention of the Communist Party can release them to the next stage), the latter sees the Third World as essentially a historical *product* of capitalism itself,[67] a product which has become a *condition* of the further development of the capitalist system on a world scale. It also rejects the Regulation theorists' perception of global inequality as a kind of large-scale historical accident which can be rectified *within* the system.

Whereas earlier accounts (so-called 'Dependency Theories') had attached all the weight to exploitation through the global mechanism of unequal *exchange*, contemporary Participation theorists put the emphasis on global *production* relations, and situating exchange and circulation in the context of these.[68] This model presents us with a global system in which the exploitation which causes and reproduces underdevelopment operates through an unequal international division of labour or, more precisely, an articulation of two different kinds of production relations: (1) the 'democratic' class relation in which (as already described) concealed exploitation takes place through a phenomenal *economic* relation (wages for labour-power), and (2) an overtly *political* class relation (with manifest exploitation) in the typical 'peripheral capitalist' Third World forms of military rule and landowner coercion, ensuring low wages and low ground rents. The two modes of production are structurally linked, with the surplus extracted in the Third World being transferred to the metropolises through various forms of commodity and financial exchange.

This model also assumes the possibility and necessity of some degree and kind of industrialization for the satisfaction of the needs of Third World peoples, but it rejects the kind of industrialization constituted *within* the confines of the global profit-based system. For example, the emergence of the Newly Industrializing Countries (NICs) such as South Korea, Taiwan and Singapore is not taken to be evidence for a continuing progressive role for capitalism, for these are only 'export processing zones' for the TNCs, which still control production, even where there is some kind of nationalization.[69] The NICs are not independent economies but dependent aspects of a world profit system, a system which is now increasingly dividing the underdeveloped countries into dependent NICs and a marginalized 'Fourth World' (e.g. Bangladesh, Sri Lanka and Sudan).

Even so-called 'socialist' states, whether in the former eastern bloc or in the Third World, are in their own way integral parts of the world economic system. The Statist Model of development with its policy of state direction of the economy (e.g. in Angola) does not differ radically from the alliances of Third World governments and TNCs (e.g. in India) which are generally considered to operate in the so-called 'free world'. Thus for Samir Amin, unlike the Soviet theorists, any Third World 'national liberation movement is a *moment* in the socialist transformation of the world and not a [national] *stage* in the development of capitalism on a world scale.'[70]

Environment

The Participatory Model entails a distinctive understanding of the environmental crisis. In general terms the crisis is seen as the result of a production system in which nature is no longer the immediate life concern of the producers (who are separated from it) but a mere *means* to the self-expansion of capital. On the evolutionary assumptions of the Market, Regulation and Statist models the environmental crisis is regarded as a transitory phenomenon associated with a certain *technological* phase of industrialization, rather than a political–economic phase. It is often suggested that this phase will be superseded by means of techno- logical developments themselves, perhaps with some assistance from more efficient management. To be sure, this notion is itself in crisis, and the Green Model is a popular and eclectic response to the growing disparity between the standard capitalist ideology and the alarming ecological evidence. But the Green Model tacitly accepts the evolutionary paradigm in its own recommendation that the line of economic growth must stop; the Third World should not industrialize.

The Participatory paradigm offers an alternative to all the other models in one absolutely fundamental respect: it is not the inter- national evolution of industry ('industrialization', 'industrialism', 'technology') which in itself is disrupting the environment but *globally divisive social relations of production* which are doing so. While the adherents of the Statist Model would also appear to recognize this in an abstract way they actually put the emphasis on the *forces* of production (i.e. technology) and accordingly derive a technocratic and authoritarian conception of development and the resolution of the environment–development conflict. The essential problem is not national economic productivity, as the Soviet theorists think, but exploitative social (i.e. human) relations on a world scale. Productivity can be improved by increasing the tech- nical content of capital, and this can be done bureaucratically, by piecemeal regulation, or by the market. This done, the twin problems of underdevelopment and ecological imbalance remain in some form or other as long as the product of labour is not democratically controlled for collective human good (i.e. as long as the relations of production are authoritarian, class-based).

As we have seen, the global articulation of the economic mode and political mode of exploitation essential to capitalism entails the impossibility of a homogeneous world capitalist order of the liberal and integrated kind found in Europe and the USA. (In fact this is not a *kind* of capitalism, but is an aspect of the global profit-based order.) This impossibility has nothing to do with ecology, and here the Greens are quite wrong. It is socio-economically impossible under capitalism (whether of the western or eastern statist varieties). The global articulation of modes of production which constitutes capitalism entails ecological crisis by the same token that it entails underdevelopment.

The contemporary Participatory Model shows how the division of the Third World into NICs (plus OPEC capital-surplus economies such as Saudi Arabia) and a Fourth World involves two distinct aspects of the ecological crisis as it is developing in Asia, Africa and Latin America. On the one hand, the export-processing zones (and oil exporters) create a tremendous output of pollutants. As André Gorz has argued, the TNCs of the metropolises are exporting their dirty and dangerous manufacturing industries to the Third World, while the metropolises themselves increasingly enjoy a society of high finance, services, countryside conservation and leisure.[71] On the other hand, a quarter of the world's population is so marginalized and impoverished by exploitation and neglect that it is forced to destroy forests and degrade the soil on an unprecedented scale in search of a livelihood. For example, what we might call the neo-feudal land tenure system in parts of Latin America plays an integral role in the world profit system at the expense of small farmers who are forced to overwork steep slopes or unsuitable forest soil where severe erosion is taking place as a result.[72]

As regards Third World food production, unequal exchange is at work once again. Self-expanding capital treats food in the same way as any other item through which profit may be realized.[73] Food-producing land in the Third World is taken over for the production of non-food cash crops for export (tobacco, cocoa, oil palm, rubber, etc.) under unequal exchange to the metropolises. The accumulated wealth of the latter allows capital-intensive agriculture with a very high productivity which commands the global market, attracting Third World food importers and creating dependency on unequal agricultural exchange. Where domestic food is grown in the Third World this is increasingly oriented to the demands of profit – for the market – with high demand guaranteed by the dense population of the urban centres. This situation creates the 'need' for imported fertilizers and pesticides in the Third World, with their ecologically damaging effects.[74]

The Participatory Model attaches central importance to the

TNC as the autocratic agent, or institutional embodiment, of capital in this new corporate world system, and thus its centrality to the ecological crisis is also stressed. The relationship between the TNC and ecological damage still needs to be worked out in detail, but there can be no doubt that, for example, TNCs have been irresponsibly clearing forests in Central America to make way for hamburger cattle ranches, and are responsible for tearing thousands of acres of timber out of west African, Indonesian and Malaysian forests and for causing soil erosion in places such as Senegal by intensive cultivation of export crops.[75]

The Participatory conception of the remedy for underdevelopment is more complex and open than the Statist Model. In particular it puts the emphasis on the *globality* of the solution while recognizing the division and diversity of the Third World; it stresses mass participatory politics as opposed to authoritarian party-directed solutions; and it characterizes the resolution of the environmental crisis as essentially a global *political* resolution. It is true that participatory democracy is a theme in many Green writings, but it largely remains on the level of individual morality rather than recognizing the class divisions, and divisions of labour, which already exist. Class divisions cannot be wished away simply by asserting that they are 'outdated'. The Participatory Model grounds participatory politics in the realm of industrial production, not in consumption as with the Greens (although I recognize that Greens often do also support small-scale participatory production ventures).

The struggle to make collective human good the end of production, not a mere means for it, must encounter resistance from both the TNC and typically the state, and increasingly from the organs of a world capitalist state such as the World Bank, the IMF, the Trilateral Commission and the Organization for Economic Co-operation and Development. This essentially is what contemporary class conflict is all about, a conflict which the Greens would turn their backs on. Yet under conditions of the new transnational corporate order the clash of class interests too is increasingly a global, not merely a national, occurrence. Thus, for example, workers' protests against the conditions of work on a merely local level are increasingly futile when the employer can at a moment's notice transfer plant to another country. Perhaps this indicates the need for the transnationalization of trade unions and other organizations of resistance to TNCs and their policies.[76]

Thus when Union Carbide, a TNC which has more than 500 factories, mines and mills operating in 36 countries and employing over 100,000 people, threatens life and environment with toxic chemicals in Bhopal this is not a problem for Indian workers and ecology alone. It is a problem for everyone affected by Union Carbide's profit-maximizing activities globally.[77] Not only members of the working class are affected, for example, by the current irresponsible use of chemical pesticides on a huge scale (in which Union Carbide is implicated), for in fact everyone on the planet is affected, however indirectly. Thus the Participatory Model implies that the concept of 'class resistance' itself needs expanding beyond the vulgar Marxist understanding to involve all social movements resisting various aspects of capitalist society – in this country environmental movements such as Friends of the Earth and Greenpeace, and other movements such as the Campaign for Nuclear Disarmament, Charter 88, the Anti-Apartheid Movement and feminist groups.[78] In this connection André Gorz has spoken of 'the revolt of civil society' in the metropolises, meaning the growing opposition to the capitalist state of new formations springing from the 'whole web of self-regulating and non-institutional social relations' of capitalist society: 'Against the centralizing and totalitarian tendencies of both the classical Right and the orthodox Left, ecology embodies the revolt of civil society and the movement for its reconstruction.'[79] While this might appear to be a typical Green statement (and admittedly Gorz's work is not without ambivalence) the context would seem to indicate that Gorz uses 'ecology' very broadly to mean all forms of resistance to the pursuit of profit, and his analysis is still rooted in *class* resistance. The revolt of civil society in the metropolises may well develop increasingly in solidarity with the mass movements against neo-colonial governments in the Third World, governments which are the intermediaries in the TNC exploitation of the workers, peasants and tenant farmers.

In the Participatory Model the environmental crisis will not be resolved by creating an *alternative* alongside or within profit-based society, but by *transforming* that society politically, a transformation which it assumes can only be finally achieved on a world scale. The model, like the Statist one, has optimism built into it. In the historical movement towards this resolution there will be many different kinds of conflict, at different levels in different circumstances, but the general drift of these conflicts is to create the conditions for an end to double separation and autonomous appropriation and the establishment of a global participatory control of production for collective human good. But this model breaks with the inevitabilist assumptions of the vulgar conception. For we may yet be annihilated in a nuclear holocaust, suffocate in our own effluent or relapse into a prehistoric condition.

It is assumed in this model, and this certainly needs further elaboration, that *if* the structural political–economic tensions are resolved (or, *as* they are resolved) conditions will be created for resolving the *technical* problems. Various ecologically benign forms of energy such as wind, hydroelectric and solar (and possibly fusion, if proved to be reasonably safe) can be given all the necessary resources and attention as profit is increasingly replaced by collective human good as the end of production. The same goes for the vast potential of ecologically benign biotechnology in all areas of pest control, natural fertilizing of the soil and pollution-free manufacture, as well as the genetic engineering of plants able to recover the lost ground of deserts and deforested and eroded areas.[80]

CONCLUSION

The answer to our question 'Is there a conflict between environment and development?' is *Yes*, if development is (or is based on) economic growth, and economic growth is essentially the self-expansion of capital. The answer to the question is *No*, if development is the increasing control of economic growth in the form of self-expanding capital and its replacement with the participatory–democratic control of production to serve collective human good, if it is the development of the free creative powers of each as the condition of the freedom and welfare of all.

We may also choose to call the expansion of the product of human creativity under these new conditions 'growth', a growth within the bounds of ecological and human harmony.

NOTES

This chapter ultimately has its origin in a paper presented at the Annual Conference of the Society for Applied Philosophy with the theme 'Environment', held at Chelwood Gate, Sussex, in May 1986, and I wish to thank participants for their criticisms. It has gone through several revisions as the result of seminar presentations. Robin Attfield, Andrew Belsey and Barry Wilkins at the University of Wales College of Cardiff gave me comments and encouragement for which I am grateful.

1 Peter Bartelmus, *Environment and Development*, Boston, MA: Allen & Unwin, 1986. See my critical review in *Explorations in Knowledge*, V, 1, 1988, pp. 52–6.

2 An international consensus on the idea of a conflict between development and environment seems to have emerged with the 1978 United Nations Environment Programme review, and this defined the problem area which resulted in the formulation of 'ecodevelopment'.

3 Massachusetts Institute of Technology Study of Critical Environmental Problems, *Man's Impact on the Global Environment: Assessment and Recommendations for Action*, Cambridge, MA: MIT, 1970; Susan George, *How the Other Half Dies: The Real Reasons for World Hunger*, revised edn, Harmondsworth: Penguin, 1977, pp. 312–17.

4 Wilfred Beckerman, *In Defence of Economic Growth*, London: Cape, 1974, p. 98.

5 'Ecodevelopment' claims to be a reconciliation of the conflict but it remains, I think, unrealizable except for small programmes relatively isolated from national/global dynamics. See my discussion of the Green Model on pp. 124–8.

6 See my 'Two methodological paradigms in development economics', *The Philosophical Forum*, XVIII, 1, 1986, pp. 52–68.

7 See Erik P. Eckholm, *Losing Ground: Environmental Stress and World Food Prospects*, Oxford: Pergamon, 1978. For a general survey of the environmental crisis see Charles H. Southwick (ed.), *Global Ecology*, Sunderland, MA: Sinauer, 1985.

8 P. T. Bauer, *Dissent on Development*, London: Weidenfeld & Nicolson, 1971; *Equality, the Third World and Economic Delusion*, London: Weidenfeld & Nicolson, 1981; and *Reality and Rhetoric: Studies in the Economics of Development*, London: Weidenfeld & Nicolson, 1984.

9 This position has re-emerged in the neo-*laissez-faire* monetarist era of the 1980s and early 1990s, and has even been adopted by the United Nations. Thus at the UN Special Session on Africa in June 1986 the final communiqué emphasized free market policies and private enterprise as the solution to the African crisis.

10 Bauer, *Equality, the Third World and Economic Delusion*, op. cit., p. 81.

11 *North–South: A Programme for Survival* (the Brandt Report), London: Pan Books, 1980, and *Common Crisis North–South: Co-operation for World Recovery*, London: Pan Books, 1983. See also the useful *Handbook of World Development: The Guide to the Brandt Report*, Harlow: Longman, 1981.

12 This tension appears in GATT, which was meant to open up international trade; its article 19 allows trade restrictions where imports damage domestic production, but this has increasingly provided an excuse for protectionist measures. The Brandt Commission wanted to limit appeal to this article.

13 Beckerman, op. cit., pp. 18–20.

14 ibid., p. 98. Beckerman maintains that growth is necessary but not sufficient for improving living standards, p. 245.

15 ibid., p. 34.

16 Brandt Commission, *North–South*, op. cit., p. 115.

17 See *Handbook of World Development*, op. cit., pp. 43–4, on 'mutual interests', and Brandt Commission, *Common Crisis*, op. cit., p. 126.

18 Their grounds are quite different. See: 'Participatory model', pp. 133–44.

19 Brandt Commission, *North–South*, op. cit., pp. 81, 94, and *Common Crisis*, op. cit., pp. 121, 126; *Handbook of World Development*, op. cit., pp. 5–6.

20 *Politics for Life: The Green Party Manifesto*, London: Green Party, 1985, pp. 22–3. E. J. Woodhouse predicted the Brandt Report and prefigured the Green response to it in his 'Re-visioning the future of the Third World: an ecological perspective on development', *World Politics*, XXV, 1, 1972, p. 29.

21 See Rudolf Bahro, *Socialism and Survival*, London: Heretic, 1982; *From Red to Green*, London: Verso, 1984; and *Building the Green Movement*, London, Heretic, 1986; Jonathon Porritt, *Seeing Green*, Oxford: Blackwell, 1984; C. Spretnak and F. Capra, *Green Politics*, London: Paladin, 1985; *Programme of the German Green Party*, trans. of 2nd German edn, preface by Jonathon Porritt, London: Heretic, 1983; and *Politics for Life*, op. cit.

22 Bartelmus, op. cit.; Rajni Kothari, 'Environment and alternative development', *Alternatives*, V, 1979–80, pp. 427–75; Ignacy Sachs, 'Environment and development revisited', *Alternatives*, VIII, 1982, pp. 369–78.

23 Bahro, *Socialism and Survival*, op. cit., p. 151, and *From Red to Green*, op. cit., pp. 145–6.

24 See e.g. *Politics for Life*, op. cit., p. 4, and Bahro, *From Red to Green*, op. cit., pp. 179–80.

25 Bahro, *Socialism and Survival*, op. cit., pp. 126 and 150 respectively.

26 ibid., p. 129.

27 ibid., p. 143.

28 Cf. Porritt, op. cit., pp. 120, 136; Spretnak and Capra, op. cit., pp. 83–5; *Programme of the German Green Party*, op. cit., pp. 10, 28.

29 Porritt, op. cit., e.g. pp. 45, 105.

30 Bahro, *Socialism and Survival*, op. cit., pp. 21, 27–33, 82.

31 Bahro, *From Red to Green*, op. cit., pp. 148–9, 175–9, on cultural revolution, and *Socialism and Survival*, op. cit., pp. 22, 71, 82, on religious conversion.

32 Porritt, op. cit., pp. 115–16; see also pp. 118, 226 and the remark on p. 4 of his preface to the German Programme.

33 See Bahro, *Socialism and Survival*, op. cit., pp. 43–5, 65, 73, and *From Red to Green* op. cit., p. 117.

34 Bahro, *From Red to Green*, op. cit., pp. 133, 184–6.

35 In fact, Bahro himself abandoned the German Green Party in June 1985 complaining: 'The Greens have identified themselves – critically – with the industrial system and its political administration. Nowhere

do they want to get out' (*Building the Green Movement*, op. cit., p. 210). Bahro still fails to grasp the fundamental inconsistencies in the Green position itself and only counterposes to Green party practice a Green fundamentalism. See also Bahro, *From Red to Green*, op. cit., pp. 170–1.

36 Porritt, op. cit., p. 48; *Politics for Life*, op. cit., pp. 11, 14; Spretnak and Capra, op. cit., pp. 93–4.
37 Porritt, op. cit., p. 190, his emphases.
38 Bahro, *Socialism and Survival*, op. cit., p. 41; see also p. 28.
39 Porritt, op. cit., p. 188.
40 *Politics for Life*, op. cit., p. 23.
41 *Programme of the German Green Party*, op. cit., p. 29.
42 Bahro, *Socialism and Survival*, op. cit., p. 130.
43 Bahro, *From Red to Green*, op. cit., p. 211.
44 For Bahro's rejection of Third World industrialization see Bahro, *Socialism and Survival*, op. cit., pp. 27, 129, 150, and *From Red to Green*, op. cit., p. 211. Cf. André Gorz, *Ecology as Politics*, Boston, MA: South End, 1980, p. 65, where he endorses the idea of the impossibility, on ecological grounds, of the 'Americanization' of global standards of living.
45 Bahro, *Socialism and Survival*, op. cit., pp. 130–1. In his discussion of self-reliant regionalism Bahro suggests that about 90 per cent of goods could be produced within a self-sufficient locality of 5,000 sq km with only 1–10 per cent obtained through foreign trade (*From Red to Green*, op. cit., pp. 179–80).
46 Porritt, op. cit., p. 217. In 1972 the Club of Rome had already argued that Third World industrialization would be unwise, assuming an imminently critical level of resource depletion and pollution.
47 See Stephen Clarkson, *The Soviet Theory of Development: India and the Third World in Marxist-Leninist Scholarship*, Toronto: University of Toronto Press, 1978, and London: Macmillan, 1979; R. Bideleux, *Communism and Development*, London: Methuen, 1985.
48 See P. N. Rosenstein-Rodan, 'Problems of industrialization of eastern and south-eastern Europe', *Economic Journal*, 1943, pp. 204–7; excerpt in G. M. Meier (ed.), *Leading Issues in Development Economics*, Oxford: Oxford University Press, 1964, pp. 431–6.
49 In classical Marxist theory this is because competition entails an effort to increase productivity, and this has the consequence of increasing the amount of fixed capital (machinery, etc.) per worker. Thus the ratio of surplus-value appropriated to the total capital employed tends to decline.
50 There is considerable debate within Marxist circles about the meaning of the 'falling rate of profit'. The neo-Marxist Samir Amin, for example, thinks it is not required in order to explain imperialism; for him it is sufficient that greater profits could be made overseas.
51 On the Soviet version of the theory of unequal exchange see Clarkson, op. cit., p. 186.
52 Soviet analysts now admit that in the Third World this may be very difficult and that there are no universal solutions. Some countries

may be able to do no more than struggle to provide some of the conditions for a future industrialization, e.g. by building infrastructures (electrification, piped water, roads, etc.) and developing the export sector. See Clarkson, op. cit., p. 91.

53 V. G. Solodnikov, *Some Problems of Economic and Social Development of Independent African States*, Moscow, 1967, cited in Clarkson, op. cit., p. 201.

54 Boris Komarov, *The Destruction of Nature in the Soviet Union*, London: Pluto Press, 1981, p. 7.

55 ibid., p. 139.

56 ibid., p. 119.

57 ibid., p. 109. Komarov was writing before *perestroika*, of course.

58 Bahro, *Socialism and Survival*, op. cit., pp. 123–37.

59 See Samir Amin, *Unequal Development: An Essay on the Formations of Peripheral Capitalism*, New York: Monthly Review Press, 1976, and *Class and Nation: Historically and in the Present Crisis*, New York: Monthly Review Press, 1980; Immanuel Wallerstein, *The Modern World System*, vol. 1, New York: Academic Press, 1974, and *The Capitalist World Economy*, Cambridge: Cambridge University Press, 1980; André Gunder Frank, *Latin America: Underdevelopment or Revolution*, New York: Monthly Review Press, 1969, *Crisis: In the World Economy*, New York: Holmes & Meier, 1980, and *Crisis: In the Third World*, New York: Holmes & Meier, 1981; André Gorz, *Ecology as Politics*, Boston, MA: South End, 1980 (first French edn 1975), may be considered neo-Marxist although some of his themes are typically Green and do not really cohere with the neo-Marxist model of contemporary capitalism. The neo-Marxist model of development is generally said to originate with Paul Baran, *The Political Economy of Growth*, New York: Monthly Review Press, 1967; first pub. 1957. Note that I depend more heavily on Samir Amin's version than any other, even though it is distinctive in some secondary respects. For criticisms of the neo-Marxist model see Peter Limqueco and Bruce McFarlane (eds), *Neo-Marxist Theories of Development*, New York: St Martin's Press, 1983.

60 On the emergence of liberal ideology from the dominance of exchange relations see my 'Hegel and economic science', in B. Cullen (ed.), *Hegel Today*, Aldershot: Avebury, 1988, pp. 61–87, and my 'The development of the concept of civil society in Marx', *History of Political Thought*, VIII, 2, 1987, pp. 263–76. For more on the ideological character of the Green Model see Hans Magnus Enzensberger, 'A critique of political ecology', *New Left Review*, 84, 1974, pp. 3–31. On ideology in economic theory see M. Dobb, *Theories of Value and Distribution since Adam Smith: Ideology and Economic Theory*, Cambridge: Cambridge University Press, 1973; and M. de Vroey, 'The transition from classical to neo-classical economics: a scientific revolution', in W. J. Samuels (ed.), *The Methodology of Economic Thought*, New Brunswick, NJ: Transaction Books, 1980.

61 For an ideological defence of 'basic needs' see Paul Streeten, *Basic Needs*, Washington, DC: International Bank for Reconstruction and

Development (World Bank), 1977; and for a critique R. H. Green, 'Basic human needs: concept or slogan, synthesis or smokescreen?', *Institute of Development Studies Bulletin*, June 1978.

62 Karl Marx, *Capital*, vol. 1, cited in H. L. Parsons (ed.), *Marx and Engels on Ecology*, Westport, CT: Greenwood Press, 1977, pp. 174–5.

63 André Gunder Frank says: 'the so-called socialist world has not escaped from the historical process of world capitalist development or even from the operation deep within the socialist economies of the capitalist world's law of value' (*Critique and Anti-Critique*, London: Macmillan, 1984, pp. 282–3). Cf. Samir Amin, *Class and Nation*, op. cit., pp. 218–24, on the 'statist' mode of production.

64 See Osvaldo Sunkel, 'Transnational capitalism and national disintegration in Latin America', *Social and Economic Studies*, XXII, 1, 1973, pp. 132–76, and 'The transnational corporate system', *Links*, 24, 1986, pp. 7–9 (reprinted from the *CTC Reporter*, autumn 1985). Also relevant and informative is Folker Fröbel, 'The current development of the world economy: reproduction of labour and accumulation of capital on a world scale', *Review*, V, 4, 1982, pp. 507–55. Note that from 1977 Third World exports have been principally *manufactures*, and the composition of Third World imports has shown a declining proportion of consumer goods and an increasing proportion of *capital* goods. (See GATT trade figures for 1977 and later.) Of course, a very few NICs are involved.

65 One principal methodological difference (unity–diversity) between liberal and Marxist theories is discussed in my 'Two methodological paradigms in development economics', op. cit., note 6 above.

66 The pro-colonialist consequences of an earlier version of naturalistic Marxism are discussed in my 'Antonio Labriola, evolutionary Marxism and Italian colonialism', *Praxis International*, 7, 3–4, 1987–8, pp. 340–59.

67 Thus for neo-Marxists there is no 'traditional society' in Africa and the rest of the Third World: 'we have to conclude that there are no traditional societies in modern Africa, there are only dependent peripheral societies' (Samir Amin, 'Underdevelopment and dependency in Black Africa', *Social and Economic Studies*, XXII, 1, 1973, pp. 177–96). See Samir Amin's remarks on the linear paradigm in both liberal and statist theories in *Class and Nation*, op. cit., pp. 133–4.

68 André Gunder Frank's *Capitalism and Underdevelopment in Latin America*, New York: Monthly Review Press, 1967, presented this 'exchange relations' position, and it was first cogently criticized by Ernesto Laclau in 'Feudalism and capitalism in Latin America', *New Left Review*, 67, 1971, reprinted in his *Politics and Ideology in Marxist Theory*, London: Verso, 1979. For the standard neo-Marxist 'exchange relations' account see A. Emmanuel, *Unequal Exchange*, New York: Monthly Review Press, 1972. The early neo-Marxist position of Frank *et al.* was probably, in some respects less, not more, advanced than the standard Soviet theory which at least emphasized production relations in its own peculiar and unelaborated way. For the

contemporary model I am describing see Amin, *Unequal Development*, op. cit., and *Class and Nation*, op. cit., ch. 6.

69 See F. Fröbel, J. Heinrichs and O. Kreye, *The New International Division of Labour*, Cambridge: Cambridge University Press, 1980. The hypothesis that capitalism is still progressively industrializing the Third World is defended by a more traditional Marxist, Bill Warren, in his *Imperialism: Pioneer of Capitalism*, London: New Left Books, 1980. For a recent contribution to the debate on the 'progressiveness' of capitalism see Haldun Gülap, 'Debate on capitalism and development: the theories of Samir Amin and Bill Warren', *Capital and Class*, 28, 1986, pp. 139–59.

70 Amin, *Class and Nation*, op. cit., p. 131, my emphasis.

71 Gorz, op. cit., p. 85.

72 For figures on Latin America see Piers Blaikie, *The Political Economy of Soil Erosion in Developing Countries*, London: Longman, 1985, pp. 31–2. The complexity and diversity of the economic, political, social and geographical causes of soil erosion are emphasized and illustrated by Blaikie in this most illuminating book. His chs 6, 7 and 8 present an essentially neo-Marxist analysis of global soil erosion.

73 On the relation of subsistence agriculture and capitalism see C. Meillasoux, 'Development or exploitation: is the Sahel famine good business?', *Review of African Political Economy*, I, 1, 1974, pp. 27–33.

74 On the role of the TNCs and the Food and Agriculture Organization in forcing pesticides on the Third World see the merciless indictment by Marcus Linear in *Zapping the Third World: The Disaster of Development Aid*, London: Pluto Press, 1985.

75 See Blaikie, op. cit., pp. 138–46.

76 Stuart Howard, 'When the bosses are international, we've got to be international too', and Stuart Bell, 'Corporate campaigning', *Links*, 24, 1986, pp. 26–7 and 28–31 respectively.

77 See Alex Hughes, 'Corporate killers: Union Carbide in India', ibid., pp. 16–19.

78 The vulgar Marxist viewpoint misses the structural and historical significance of the 'new social movements', thinking of them only as shallow movements with which the 'true representative' of the 'proletariat', namely the Communist Party, may only tactically co-operate. See e.g. Ernst Wimmer, 'Ideology of the "New social movements" ', *World Marxist Review*, 28, 7, 1985, pp. 36–44.

79 Gorz, op. cit., pp. 36–40. I have argued elsewhere that it is vital to distinguish between a critical and an uncritical concept of 'civil society'. See 'The development of the concept of civil society in Marx', op. cit., and my 'Gramsci, civil society and bureaucracy', *Praxis International*, 6, 2, 1986, 206–19.

80 On the biotechnological possibilities in mining, the food and chemical industries, agriculture, and so on, see Steve Prentis, *Biotechnology: A New Industrial Revolution*, London: Orbis, 1984.

Chapter 7

Development and environmentalism

Robin Attfield

The days are receding when advocates of Third World development maintained that concern for the environment was a luxury
which only developed countries could afford. A similar view
sometimes surfaces from British Conservative politicians, when
they claim that conservation and preservation can only be afforded
out of the proceeds of development, as if at least the early stages
of development could take place in their absence. There is, however, an increasing realization that the kind of 'development'
which pollutes and sometimes undermines life-support systems is
inimical to any development worthy of the name. In this more
enlightened approach, human interests tend to be paramount, but
there is concern for the protection of the natural world, if only
for prudential reasons.

Environmentalists, meanwhile, frequently regard development
and its advocacy as the enemy which is to be opposed at all costs,
or at least as often as possible. While this is not the posture of
groupings such as the Green parties of Britain and Germany, it
is often encountered in British environmentalist circles, and is
even more prevalent among environmentalists in North America
and Australia. How deep this attitude goes depends in part on
the underlying value-theory and ethic professed or taken for
granted, and partly on the locally accepted understanding of the
causes of ecological problems and of the social and political conditions necessary to solve them. Accordingly, the ranks of
environmentalists include some who recognize poverty as one of
the causes of environmental deterioration and welcome sustainable
development in the Third World. Yet the advocates of development still come in for criticism for caring about nature largely in
the human interest.

In this chapter I shall try to explain why even the 'deeper' strain of environmentalists should support sustainable development (as opposed to undifferentiated growth), and are required to do so by their own principles, in so far as they are defensible. I shall also try to explain why developmentalists should equally support environmentalism, and support not merely its 'shallower' but also some of its 'deeper' versions,[1] and will do so if they are consistent. This double project will also involve comparing and relating the critiques of current evils propounded by the two camps: the developmentalist critique of underdevelopment and its economic causes, and the deep environmentalist critique of anthropocentrism. Critiques improve by taking greater ranges of factors into account, and I shall claim that each of these critiques is in danger of neglecting the factors stressed by the other.

A WAY OF PRESERVING THE INDONESIAN RAINFOREST: BUTTERFLY RANCHING

Applied philosophy can contribute to issues such as these by close attention to concepts and principles, and by tracing their implications. But to prevent the intricacy and complexity of the circumstances to which the concepts and principles must be supplied being overlooked, I shall begin my discussion of what development involves by reference to an example drawn from *Orbit*, the magazine of the British organization, Voluntary Service Overseas. There a volunteer in the cause of overseas aid to the Third World, Ian Craven, who worked for three years in Indonesia as an environmental officer for the World Wide Fund for Nature, adduces his own experience in rejecting the kind of conservation which would involve 'the total exclusion of any resource utilization' or 'the segregation of land from the local population for nature's protection in certain over-stressed regions'. Granted the poverty of the tribal people of the Arfak Mountains with whom he was working, and the risk that, without some financial return from the forest, they would succumb to external economic pressures (presumably from timber companies), the establishment of a nature reserve there required, and in Craven's view justifies, the participation of local people in its management and in particular the collection for export of butterflies. Butterfly ranching involves the collection of 'eggs, caterpillars or cocoons . . . from areas enriched with the butterflies' plant foods'; they are then 'shipped to butterfly zoos, collectors, taxonomists and scientists around the world'. Since the butterflies are forest reliant and the local people know this, they thus have a strong interest in preventing the destruction of the forest. Craven's short article is entitled 'Profit for the poor'.[2] (The role of timber companies in Indonesia is explained on the next page of the same number in an article by Jasper Zjilstra entitled 'Rainforest reality'.[3])

Many developmentalists would be likely to applaud Craven's plan unreservedly, on the counts that the basic problems of Indonesia are poverty and exploitation, and that for the tribal people in question this plan appears to alleviate poverty in some degree without the further exploitation which would be involved in the destruction of their native habitat and thus their way of life. The plan also involves their active participation, another hallmark of development which is of value both in itself and because of the self-respect and the increased autonomy of previously disadvantaged people which it is likely to bring. And developmentalists who are not apologists of timber companies would add the pertinent point that the plan would help secure the forest for future generations of Indonesians, and may well be the only way in which that can be achieved.

Others, whether environmentalists or not, would want to ask a number of questions, for example about the extent to which the plan really does save the forest ecosystem from destruction. In particular we are not told how (if at all) it is proposed to ensure that the butterfly species in question do not become extinct, at least as far as sites in the Arfak Mountains are concerned. For if they were to become extinct the forest would have been impoverished and at the same time the benefits to local people would prove not to be sustainable;[4] in other words, they would be thrust back into the same problem as at the outset. Thus the plan could be counter-productive even from a purely developmentalist viewpoint.

Environmentalists of a quite moderate persuasion might well add a number of points. Thus we are not told what other forest species depend, whether through pollination or predation, on the presence of the butterflies, and should need to know this to discover to what extent the forest genuinely escapes destruction. This relates to a more general question: how much 'resource utilization' is consistent with conservation? And even if the answer turns out to be 'quite a lot in this case', very little follows about whether conservation should not sometimes exclude the consumption of resources, and sometimes exclude even the use of non-consumable resources, and thus an actual prohibition of the human use of certain habitats. Anthropocentric (i.e. human-centred) reasons could sustain all these possibilities, but they become stronger still when the interests of non-human species are taken into account, as advocated by environmentalists of 'deeper' persuasions.

Some readers, particularly if they are also environmentalists, may by now be aghast at any amount of consideration at all being given to the cause of development, as opposed to none at all, especially if it can adopt such manifestations as this. But this is where the concept of development and the related moral obligations need to be brought into prominence. For I shall be arguing that there are obligations here to support and foster development which in any case cannot be disowned.

WHY ENVIRONMENTALISTS SHOULD SUPPORT DEVELOPMENT

In social and economic connections it is easier to define under-development than development. Underdevelopment is a condition of society where several of the following factors reinforce one another: malnutrition, high infant mortality, low levels of liter-acy, relatively high morbidity among the young and the middle-aged, poor medical facilities, poor educational facilities, low levels of income per head and low levels of productivity per head. Development may be taken, relatedly, as either the process or the condition resulting from the process of moving away from the cycle of underdevelopment.

But not just any departure from one of the mentioned variables amounts to development. The obvious example is productivity; for mere economic growth need not, as such, involve or indicate development of any kind. A number of other implications flow from the definition, such as the need for the active participation of the people concerned in the process of development if that process or its outcome is to be worthy of the name. But I have written about these matters elsewhere,[5] and should here move to a centrally relevant aspect of development (as just now defined), namely its necessary connection with justice. For injustice prevails where people's basic needs are avoidably unsatisfied; and except where underdevelopment is out of people's control, many people's basic needs are precisely unsatisfied, and avoidably so too, in the circumstances of underdevelopment. There is thus a strong moral obligation incumbent upon those who have the ability to help or hinder the process anywhere (whether by action or by inaction) to promote some form of development, for not to do so is to perpetuate injustice. This obligation is obviously particularly strong in the cases of the members of the society in question; but, short of stronger countervailing obligations, it is also a strong one for members of other societies who (individually or in concert) have the ability (whether by action or inaction) to help or to hinder the process.

To say this is certainly to assume that there can be relations of justice and injustice not only between members of one and the same society but also between different societies and their members. But this assumption cannot seriously be denied by anyone prepared to enter into moral discussion at all. For if the basic needs of anyone count, so do the basic needs of anyone else, in so far as an agent can make any difference to them. The fact that the one person is a member of the same society and another is not makes no difference at all in this regard. Certainly there are further moral rules requiring agents to pay special consideration to the needs e.g. of members of their family, and rules at that which make good moral sense; but the nature of these obligations in no way implies that all obligations depend on some special relationship or other.

Correspondingly there is a like obligation to help remove oppression wherever it is to be found, to the extent of one's power, and in so far as this does not conflict with stronger obligations. But where underdevelopment is avoidable, there, whether known or unknown, oppression exists. Accordingly, at least where other things are equal (and quite often when they are not), there is a strong obligation to combat oppression. But this is a further way of showing that it is a moral obligation to support development wherever avoidable underdevelopment is to be found. It would not be obligatory to support any and every form of development, as there are alternative forms, and some are arguably better than others. (Thus there is no general obligation to support schemes to develop tribal societies in ways which would undermine their inherited cultures.) But it is morally obligatory to support some form of development in each avoidably underdeveloped society.

But if so, the needs of the poor in Indonesia must be taken seriously, whatever our beliefs as environmentalists may be. It is morally unacceptable to claim, for example, that the needs of future generations for intact rainforest there justify us in disregarding these current needs. For if future people's needs count, so do the needs of our contemporaries. Nor is it satisfactory to maintain that what fundamentally matters in morality is the integrity and stability of the biosphere, and that as human beings sometimes subvert this integrity and stability their interests can be disregarded for the sake of the greater good. This kind of misanthropy is sometimes to be found among ecological writers;[6] but everyone should be clear that it involves disowning the intrinsic value and moral significance of the well-being of every individual, and the valuing of everyone and everything according to its relation to the biosphere instead. In other words, it is an attempt to disown all the requirements of justice. But it is hard to believe that even those who from time to time swallow this ethic can seriously employ it in their own interpersonal dealings, much less in their attitudes to themselves.

In any case, misanthropy of this kind is no part and no implication of what Arne Naess has called 'Deep Ecology', one tenet of which concerns the equal right of all creatures to live and blossom.[7] While I should not seek to defend his 'biospherical egalitarianism'. I want to draw attention to some of its less problematic implications. For the creatures which are said to have the right to live and blossom certainly include non-human creatures, and thus insects such as butterflies. But they also include human beings, with their more complex possibilities for self-realization. According to this approach, then, while the different interests must sometimes be weighed up against one another, there is a strong case for upholding the interests of each and every human being, especially (as in conditions of underdevelopment) where these interests are significantly unsatisfied at present. Indeed, Naess explicitly maintains that the Deep Ecology movement takes into account the needs of the Third World, alongside the interests of future generations and of non-human species.

Some environmentalists, however, will now maintain that all this stress on the needs of human beings exhibits species discrimination, and thus reinforces the central, underlying source of oppression, namely anthropocentrism. Why, it will be asked, should the problems of people be singled out as they have been above, to the neglect of non-humans (and in particular those sentient non-humans whom human beings exploit for food and in experiments)? A failure to recognize anthropocentrism for what it is fundamentally vitiates any ethic and any social programme, it will be alleged. Later in this chapter I shall try to explain that there is a great deal to be said in favour of this appraisal of anthropocentrism. Here it is more relevant to point out that drawing attention to unsatisfied human needs is quite compatible with concern for the needs of non-human creatures, and need not involve neglect of them. Thus the humanitarian tradition has historically made a point of protesting not only at slavery, excessive working hours and the oppression of women and children, but also at the maltreatment of animals.

But no movement should allow itself to supply too one-dimensional a critique of oppression. I shall be returning to this point in a later connection, but in the present context its bearing is that those who recognize the evils of anthropocentrism have a distorted vision if they ascribe the world's evils to anthropocentrism alone. Such a critique neglects such other sources of oppression as economic exploitation, racism and sexism. Warwick Fox has some salient remarks about one-dimensional critiques of oppression, of which mention is now in place.[8]

Such simplistic critiques, according to Fox, suffer from two major weaknesses, in respect of which they are 'not merely descriptively poor and logically facile' but also 'morally objectionable'. One of these is 'scapegoating', by which all members of a particular class are targeted for criticism to an equal degree, whereas in fact some subclasses are much more responsible for oppression than others, and some subclasses of the targeted class are actively working to challenge ecological destruction or whatever form of oppression is envisaged. By targeting all members of the class which (in the short term) stands to gain from discrimination, scapegoating is objectionably 'over-inclusive'.

At the same time, simplistic critiques suffer from what Fox calls 'inauthenticity' and at the same time 'under-inclusiveness'. For such analyses can lead to a denial of responsibility in cases where some responsibility should be accepted. Fox has in mind here critiques which focus in an uni-dimensional manner on capitalism or, again, on patriarchy; for such critiques can serve to exonerate e.g. trade unionists or women of all responsibility for oppression of any kind; but his point is not without relevance to any critique which focuses simply on anthropocentrism, and thus fails to ascribe responsibility for oppression to those human groups and individuals (not excluding some unionists and some women) who have the power to act oppressively and do not hesitate to use it so.

Fox's points here are well taken; a critique of global problems should neither be so blunt as to bestrew blame indiscriminately nor be so unsubtle as to distract attention from genuine major sources of oppression, and tacitly to exonerate them accordingly. What is needed in a critique of social or of global problems is the kind of intelligent approach which takes into account a plurality of seats of power and sources of oppression, a variety of degrees of complicity and a range of would-be legitimations of unjustified hierarchies, all of which need to be challenged. Such an approach has the tactical advantage that, instead of writing off all males or all beneficiaries of capitalism or even the vast majority of human beings, it facilitates alliances between diverse subgroups which either suffer from oppression or are prepared to campaign against it. But, tactical considerations apart, it has the intellectual and moral advantages of being more appropriate to the actual distribution of power in society (international society included) and more just.

While Fox was primarily objecting to writers and movements which neglect anthropocentrism and environmental destruction (a theme to which I shall return), his general remarks apply similarly to those who focus on anthropocentrism and environmental destruction to the exclusion of all else besides. For the same anti-discriminatory principles which underlie e.g. the Deep Ecology stance of Arne Naess apply to other instances of discrimination, of the misuse of power and of oppression also. There is, indeed, a kind of inconsistency involved in excoriating the arrogance of humankind for its chauvinist treatment of all other species besides, and lifting not so much as a finger in protest at economic oppression, sexism and racism. It is not as if these latter misuses of power involved minor discriminations within the world elite, humanity; for in many cases discrimination against humans is at least as bad as the treatment accorded to non-human animals. It is certainly true that nobody can campaign about everything, and that different people may rightly focus their energies on one campaign rather than another. But that is no justification for asserting or giving the impression that the same principles do not apply to oppression of different kinds.

The point may be reinforced by citing the definition of chauvinism given by Richard Routley (now Sylvan) and Val Routley (now Plumwood). The Routleys used this designation of 'substantially differential, discriminatory and inferior treatment by humans of nonhumans',[9] and this is a perfectly proper extension of the use of 'chauvinism'. But if this kind of treatment by humans of non-humans is chauvinism, then equally so is such treatment by humans of humans, especially in connection with discrimination of a nationalist or a racist basis, the original context of application (after all) of the term. And if substantially differential, discriminatory and inferior treatment is oppressive and unjustified in the one kind of case, so (truistically) it must also be in the other.

Thus where an environmental philosophy (or 'ecophilosophy') is partly grounded, like that of the Routleys, in opposition to unjustified discrimination, or, like that of Arne Naess, in the advocacy of egalitarianism on a global scale (at least in principle), or, like that of John Rodman, on the need for liberation,[10] the same grounds require support for opposition to injustice and oppression in inter-human relations. This remains the case even among those who maintain that the root cause of ecological problems is population growth, reluctant as the holders of this kind of theory may be to support some of the steps to development advocated by those who are not so persuaded. For even theorists of this kind would be obliged by their principles to oppose the oppression of those humans who are already alive. Their support of development programmes would, however, be more uninhibited if they came to recognize that the underlying cause of population growth is poverty, and that poverty is also one of the direct causes of ecological problems;[11] indeed, once these causal connections are granted, environmentalists have additional grounds for supporting the alleviation of poverty. But even if they are not recognized, such support is in any case obligatory on grounds of justice.

There is more of a problem, however, with environmentalists of two kinds, whose positions are prone to coincide in practice. One is the kind which regards humanity as a cancerous growth, so detrimental to other life-forms that the planet would be better off without it, or with drastically curtailed numbers. The other is the kind referred to above, which locates intrinsic value in the well-being of the biosphere as a whole, and determines the value of individuals and/or species by their contribution to this well-being, of which the leading criterion is diversity. Since most humans contribute little to the integrity of the whole, and since humanity has been diminishing planetary diversity, human beings would on this basis be either of neutral or of negative value, and should be treated accordingly. The first kind of position is sometimes supported on a consequentialist basis, in that humans are held to do more harm than good to life-forms overall; alternatively it can be harnessed to the ethical holism of the second kind. The second kind does not attach any value to the good of individual creatures or even life-forms, but derives its entire ethic from its collectivist and holist value-theory. Both kinds may fairly be described as misanthropic, and both earn the designation, coined I believe by Murray Bookchin, of 'ecofascism'.

The first kind of misanthropic environmentalism has been put forward by Dave Foreman, a supporter of Deep Ecology,[12] and has attracted from Bookchin the charge that Deep Ecology is essentially a misanthropic enterprise.[13] Foreman maintains that the best way to help Ethiopia is to let people starve, and that this will minimize suffering and death in the long term. Fox, however, is happy to see Bookchin taking Foreman to task for these 'personal, unhistorical and abhorrently simplistic views on population control', and is quick to dissociate Deep Ecology from support for them. Indeed, he quotes Naess as writing that 'faced with hungry children humanitarian action is a priority, whatever its relation to developmental plans and cultural invasion'.[14] To Fox's criticisms it may be added that any kind of positive consequentialism, in which intrinsic value is attached to worthwhile life, would be inconsistent with Foreman's conclusions; while if Foreman is appealing to negative consequentialism, a theory which would also, depending on circumstances, support the elimination of all sentient life in the cause of preventing suffering, the unacceptable implications require the rejection of any normative theory of this kind, and thus of whatever negative consequentialist theory he may happen to be appealing to. Ecofascism, in short, cannot be defended by the harm to people which it is supposed to prevent. It is only fair to grant to Fox here that he well shows that Deep Ecology does not stand for any such misanthropic position.

As for the holistic version of misanthropic environmentalism, I have already published what I believe to be fatal criticisms.[15] The central problem here is that no defensible ethic can assume the form which this kind of collectivist holism assumes, for its implications conflict with almost all the central cases of agreed ethical judgements and principles. This becomes particularly clear in connection with the instrumental approach which this position requires to be taken to all individuals. Thus whatever we say about the well-being of the biosphere and the desirability of diversity, we cannot defensibly say this. (These remarks do not, of course, subvert certain other positions in which axiological holism is combined with belief in the intrinsic value of worthwhile individual life; but there is no need to argue against such positions as these in the current connection.)

The conclusion which I draw from consideration of these two versions of environmentalism is that they are indeed misanthropic, but that there are extremely strong grounds against adherence to either of them. To put matters another way, those forms of environmentalism which are essentially opposed to development are ones which intrinsically deserve to be rejected in any case, while the remainder require some degree of support for development in so far as their supporters are consistent, not to mention the regard which they ought to have for justice.

One qualification is in place before I move on. It should be stressed that grounds for supporting development are *pro tanto* grounds for supporting sustainable development, i.e. the kind of development which avoids harm and loss to future generations and can be sustained indefinitely. Supporters of Deep Ecology are sometimes suspicious of sustainable development; but Arne Naess himself would seem to be selectively in favour of it, to judge from his article 'Sustainable development and the deep, long range ecological movement'.[16] Indeed, this is where Naess's remark about humanitarian action sometimes being a priority is to be found.

WHY DEVELOPMENTALISTS SHOULD SUPPORT ENVIRONMENTALISM

I now turn to the issue of whether supporters of development should also support environmentalism. Now there is not much of a problem about support for environmentalism in its shallower forms. Let us presume that the developmentalists in question are moderately well versed in the findings of ecological science, and also accept what is argued in *Blueprint for a Green Economy* in terms of the considerable impact of environmental factors on a country's economy as well as of the considerable impact of the latter on the former.[17] They will, if so, recognize that economic development requires not only the reduction of pollution and the conservation of natural resources, but also the preservation of a good deal of wilderness (e.g. wetlands and rainforest), all in the long-term interest of humanity. Indeed, the degradation of the natural environment would at some point make economic life unsupportable, while the loss of a species or an area of wetlands, being irreversible, involves a cost for ever to whichever humans could have benefited therefrom. Thus sustainable development calls for preservationist measures even more strongly than development does as such.

But these are just the kind of grounds which make environmentalists of the deeper persuasion suspicious, for they are compatible with an anthropocentric approach. And this may serve as a clue to the location of possible disagreement; for developmentalists are often reluctant to support campaigns conducted in the interests of non-human species or their members, particularly when so much human need remains unsatisfied. To some extent this would be a matter of priorities: non-human interests, it might be held, matter, but can wait. Others again might hold that they do not matter at all. And both schools of thought might well maintain that to focus on anthropocentrism in one's critique of the world's problems is to divert attention from significant evils such as inter-human oppression and the excesses of capitalism, and thus from the realities of power.

In practice, concern for human interests would bring such people into many a preservationist campaign. For humans have interests in preservation for the sake of scientific research as an end in itself, for the sake of its medical and agricultural applications, for recreation, contemplation and aesthetic enjoyment. Thus campaigns for the preservation of wildlife and the necessary habitats frequently have this kind of motivation. Yet in all these connections the natural world is regarded as nothing more than a resource, whether laboratory, museum, playground, temple, cathedral or art gallery. To this catalogue might be added the symbolic value of natural objects such as high mountains, cliffs (like those at Dover) and untamed rivers: nature as emblem, or perhaps as mascot. Nevertheless where human interests are paramount, other human interests will often take priority over all of these. So if preservationist campaigns are supported by some people on these grounds and by others on deeper environmentalist grounds, the alliance will be an uneasy one. Sometimes, indeed, the allies may part company, such as when preservationists urge (in Craven's words) 'the segregation of land from the local population for nature's protection'.[18] But this kind of segregation would be rejected not only by developmentalists, but also by the environmentalist movements of both Germany and India, to judge from Ramachandra Guha's excellent article 'Radical American environmentalism and wilderness preservation: a Third World critique'.[19] Indian environmentalists tend rather to support forest preservation for the sake of preventing soil erosion and flooding, and generally for the sake of human beings as well as that of forest creatures.

Nevertheless to grasp the need to support environmentalism of a deeper kind than that of anthropocentric preservationists, a developmentalist, like anyone else, would need to see the force of the critique of anthropocentrism. This would in no way involve abandoning other forms of negative critique, concerning oppression or hierarchy for instance, any more than it would involve support for the kind of segregation which debars local people from their own countryside. Rather it would supplement such a critique, and broaden appreciation of the nature of social and global problems, and of what might count as solutions to them.

There are two kinds of ways to proceed. One is to point out the inconsistency (and sometimes hypocrisy) of opposition to human suffering which stops short at opposition to comparable suffering in animals, or to argue from the intrinsic value of human health, happiness and flourishing by analogy to there being intrinsic value in the health, happiness and flourishing of non-humans, despite the differences between the natures of the different species concerned. To discriminate on the basis of species for no good ground is just as arbitrary as to discriminate on the basis of race or sex for no good ground, as Peter Singer has long been arguing;[20] and to mete out treatment which is substantially differential and inferior on no better basis amounts to what Val and Richard Routley have called 'human chauvinism'.[21] These are good liberal arguments, and none the worse for that; they deserve a hearing both from supporters of possessive individualism and from its most resolute enemies, and they call for radical changes not only at the level of individual behaviour but also at the level of public policy in matters such as agricultural methods, fisheries and land use. But there is another route by which a negative critique of anthropocentrism can be commended, at least to developmentalists, and I shall attempt to expound it now.

The critique standardly advanced by developmentalists of the causes of persistent underdevelopment concerns systems of power relations. Both within and between societies, it is held, the terms on which economic and other transactions take place are so skewed that flows of resources pass from those in economically weaker positions to those in stronger positions, in forms such as rent, debt servicing and the relative prices of raw and processed commodities. These economic relations depend on relationships of power, and are perpetuated by them; not only do governments protect business corporations, landowners and local elites, but at international level transnational corporations and the governments which support them have enough power to dictate terms to the governments of most developing countries. This system of economic and political relations sometimes actually benefits some of the poor, in that they would be even worse off without the investment and employment which it offers. But for all that it is profoundly exploitative. It is also mirrored in the power relations which often hold within families and between the sexes and the generations, and is thus prone to uphold the least desirable aspects of patriarchy and of gerontocracy.

This critique depicts a hierarchy of power relations, which does a lot to explain the persistence of poverty, and suggests that lasting solutions to social and global problems depend on a radical redistribution of power. Not all developmentalists, of course, subscribe to this critique, but very many would subscribe to at least parts of it, and this accounts for an insistence on exposing capitalism, sexism, and the like, for what they are. As the present project is to persuade developmentalists of a further point, I will assume the essential acceptability of this critique, at least for present purposes. But if that much is accepted, is it credible that the base of the hierarchical pyramid consists of rural and urban proletariats, subsistence farmers and the unemployed? At each of the higher levels interest-groups and classes profit from the humbler classes. Thus, as Bahro has been pointing out,[22] the working class in developed countries has considerably profited from the much more wretched condition of the poor of the Third World. But, as Bahro would readily agree, the lives of the poor (and to some extent of the relatively rich as well) have also benefited economically from transactions between humanity and other living creatures. Domestic animals have been used for traction, transport and food; wild animals are often hunted for their hides, fur or flesh; and forests have been eradicated for timber and for farming.

Now I am certainly not suggesting that the domestication of wild species of plants and animals is reprehensible; much less, with deep ecologists like Rodman, that domesticated animals should be phased out.[23] Technology in the forms of agriculture and medicine has contributed a great deal to making civilized life possible, and thus the liberation and flourishing of humanity. Nevertheless much civilized life has depended on the toil of animals, who, to quote St Basil, 'bear, with us, the heat and burden of the day;[24] and much has depended, and continues to depend, on animal deaths, in many cases before there has been time to develop the faculties proper to their kind, and often in unspeakable conditions. In the past, certainly, the system often gave some sort of dignity at least to some domesticated animals; and the use of wild species was sufficiently restrained as to be sustainable and to avoid too drastic damage to wilderness. But now two factors have intensified the time-honoured human use of nature: on the one hand, an increase in what the World Bank calls 'absolute poverty' and, on the other, the extension, usually driven by the profit motive, of economic activity on the part of corporations and governments to the furthest fastnesses of the globe. (Of these developments both pressures from the timber companies and the project to ranch butterflies in the Arfak Mountains are but tiny manifestations.) Population growth has exacerbated the problems caused by poverty, but as it is itself plausibly a product of poverty, there is no need to supplement the inventory of underlying problems in its regard. And as, according to the usual critique of developmentalists, poverty is itself a function of the global system of power relations, all the indications are that here we have the underlying cause, at least to the extent that the critique is to be credited.

If it is now added that human actions and policies *vis-à-vis* non-human creatures are no more inevitable or indispensable than most inter-human relations are in their present form, it becomes extremely difficult to resist the conclusion that these actions and policies often also amount to exploitation, i.e. not just use but unjustified use. The power system which pervades inter-human relations extends also to inter-species relations, and does not become any the more excusable in the latter connection. (I have hitherto avoided the use of 'exploitation' in connection with treatments of nature, as it has both a morally neutral and a morally pejorative sense; but I am now in a position to use the term without the need to qualify it.) And further, the processes which issue in exploitation within human relationships are identical with those which issue in unacceptable treatments of the natural world.

But if this is correct, then the critique adhered to by most developmentalists must itself be supplemented. For oppression turns out to be manifested not only in capitalism, sexism and racism, but also in anthropocentrism and human chauvinism. The iceberg of exploitation is even larger beneath the surface than is usually imagined; and, all along, it is habituating us to legitimize oppression, and to become hardened to it. Yet oppression is often a seamless whole, at least psychologically; when a callous disregard sets in towards any one class, the possibility opens up of the parallel unquestioning acceptance of oppression at any other level. And this symbolic factor is yet another reason for supplementing and developing the critique of the developmentalists.

There is, indeed, a close analogy of the case presented for environmentalists to broaden their critique of oppression beyond anthropocentrism alone; the developmentalist critique needs to be broadened similarly so as to include anthropocentrism. The reasons for this include the requirement to be consistent with one's own principles, the recognition that both underdevelopment and ecological problems have a common source and are causally interrelated, and the symbolic links between the different forms of oppression and, again, between the various campaigns which oppose it. A further reason would consist in the requirements of justice. This reason has not till now been deployed, as there is a widespread view (held, for example, by John Rawls[25]) that non-human creatures fall outside the scope of justice. But to the extent that the concept of exploitation has been shown to be in place, the same will apply to the concept of justice; and if so, there is yet a further similarity between the reasons why environmentalists should support development and the reasons why developmentalists should support some non-anthropocentric version of environmentalism.

As the future of the forest is apparently at stake, as well as that of numerous butterflies, it would not follow outright that butterfly farming should be rejected. But if the case which I have been making stands up, then even in that instance the grounds of environmentalists for reluctance about farming butterflies should at least be taken seriously. Those grounds turn not only on the interests of human beings, but also on those of forest creatures including butterflies.

NOTES

This chapter was presented as an address to the World Congress of Philosophy, Nairobi, in July 1991.

1 The distinction between shallow and deep ecology movements was made by Arne Naess, in 'The shallow and the deep long-range ecology movements'. A summary', *Inquiry*, 16, 1973, pp. 95–100.
2 Ian Craven, 'Profit for the poor', *Orbit*, 33, summer 1989, p. 15.
3 Jasper Zjilstra, 'Rainforest reality', *Orbit*, 33, summer 1989, p. 16.
4 Such criticisms are made by Vandana Shiva in 'Recovering the real meaning of sustainability', in David E. Cooper and Joy A. Palmer (eds), *The Environment in Question: Ethics and Global Issues*, London and New York: Routledge, 1992, pp. 187–93. But Shiva is also critical of the whole concept of sustainable development, a concept to the defence of which both Nigel Dower's chapter and this chapter in different ways contribute.
5 Robin Attfield, 'Development: some areas of consensus', *Journal of Social Philosophy*, 17, 2, summer 1986, pp. 36–44.
6 See e.g. J. Baird Callicott, 'Animal liberation: a triangular affair', *Environmental Ethics*, 2, 4, 1980, pp. 311–38. More recently Callicott's views have changed; see 'Animal liberation and environmental ethics: back together again', in his *In Defense of the Land Ethic*, Albany, NY: State University of New York Press, 1989, pp. 49–59.
7 See Naess, op. cit.
8 Warwick Fox, 'The Deep Ecology/ecofeminism debate and its parallels', *Environmental Ethics*, 11, 1, 1989, pp. 5–25.
9 Val Routley (now Plumwood) and Richard Routley (now Sylvan), 'Human chauvinism and environmental ethics', in Don Mannison, Michael McRobbie and Richard Routley (eds), *Environmental Philosophy*, Canberra: Australian National University, 1980, pp. 96–189.
10 John Rodman, 'The liberation of nature', *Inquiry*, 20, 1977, pp. 83–145.

11 See World Commission on Environment and Development, *Our Common Future* (the Brundtland Report), Oxford: Oxford University Press, 1987, ch. 4.
12 Thus Dave Foreman, interviewed by Bill Devall, 'A spanner in the woods', *Simply Living*, 2, 12, n.d., p. 43.
13 Thus Murray Bookchin, 'Thinking ecologically: a dialectical approach', *Our Generation*, 18, 2, 1987, pp. 3–40; Fox, op. cit., pp. 20f., reports finding similar sentiments in Bookchin, 'Social ecology versus "Deep Ecology" ', *Green Perspectives: Newsletter of the Green Program Project*, summer 1987.
14 Fox, op. cit., quoting from Arne Naess, 'Sustainable development and the deep long range ecological movement', published in *The Trumpeter*, 5, 4, 1988, pp. 138–42. Naess gives qualified support to sustainable development at p. 140, and stresses the priority of humanitarian action in face of the problem of hungry children on p. 141.
15 Robin Attfield, *The Ethics of Environmental Concern*, Oxford: Blackwell, and New York: Columbia University Press, 1983, pp. 179–82, also 'Methods of ecological ethics', *Metaphilosophy*, 14, 3–4, 1983, pp. 195–208, and 'Value in the wilderness', *Metaphilosophy*, 15, 3–4, 1984, pp. 289–304.
16 Naess, 'Sustainable development and the deep long range ecological movement', op. cit.; see also Fox, op. cit., p. 6 and p. 21 n. 38.
17 David Pearce, Anil Markandya and Edward B. Barbier, *Blueprint for a Green Economy* (the Pearce Report), London: Earthscan, 1989, ch. 1.
18 Craven, op. cit.
19 Ramachandra Guha, 'Radical American environmentalism and wilderness preservation: a Third World critique', *Environmental Ethics*, 11, 1, 1989, pp. 71–83.
20 E.g. in Peter Singer, *Animal Liberation: A New Ethic for Our Treatment of Animals*, London: Cape, 1976.
21 Routley and Routley, op cit.
22 Rudolf Bahro, *From Red to Green*, London: Verso, 1984.
23 See Rodman, op. cit.
24 Cited in John Passmore, 'The treatment of animals', *Journal of the History of Ideas*, 36, 1975, p. 198.
25 John Rawls, *A Theory of Justice*, Oxford: Oxford University Press, 1971, p. 512.

Chapter 8

Debt and underdevelopment: the case for cancelling Third World debts

Barry Wilkins

The 1980s are often referred to (by, among others, the World Bank) as the 'lost decade' for the development of the Third World.[1] The harsh reality behind this euphemism is that for hundreds of millions of the poorest people in the world life is getting steadily worse. James P. Grant, executive director of the United Nations Children's Fund (UNICEF), reports that 'For almost nine hundred million people, approximately one sixth of mankind, the march of human progress has now become a retreat. In many nations, development is being thrown into reverse.'[2] UNICEF further reports that since the early 1980s Latin America has experienced at least a 10 per cent drop in living standards, and Africa more than a 20 per cent drop.[3] Since these figures are averages the poorer sections of the populations in those continents have inevitably suffered an even greater deterioration in the quality of their lives.

In its *World Development Report 1990* the World Bank confirms this appalling picture, acknowledging as 'a disaster' that 'The living standards of millions in Latin America are now lower than in the early 1970s. In most of Sub-Saharan Africa living standards have fallen to levels last seen in the 1960s.'[4]

Why are conditions of life in many parts of the Third World getting worse? There are many causes. But fundamentally these causes flow from the weak and disadvantaged position of Third World countries in the world economic and political system. I will argue that in particular the Third World debt crisis plays a major role in obstructing the development of Third World countries by draining them of vital resources and finance. The debt crisis ensures that the poorest people in the world are subsidizing the incomparably richer institutions, such as banks, companies and governments, of the western world.

This chapter has three main purposes. In the first section I give a brief account of how the scale of Third World debt became so huge so rapidly. In the second section I indicate some of the consequences of this debt for the governments and, more importantly, the peoples of the debtor countries. In the third section I consider what should be done about the debt and by whom. I argue that Third World countries would be justified in ceasing the servicing of their debts to the west, but that the best solution to the Third World debt crisis would be for western institutions such as governments and banks to embark upon the wholesale and unconditional cancellation of these debts. While it is recognized that the issues are complex, adequate grounds are given for believing this conclusion to be compelling.

THE GROWTH OF THIRD WORLD DEBT

In 1990 the World Bank estimated that the total accumulated debt of the developing countries was $1,341 billion.[5] The magnitude of this sum is not easy to comprehend. Suppose that it were spread evenly throughout the underdeveloped world. Each person in the Third World would then owe several hundred dollars, which is more than the average wealth production per person in a whole year in many Third World countries. But of course the debt is not evenly spread throughout the underdeveloped world. The burdens it imposes fall particularly heavily upon some countries (especially, but not exclusively, in Africa and Latin America) and upon some people in those countries, as will become clear later.

The total debt of developing countries to western institutions – such as commercial banks, governments, the International Monetary Fund (IMF) and the World Bank – has grown rapidly.[6] In 1960 it stood at around $18 bn. It more than quadrupled to $75 bn in 1970.[7] The rate of growth accelerated dramatically in the next decade, so that by 1980 the debt had reached $639 bn, more than eight times the 1970 figure.[8] By 1990 this had more than doubled again to $1,341 bn. Thus in three decades developing country debt had grown to a staggering seventy-four times its size in 1960!

One way of assessing the seriousness of a Third World

country's debt is to compare it to the country's annual Gross National Product (GNP). Very many Third World countries, especially in Latin America and Africa, owe more than their annual total production of wealth. For example, in 1989 Argentina, Bolivia, Nigeria and Zambia all owed more than their GNP for that year. Some countries owed more than twice their annual GNP, e.g. Congo, Mauritania and Somalia. And a small number of countries owed even higher multiples of their annual wealth, e.g. Mozambique (nearly five times GNP), Nicaragua (more than six times GNP) and Guyana (more than seven times GNP).[9]

A number of factors have combined to generate the growth of these staggering levels of debt. In the space available I can briefly outline only some of the more important ones. First, there has been a long-term, serious decline in the prices which the export commodities of the Third World can obtain on the world market. Consequently, it has become increasingly difficult for the underdeveloped countries to obtain resources by trade. Commodity prices at the end of 1986 were the lowest in real terms for fifty years. The World Bank estimated in 1988 that by the end of the century prices would rise only modestly. According to the *Financial Times*, if this estimate is correct then commodity prices will have halved in real terms during the period 1950–2000.[10]

For Africa, the decline in commodity prices has been even sharper. In 1988 the World Bank also calculated that 'a typical basket of African exports now buys a third fewer imports than 10 years ago; if oil exports are excluded, the loss in purchasing power climbs to 50 per cent'.[11] Furthermore, earnings from oil exports also shrank during the 1980s as world oil prices fell. In 1990 the oil exports of Nigeria (Africa's principal oil producer) were worth less than half of what they had been in 1980.[12]

Second, the growing trade protectionism in the advanced capitalist world makes it harder for Third World countries to gain access to markets for their exports. Protectionism is on the increase as governments impose yet more tariffs, quotas, and the like, on the exports of other countries. This hits the Third World particularly hard. The way the system operates greatly hinders Third World countries from earning finance through processing their own natural resources, as Ben Jackson explains:[13]

The further Third World countries go up the scale of processing, the greater the efforts of rich countries to keep their products out. . . . Rich countries know they're on to a good thing, and allowing poor countries to do their own processing would threaten their ability to reap most of the profits. The greatest trade barriers put up by rich countries tend to be concentrated on the basic industries which Third World countries can most easily set up to process their natural resources. . . . Eighty per cent of poor countries' manufactured exports to the European Community are in sectors facing protectionist barriers (and 56 per cent in the United States).

Susan George, drawing upon a 1987 General Agreement on Tariffs and Trade (GATT) report, indicates that a decreasing percentage of the advanced world's imports are coming from the Third World. The result is that 'While less developed countries held 28 per cent of world trade in 1980, by 1986 their share had dropped to 19 per cent.'[14] Once again, Africa is especially hard hit. While comprising approximately 12 per cent of the world's population, its share of world trade had declined to 2.5 per cent by 1990.[15]

The combined effect of the two factors discussed so far has been to diminish the value of Third World exports and to obstruct Third World efforts to maintain export revenues by increasing the volume of exported goods. But simultaneously, the Third World has faced two further pressures. The growth of industrialization and urbanization in many underdeveloped countries, together with improvements in mass communications, has contributed to raising the expectations and aspirations of the poor for a better quality of life. Third World governments have thus come under increasing pressures to satisfy the rising demands of their peoples. Inevitably this has tended to increase the flow of imported goods from the developed world.

Furthermore, the cost to the Third World of imported manufactured goods has steadily increased. For example, when the Organization of Petroleum Exporting Countries (OPEC) substantially raised the price of oil in 1973, and again in 1979, these increases were passed on by companies in the developed world in the form of higher prices of manufactured goods. (Also the oil price rises themselves added to the import bills of those Third World countries – the vast majority – which are oil importers.) An additional factor increasing import costs has been pressure from the IMF upon Third World governments to devalue their currencies. (The effect of such devaluation is to make exports cheaper, but to make imports more expensive.) Often the IMF has insisted upon this (together with other measures which are discussed in the next section) as a condition of providing any financial resources to a Third World country.[16]

Thus the Third World was caught between declining export revenues and increasing import costs. This created a need for finance which western banks became eager to meet. From the early 1970s onwards western banks began substantially to increase their loans to the Third World, especially Latin America. In the belief that 'Countries simply could not go bankrupt'[17] and that a Third World nation could be relied upon to continue servicing its debts, the banks regarded the Third World loan business as highly profitable. Consequently, 'No one wanted to be left out. Immense effort went into selling loans to the Third World.'[18] Until the late 1970s interest rates were relatively low, and this increased the attractiveness to Third World countries of bank loans. But mostly these loans were commercial arrangements at variable rates of interest. When interest rates rose, as they did from 1977–1981, and (following a brief period of declining rates in the mid–1980s) again in the late 1980s,[19] further debts were piled up for those Third World countries which owed a high proportion of their debts to the banks.

Two preliminary conclusions are supported by the evidence and analysis which I have so far presented. First, the Third World as a whole, and Latin America and Africa in particular, occupies a position of structural weakness in the world economic and political system, in which it is especially vulnerable to the policies of the institutions of the advanced capitalist world regarding such matters as trade and interest rates. Second, the institutions of the advanced capitalist world have reaped many benefits from the weak position of Third World countries. Declining Third World commodity prices, growing trade protectionism to control imports from the Third World, increased prices of manufactured goods exported to the Third World and the development of a profitable Third World loans business[20] have all helped to support the institutions and economies of the advanced capitalist world at the very same time as piling up the financial burden on the Third World.

A final factor in increasing debt which must be considered is the role of Third World governments and political leaders.

Undoubtedly they have often contributed to the social and economic crises in their countries. The plight of the peoples over whom they rule has all too often been worsened by errors of political and economic judgement and by outright greed and corruption. But the errors, or crimes, of such governments and leaders are not the primary and fundamental causes of the crises in their Third World countries. This is not, of course, to whitewash the rule of such figures as Somoza, Marcos and Pinochet. By becoming the willing junior partners to the financial and political leaders of the advanced capitalist world they benefited from the disadvantaged position of their countries in the world economic and political system. But they were not responsible for that weak structural position in the first place. The main cause of the general plight of the Third World, and the debt crisis in particular, is the seriously disadvantaged position of the underdeveloped countries in the world economic and political system, and the domination of that system by the banks, companies and governments of the advanced capitalist countries in their own interests.

CONSEQUENCES OF THE DEBT FOR THE THIRD WORLD

The consequences of the debt for the countries and peoples of the Third World are devastating. First, a huge amount of resources has to be committed to servicing the debt. For example, according to the World Bank, in the seven years from 1983 to 1989 the developing countries spent in excess of $908 bn just on servicing their debts.[21] Yet in that same period the total debt grew from $893 bn to $1,261 bn.[22]

One reason for the continued growth of the debt despite the colossal level of debt servicing is that many Third World countries were forced to borrow more money, not only for the reasons explained in the previous section, but also in order to be able to continue to service their existing debts. Western banks had been happy to oblige with further loans as long as continued debt servicing remained secure and the loan business remained profitable. Until 1982, when the Mexican government declared a unilateral moratorium on its debt servicing, the Third World loan business *was* extremely profitable for the banks.[23] But from 1983 onwards, the commercial banks have grown increasingly reluctant to lend further amounts, as they have become aware of both the problems of Third World countries in maintaining their debt servicing and the popular pressures in the Third World to scale down or even halt such transfers of financial resources to the west.[24]

The reduction in the flow of commercial bank lending to the Third World since 1982 had the effect that in 1983 the net transfer of resources in relation to the debt between the developed capitalist countries and the Third World *went into reverse*. Every year since 1983 the Third World has suffered a huge net financial loss to the institutions of the western world through the mechanisms of debt servicing. The following World Bank figures represent net transfers from developing countries to the developed world solely in relation to debt:[25]

1983 $2.8   bn
1984 $21.7 bn
1985 $36.7 bn
1986 $38.3 bn
1987 $41.3 bn
1988 $42.1 bn   *people could not pay.*
1989 $39.8 bn
1990 $27.5 bn (projection)

Thus, in relation to their debts the developing countries from 1983 to 1989 transferred to the advanced capitalist world a net total of $223 bn. This is a gigantic transfer of resources from the Third World to the institutions of the developed world. It fully justifies Susan George's judgement that 'Third World debt . . . is a mechanism by which the poor in the poor countries can be forced to finance the rich in the rich countries.'[26]

The above figures indicate that the problem of the debt-related net loss of Third World resources to the west increased each year from 1983 to 1988. Does the slight reduction for 1989, and the more substantial reduction projected for 1990, suggest that the position of the Third World is now beginning to improve? Unfortunately not. It mainly reflects the rapid growth in arrears on debt servicing payments. Total arrears have grown from $27 bn in 1985 to $79 bn in 1989, and are projected to increase still further.[27]

The World Bank points out that for Third World countries there is 'financing implicitly provided by the accumulation of arrears', but despite this reports that it has not led to any increase in investment or growth in those countries which have accumulated arrears.[28] Yet this is hardly surprising. For many countries falling into arrears on their debt servicing, there is not a conscious choice to reallocate those resources elsewhere in the economy, but rather an inability to continue to transfer that level of resources to their creditors.

As it became more difficult, from 1983 onwards, for Third World governments to arrange further loans, they faced the question of how else they could gain the foreign currency needed to maintain debt servicing. Although some expansion of exports took place, for reasons explained in the previous section there were limitations to the progress which was possible. Only two main methods remained. First, the government could commit an increasing proportion of its export earnings to debt servicing. Second, large cuts in imports could be imposed.

Many indebted countries now spend a very large proportion of their export earnings on debt servicing. Hard-won foreign currency, which could be spent on development, is instead being sent back to the west. Many Latin American countries spend between a quarter and a half of their export earnings in this way.[29] For some African countries the problem is as bad or worse. Ghana spends a half of its export earnings on debt servicing, and Algeria more than two-thirds.[30] Only the accumulation of substantial arrears has saved many other African countries from a similar position. Melvyn Westlake has calculated that ten African countries would have to spend four-fifths of their export earnings on debt servicing if they were to meet all of their scheduled payments.[31]

Many Third World countries have also resorted in the 1980s to substantial reductions in imports to save money for debt servicing.[32] For Latin America and the Caribbean as a whole the level of imports in 1980 was regained only in 1989.[33] Some countries in the region (e.g. Brazil, the Third World's biggest debtor) did not even manage this.[34] In sub-Saharan Africa the situation was much worse. In the region as a whole imports in 1989 had still not regained their 1980 level,[35] and for Nigeria, the largest debtor in this group, 1989 imports had collapsed to just over a third of those in 1980.[36]

These two methods of accumulating foreign currency for debt servicing have very similar effects. The expenditure of a large proportion of export earnings on debt servicing rather than imports is entirely unproductive in terms of the development of a Third World country. A good deal of the finance which the country has earned through trading its products is thereby not available to benefit the people of that country but is transferred straight back to the developed world. Similarly, substantial cuts in imports reduce the quality of life of most of the people in a Third World country by depriving them of goods not available from domestic production, e.g. many manufactured products. Additionally, such cuts also hinder the economic and social progress of the country by making it harder to obtain the materials necessary for industrial, agricultural and infrastructural development.

Many Third World governments in difficulties with their debts have sought help from the IMF. In return for its financial assistance the IMF insists upon the government adopting such policies as currency devaluation (discussed earlier), cuts in government spending, privatization of state enterprises, abolition of price controls and the reduction of inflation through cutting domestic consumption (by, for example, increasing taxes and interest rates).[37] A package of such policies, tailored for an individual country, is referred to as an 'adjustment programme'. The adoption of such a programme by a Third World government at the behest of the IMF not only brings some IMF financial assistance; perhaps more importantly, other institutions such as governments, commercial banks and the World Bank take this as a symbol of the government's financial responsibility, and it can therefore lead to further loans from these sources.

However, 'adjustment programme' is another euphemism; in reality it means austerity and privation for the people of a Third World country. This is not a controversial claim. It is acknowledged by no less a person than the managing director of the IMF, Michel Camdessus, when he describes IMF programmes as 'very tough [and] harsh'.[38] The effects of such programmes are to hold down the standard of living of the country's people through, for example, lower real wages, cuts in government spending on health, education and social programmes, and cuts in subsidies on basic foodstuffs.[39] The results for large sections of the population are rising levels of unemployment, hunger, malnutrition, illness and illiteracy. But, as Ben Jackson explains, the burden of all this falls particularly heavily upon women:[40]

[T]he victims of debt are the poor. And within their ranks, women and children suffer most. Women have to cope and devise survival strategies when the country's debt-stricken economy means that household incomes fall and prices rise. Already, women are overstretched by their dual role. They are producers of both goods and services – as farmers, market traders, industrial workers. On top of this they do most of the unpaid household work, like gathering fuel and water (often from far away), caring for children, nursing the sick and managing the household. As debt and austerity programmes bite deeper, the economic pressure on women increases. . . . Yet at the same time they are expected to fill the gap as carers after health and social service cuts.

The effects of adjustment programmes are examined in detail by UNICEF in *The State of the World's Children 1989*. The evidence and arguments produced by UNICEF fully confirm Jackson's analysis, as well as highlighting the tragic effects upon Third World children:[41]

As the social effects of adjustment processes become more obvious, it can also be seen that the heaviest burden is falling on the shoulders of those who are least able to sustain it. It is the poor and the vulnerable who are suffering the most. . . . With some honourable exceptions, the services which have been most radically pruned are health services, free primary education, and food and fuel subsidies – the services on which the poor are most dependent and which they have least opportunity to replace by any other, private, means. . . . [I]n the 37 poorest nations of the world, spending per head on education has fallen by nearly 50% and on health care by nearly 25% in the last 10 years. . . . UNICEF's staff know from first-hand experience that in most countries the real cost of such cuts is being paid, disproportionately, by the poor and by their children.

To conclude this section, the consequences of the debt crisis for the Third World may be briefly summarised as follows. It is not the minority rich elite which bears the burden of debt, but rather the poor majority. It is they who are driven deeper into poverty, hunger and illness. The effects of the debt are particularly severe for Third World women, whose oppression and

Rawls

exploitation are thereby intensified. Finally, the debt crisis bears down especially heavily upon the most vulnerable human beings in the entire world, namely the children of the Third World poor.

PROPOSED SOLUTIONS TO THE DEBT CRISIS

Many ideas and proposals have been put forward as to how the problem of Third World debt should be solved. In this section I will outline and briefly assess eight such proposals. First is the view that Third World countries should continue to service all of their debts, on the grounds that these are contractual obligations which were freely entered into by the governments of such countries. This view was official western policy until 1988. But as arrears of debt servicing payments accumulated, and as economic and social conditions deteriorated in Latin America and Africa, western banks and governments abandoned this policy as no longer feasible.

Before moving on to examine the policy which the west has since adopted it is worth pointing out the chief weakness in this first view. Given the position of structural inequality which Third World countries occupy within the world economic and political system, and their extreme vulnerability to economic and political forces entirely beyond their control, it is quite implausible to claim that most Third World debt was freely entered into. As I explained in the first section of this chapter the debt grew in response to the *increasing* disadvantages faced by the Third World. The model of two parties on a more or less equal footing freely entering into a mutually binding contract is quite simply inappropriate here.

Since 1988 the new western policy has been to favour limited debt relief. This was heralded by the Toronto initiative on African debt (1988) and followed by the Brady plan (1989).[42] This second view marks a small step forward in recognizing that even with huge sacrifices many parts of the Third World cannot even meet interest payments on debts, let alone begin to repay the debt itself. In so far as the *principle* of debt cancellation has been conceded this is to be welcomed.

But great care has been taken in the formulation and implementation of these plans to set stringent limits to the debts to be cancelled. Consequently, only a small fraction of Third World debts has so far been cancelled.[43] In its 1990 survey of the world economy the *Financial Times* commented that with regard to the Toronto plan on African debt 'the benefits are so small', and as for the Brady plan 'the financial benefits have fallen short of expectations'.[44] This assessment is confirmed by the World Bank's report that the estimated increase in the developing countries' total debt from 1989 to 1990 is 'projected to exceed debt reductions under the Brady Initiative and other programs of debt relief and reduction'.[45] The current plans for debt 'forgiveness' are so modest that far from reducing total Third World debt they are allowing it to increase still further.

The third proposal requiring discussion is that of 'debt-for-equity swaps'.[46] The essential feature of this scheme is that a country pays off part of its debt by transferring the ownership of a share of one or more of its industries to institutions in the advanced capitalist world. Institutions which are owed money by a Third World country, such as commercial banks, or transnational corporations to whom the banks have sold some of the debts they are owed, then acquire property (equity) in the industries of that country. This method of paying debts became increasingly used in the late 1980s, with $9 bn of debt being swapped in 1988.[47]

However, this is a recipe for the loss of Third World financial resources by different means. It is a method by which western institutions can acquire a growing stake in the industries and economies of the Third World (and yet more 'leverage' over how those economies operate). A proportion of the profits made in such Third World industries are then returned to those western institutions according to the size of the stake which they have acquired. Even the World Bank has been moved to sound a muted warning that Third World countries are creating a future problem of growing profit remittances to the developed world.[48] Susan George quite rightly characterizes this method as 'neo-colonialist'.[49] Instead of running Third World countries by direct political rule, as in colonialism, the interests of governments in the advanced capitalist countries can now be pursued instead by the economic power wielded over the economies of those countries.

The fourth proposal for solving problems of debt is 'debt-for-nature swaps'.[50] With this method an organization with a concern for environmental conservation (e.g. the World Wildlife Fund) relieves a Third World government of part of its debt in exchange

cancel
part of
the
✗
debt

for that government agreeing to carry out certain conservation
projects. For example, in 1987 the Bolivian government was
relieved of $650,000 of its debt in return for agreeing to finance
and organize the Beni Biosphere Reserve.

One criticism of such swaps is that they ignore, or even violate,
the rights of the inhabitants of the area to be conserved. Ailton
Krenak, president of the Forest Peoples' Alliance in Latin
America, made such a criticism of the Beni Biosphere Reserve
agreement, claiming that it had involved 'the most brazen disregard for the rights of the indigenous inhabitants'. He argued that
'Debt for nature swaps put the environmentalist organizations in
the position of negotiating with our governments for the future
of our homelands.'[51]

If, in this particular case, these criticisms are well founded, it
does not follow that debt for nature swaps must necessarily ride
roughshod over the interests of local peoples. The Co-ordinating
Body for the Indigenous Peoples of the Amazon Basin has put
forward debt swap proposals which incorporate recognition of
the rights of the indigenous peoples in the Amazon region to
maintain their traditional ways of life and manage their own
land and resources.[52] (Whether such proposals are agreed by the
governments in the region is, however, another matter.)

A more fundamental weakness of the 'debt-for-nature swaps'
method is that it has relieved only a minute amount of Third
World debt[53] and is projected to save only comparably tiny sums
in the future.[54] Therefore, as Ben Jackson argues, there is a serious
danger that such projects distract attention away from the prime
issue in the debt crisis, namely the urgent need to tackle the
problems posed to Third World countries by the massive scale
of debt servicing they are expected to carry out.

The fifth proposal which I want to consider is that put forward
by Susan George in *A Fate Worse than Debt*. She calls this 'creative
reimbursement' or 'debt, development and democracy'. The
essential features of her proposal are that Third World countries
should pay their debts, but in local currencies rather than those
of the creditor nations, and also through 'reimbursement in kind'
by which she means the conservation of their natural resources
and cultural heritages for the benefit of all humanity.[55]

George recognizes that if western institutions were ever to
accept these terms they would be making huge concessions to
the Third World. She proposes that in return for these concessions

the west should require Third World countries to establish democratic governments, and to achieve greater social equality by
implementing a process of development especially aimed at the
poorest layers of society.

This is a disappointingly weak conclusion for George to come
to after the power and incisiveness of her analysis of the debt
crisis throughout the rest of the book. Indeed, it is open to a
number of serious objections. First, the debt still has to be paid,
albeit in a different form. Therefore, the burden of debt will
continue to weigh (if slightly less heavily) upon the peoples of
the Third World. Second, the west retains a coercive relationship
to Third World countries by demanding political and social
changes from them in return for the concessions made in the
forms which repayments may take.

As against this, I want to argue that the west has no moral
authority to impose this coercion upon the Third World. Very
often Third World resources (e.g. tropical rainforests) have been
squandered and exploited precisely because of the demands of the
developed world (e.g. for debt repayments).[56] Furthermore, the
west has supported (and often installed) countless Third World
dictators when it has suited the interests of western governments.
Iraqi President Saddam Hussein, for example, was backed and
armed by the west throughout his eight-year war against Iran.
And when Third World countries have democratically elected
governments which are not acceptable to the west (e.g. the
Allende government in Chile, the Sandinista government in Nicaragua) leading western governments, such as the United States,
have actively sought their downfall, often by illegal means. The
idea that the leading governments of the developed western world
would have the necessary moral authority to coerce the Third
World into the debt, development and democracy strategy is
nothing short of preposterous.

George recognizes that in order to achieve her proposed solution considerable public pressure upon western governments
would need to be mobilized and 'greater unity among the debtors
themselves, would be required.[57] However, I will argue that
public pressure in the west, and greater co-operation in the Third
World, would be more fruitfully directed at achieving the cancellation of Third World debts rather than their transmutation into
a more diplomatic form.

Sixth is the idea that individual Third World countries should simply renounce their debts and refuse to pay any further debt servicing. Although understandably attractive to Third World governments in desperate straits this would be a very risky strategy for an individual debtor country to embark upon. Enormous pressures would be imposed by western institutions to bring such a government back into line.

However, the ability of the governments of the advanced capitalist countries to ensure continued debt servicing would be considerably reduced if a number of major debtors were collectively to agree to halt their debt servicing. As we saw earlier, this is already happening in a partial and unplanned way, as the inability to pay leads to accumulating debt servicing arrears. But it has yet to be transformed into a collective, deliberate plan on the part of several major Third World debtors to repudiate their debts (the seventh proposal).

The evidence and arguments presented in this chapter strongly support the view that Third World governments would be justified in adopting such a plan. Their debts add considerably to the structurally disadvantaged position they already occupy in the world economic and political system. They lead to increasing privation and exploitation of Third World peoples, and hinder the economic and social development of Third World countries. Nevertheless, there would still be risks for those Third World governments participating in a collective refusal to repay debts. While the advanced capitalist world would probably not be able to force them back into compliance it could still inflict damaging retaliatory blows on their societies (for example by depriving them of western exports such as medicines and food).

Therefore, a far preferable solution to the Third World debt crisis, if it were possible to achieve it, would be for the governments of the advanced capitalist world to embark upon wholesale and unconditional debt cancellation. That they have a moral obligation to do so follows from the arguments already presented in this chapter. The debt crisis causes untold suffering in Third World countries, and also obstructs their future development. The obligation to cancel debts flows from the most minimal requirements of international justice, namely that the poorest and most oppressed people in the world ought not to have their predicament made even worse by institutions with far greater financial resources and political backing.

My argument therefore does not depend upon the probability

or otherwise that following western debt cancellation Third World governments would redirect financial resources currently spent on debt servicing into the economic and social development of their people. (Some would and others wouldn't.) The argument turns rather upon the obligation to relieve Third World debtor countries of an unjust burden which currently obstructs their development. While not a sufficient condition for real progress on Third World development, the cancellation of debt is certainly a necessary one.[58]

It should be noted that in addition to the plans for limited debt relief discussed earlier, western governments do cancel more substantial debts when in individual cases it suits their purposes. The United States government cancelled $7 bn of Egyptian debt in return for the Egyptian government's support in the 1991 Gulf War.[59] A further substantial debt write-off came when a group of western governments (the 'Paris Club') cancelled up to $16 bn of Poland's debt in order to assist Poland's transition to a market economy.[60]

Debt cancellation can also be offered to a Third World government to pressure it into a course of action in the interests of a western government. For example, in September 1991 the United States government sought to 'persuade' the government of the Philippines to retain a US military base by extending the treaty which expired in that month. If forthcoming, Philippine agreement 'directly opens the way for funds from the US Treasury that can be used for debt relief. The US will also be influential in securing funding from the International Monetary Fund, World Bank, and the Japanese government.'[61] (However, the Philippine senate decided to resist this pressure and rejected the US proposals.)

These types of debt cancellation which are tied to the interests of western governments have little or nothing to do with the real needs of Third World peoples and the pursuit of international justice. Rather, such cancellations pursue the continuing domination of the world economic and political system by the governments of the advanced capitalist countries. Given the historical record of these governments only the unconditional cancellation of Third World debts, for which I have argued in this chapter, could begin to free Third World nations from western-imposed obstacles to their economic and social development.

One objection often made to proposals for wholesale cancellation of Third World debts is that this would be a traumatic shock to the economies of the advanced capitalist countries. Two points may be made in reply. First, the economies of the advanced capitalist countries are far better placed than those of the Third World to absorb the burden of Third World debt. The annual production of wealth in the *whole* of the Third World is less than two-thirds of that in the USA alone! The member states of the Organization for Economic Co-operation and Development (OECD, a grouping of the most advanced capitalist countries) have a combined annual production of wealth which is more than four times greater than that of the Third World.[62] Total Third World debt is approximately 8 per cent of this annual OECD wealth.[63] These startling disparities between the financial resources of the developed and the underdeveloped countries show quite clearly that while total debt is a huge amount relative to Third World resources, it is a very much smaller proportion of the wealth of the advanced capitalist world.

Second, even if it were true that debt cancellation would disrupt the economies of the advanced capitalist countries, this would not show that the Third World should continue to service its debts. Rather it would be yet a further indication of the injustice of a world economic system whose richest members depended on net financial transfers from its poorest ones in order to support their economies.

A further objection to wholesale debt cancellation is made by Georges Enderle, one of the very few philosophers to have discussed the ethics of Third World debt.[64] Enderle accepts that (as I have argued) 'From the perspective of the industrial countries, a total cancellation could be realized without creating big problems.' Nevertheless he argues that such total cancellation is not ethically justifiable: 'debt cancellation would violate the principle of commutative justice in so far as those debtor governments or population groups who have profited from credit-taking would not have to pay back the debt burden'.[65]

Enderle's argument is flawed in two fundamental ways. First, it is misleading to talk in general terms of debtor governments or populations having benefited from credit-taking. As was explained earlier in this chapter, much Third World debt was incurred simply in order for Third World countries to cope for a little longer with their increasingly disadvantaged position in the world economic system. In retrospect it may have been a short-sighted policy, in that it landed Third World governments with a huge debt servicing burden. However, many Third World governments had little choice but to build up these debts. They were certainly encouraged to do so by the governments of the advanced capitalist countries, who 'bear a heavy responsibility' for the debt crisis.[66]

It is also misleading for Enderle to suggest that debt cancellation would mean that the Third World 'would not have to pay back the debt burden'. Rather, the cancellation of Third World debt would bring to an end a process of repayment which has gone on for more than thirty years. As this chapter has explained, the governments and peoples of the Third World have *already* repaid vast amounts of finance to the developed world, and are continuing to transfer to the west huge net flows of precious resources each year.

The argument developed so far, that western institutions ought unconditionally to cancel Third World debts, has a practical significance. Given the record of western governments and other institutions it is virtually inconceivable that they would embark upon wholesale, unconditional debt cancellation out of the goodness of their hearts. Enormous pressures would need to be brought to bear upon them to achieve such action. A number of campaigns exist which seek to build up such pressures, and the arguments presented in this chapter can help to strengthen the case which such campaigns advocate.

However, a very large difficulty remains. While the western unconditional cancellation of debt is (I have argued) the preferable solution to the Third World debt crisis, it is scarcely imminent. Realistically, it may take a long time before western governments and banks are pressured into such cancellations on a scale large enough to bring real benefits to the peoples of Third World debtor nations. But the burdens imposed upon the Third World by the debt crisis are far too severe for Third World countries simply to wait for public pressure to bring a change of policy in the west. Granted, then, the unavailability (for the present) of the preferred solution, what can the governments and peoples of the debtor nations do?

In response to this problem, and to conclude this chapter, I will briefly consider the views advanced by Sue Branford and Bernardo Kucinski in the final chapter of *The Debt Squads: The US, the Banks and Latin America*. They argue that 'Far from having a moral obligation to the creditors to go on paying the debt, the governments of Latin America have a moral obligation to their people to stop paying the debt.'[67] How this obligation should be carried out is, they suggest, a matter on which 'governments must be pragmatic',[68] since the best tactics to adopt in dealing with the west will depend upon the specific circumstances of each debtor country.

In developing their argument Branford and Kucinski draw upon the work of Anatole Kaletsky, who has made one of the most detailed studies to date of Third World government default as a possible response to growing indebtedness.[69] It is impossible to present the details of Kaletsky's analysis here. Briefly, he argues that debtor nations have more options available to them than either continued debt servicing or outright repudiation of their debts. Kaletsky coined the concept of 'conciliatory default'[70] in accordance with which a debtor government would not seek to provoke the west by an explicit repudiation of its debts, but rather would default on some of its debts, particularly those to commercial banks, while adopting a non-provocative and conciliatory manner to other western institutions, especially the governments concerned. By such a method a Third World debtor could avoid uniting its creditors against it:[71]

> One of the misconceptions which arises from failing to distinguish between conciliatory default and provocative repudiation is the belief that all the foreign economic interests in a debtor country will unite in boycotting it if it defaults. In reality, they may have no incentive to do so; for a default on medium-term bank debts which was carefully planned and presented in a conciliatory manner could leave unscathed the interests of foreign traders, multinational direct investors, and providers of trade finance.

Kaletsky further argues that the western governments concerned would be unlikely to resort to damaging retaliation in the event of a conciliatory default.[72] He gives a number of reasons for thinking that such retaliation to a conciliatory default would not be in the interests of governments in the advanced capitalist world, e.g. the possibility that western retaliation could provoke an outright repudiation by a Third World government of all of its debts.[73]

Branford and Kucinski argue that Kaletsky's analysis is

particularly suited to the predicament of Latin American debtor governments since the majority of their debts are owed to the commercial banks. Therefore, they suggest, a Latin American government could default on its bank debts while maintaining a conciliatory attitude to the western government(s) concerned, and ensuring that the default is 'presented regretfully as a painful necessity, not as a political challenge to the world's financial system'.[74]

As long as wholesale, unconditional debt cancellation is not forthcoming from the advanced capitalist governments the method of 'conciliatory default' is perhaps the best option available to those Latin American governments seeking substantial reductions in the burdens which debt imposes on their peoples. Damaging consequences from retaliatory action by western governments could almost certainly be avoided by skilful deployment of this approach.

Is the method of conciliatory default relevant to solving the debt crisis in African countries, where the majority of debt is not to the commercial banks but to western governments and also to international institutions such as the IMF and the World Bank?[75] There may be rather less scope here for defaulting on some debts while maintaining relations with other creditors. The rapid accumulation of debt servicing arrears in Africa is, in a way, conciliatory default; the debtor nations do not repudiate their debts, they simply cannot afford to pay them. But as noted earlier the scale of arrears so far has been insufficient to ease the burdens imposed by the debt to any substantial extent. Perhaps ways could be devised of applying the method of conciliatory default to the specific circumstances of the African debtor nations, and perhaps these would include the further accumulation of arrears. However, to provide sufficient resources both to benefit the peoples of these countries and to begin to develop their devastated societies will require reductions in debt servicing on a far greater scale than have so far been achieved.

Finally, however successful conciliatory default might be at lessening the burden of debt on Third World countries, as a solution to the Third World debt crisis it is still second best. It reduces rather than ends the servicing of debts. Therefore, it may slow down but it cannot halt the loss of precious resources and hard-won finance which the Third World desperately needs to retain for the benefit of its peoples and the development of their societies. My conclusion is that the unconditional cancellation of Third World debt by the institutions of the advanced capitalist countries must remain the best solution. The initiative for achieving this solution lies with the peoples of the advanced capitalist countries. Through campaigns and struggles in solidarity with the peoples of the Third World, western governments and other institutions must be made to bring the Third World debt crisis to an end with a programme of wholesale and unconditional debt cancellation.

NOTES

I would like to thank Robin Attfield and Neil Thomas for their helpful comments on an earlier draft of this chapter.

1 World Bank, *World Development Report 1990*, Oxford: Oxford University Press, 1990, p. 7.
2 UNICEF, *The State of the World's Children 1989*, Oxford: Oxford University Press, 1989, p. 1.
3 Ben Jackson, *Poverty and the Planet: A Question of Survival*, Harmondsworth: Penguin, 1990, p. 90, drawing upon information in UNICEF, *The State of the World's Children 1990*, Oxford: Oxford University Press, 1990, p. 8.
4 World Bank, op. cit., p. 7.
5 World Bank, *World Debt Tables 1990–91*, Washington, DC: World Bank, 1990, vol. 1, *Analysis and Summary Tables*, p. 12. (I follow the standard practice in the literature on Third World debt of giving all monetary amounts in US dollars, and by using 'billion' to mean 1,000 million.)
   The World Bank includes in 'developing countries' seven of the poorer countries in Europe and the Mediterranean which are not normally considered to be part of the Third World, e.g. Portugal and Turkey. However, if the debt of these countries is subtracted, the estimated total 1990 debt for Third World developing countries stands at almost $1,200 bn.
6 I include the IMF and World Bank under the description 'western institutions' since although their governing bodies include representatives from the Third World and the non-capitalist world, effective control of these institutions lies in the hands of the major contributors, namely the governments of the advanced capitalist countries, particularly the United States. See Susan George, *A Fate Worse than Debt*, Harmondsworth: Penguin, 1988, pp. 54–7; and Peter Körner, Gero Maass, Thomas Siebold and Rainer Tetzlaff, *The IMF and the Debt Crisis*, London and Atlantic Highlands, NJ: Zed Books, 1987, pp. 42–51.
7 Körner, *et al.*, op cit., p. 5.
8 World Bank, *World Debt Tables*, op cit., vol. 1, p. 12.

9 This information is derived from ibid., vol. 2, *Country Tables*, which gives details of the external debts of 107 developing countries.

10 Survey of the world economy, *Financial Times*, 28 September 1988. See also World Bank, *World Development Report*, op. cit., pp. 12–16.

11 *Financial Times*, 30 September 1988.

12 *Financial Times*, 24 September 1988; and survey of Nigeria, *Financial Times*, 12 March 1991.

13 Jackson, op. cit., p. 76.

14 George, op. cit., p. 73.

15 *Financial Times*, 13 August 1990.

16 George, op. cit., ch. 3. See also Harold Lever and Christopher Huhne, *Debt and Danger: The World Financial Crisis*, Harmondsworth: Penguin, 1987, pp. 67–8; and Körner *et al.*, op. cit., pp. 51–9.

17 Lever and Huhne, op. cit., p. 53.

18 ibid., p. 58.

19 World Bank, *World Development Report*, op. cit., p. 15.

20 Commercial bank lending to the Third World became less profitable after 1982, for reasons explained in the next section.

21 This figure is calculated from information in World Bank, *World Debt Tables*, op. cit., vol. 1, p. 126. It does not include the debt servicing payments of forty-five developing countries outside of the World Bank's Debtor Reporting System (but estimates of these countries' debts *are* included in the World Bank's estimate of the total debt of developing countries).

22 ibid., p. 12.

23 See Sue Branford and Bernardo Kucinski, *The Debt Squads: The US, the Banks and Latin America*, London and Atlantic Highlands, NJ: Zed Books, 1988, pp. 74–5; and Lever and Huhne, op. cit., p. 13.

24 For example, in Brazil the candidate of the Workers' Party, whose policies include opposition to the servicing of Brazil's debt, gained 31 million votes (47 per cent of the total valid vote) in the December 1989 presidential election (*Keesing's Record of World Events*, 35, 12, December 1989, p. 37, 117).

25 World Bank, *World Debt Tables*, op. cit., vol. 1, p. 126.

26 George, op. cit., p. 253.

27 World Bank, *World Debt Tables*, op. cit., vol. 1, p. 22.

28 ibid.

29 ibid., vol 2, passim.

30 ibid., pp. 2 and 130.

31 Melvyn Westlake, 'Why a continent suffers in silence', *Guardian*, 5 February 1991.

32 Lever and Huhne, op. cit., pp. 33–6; and Jackson, op. cit., p. 108.

33 World Bank, *World Debt Tables*, op. cit., vol. 1, p. 142.

34 ibid., vol. 2, p. 34.

35 ibid., vol. 1, p. 130.

36 ibid., vol. 2, p. 266.

37 See George, op. cit., ch. 3; Lever and Huhne, op. cit., ch. 5; and Körner, *et al.*, op. cit., chs 2–4.

38 Interview with Michael Camdessus, *Financial Times*, 24 September 1990.
39 See Jackson, op. cit., ch. 5; and UNICEF, *State of the World's Children 1989*, op. cit., pp. 15–19.
40 Jackson, op. cit., pp. 91–2. See also UNICEF, *State of the World's Children 1989*, op. cit., pp. 40–1 and 55.
41 UNICEF, *State of the World's Children 1989*, op. cit., pp. 16–17.
42 For details see Jackson, op. cit., pp. 118–24; and World Bank, *World Debt Tables*, op. cit., vol. 1, pp. 31–42.
43 See Melvyn Westlake, op. cit., and 'Recession puts the brakes on recovery', *Guardian*, 4 February 1991.
44 Survey of the world economy, *Financial Times*, 24 September 1990.
45 World Bank, *World Debt Tables*, op. cit., vol. 1, p. 3.
46 See Jackson, op. cit., pp. 121–2; and George op. cit., pp. 203–5.
47 Jackson, op. cit., p. 122.
48 World Bank, *World Debt Tables*, op. cit., vol 1, pp. 36–7.
49 George, op. cit., p. 205.
50 See Jonathan Burton, 'Back to nature – the financial way', *The Banker*, 138, 754, December 1988, pp. 22–5; and Jackson, op. cit., pp. 122–3.
51 *Guardian*, 13 April 1990.
52 *Financial Times*, 15 May 1990.
53 According to Ben Jackson, op. cit., p. 123, the total value of all debt for nature swaps by 1990 amounted to less than $100 million (i.e. $0.1 bn) of debts to commercial banks.
54 Burton, op. cit., p. 25.
55 George, op. cit., pp. 236–43.
56 Jackson, op. cit., p. 97.
57 George, op. cit., p. 236.
58 See also Jackson, op. cit., p. 98.
59 Survey of Egypt, *Financial Times*, 24 June 1991.
60 Survey of Poland, *Financial Times*, 2 May 1991.
61 *Financial Times*, 4 September 1991.
62 These comparisons are calculated from 1988 Gross Domestic Product (GDP) figures for 121 countries given in World Bank, *World Development Report*, op. cit., pp. 182–3.
63 This figure is calculated by comparing the OECD total GDP for 1988 (World Bank, *World Development Report*, op. cit., p. 183) with the total 1988 Third World debt. Following the method explained in note 5 above I have calculated the 1988 Third World debt by subtracting from the 1988 total debt of the developing countries the debts of the European and Mediterranean developing countries for the same year (World Bank, *World Debt Tables*, op. cit., vol. 1, pp. 12 and 138).
64 Georges Enderle, 'The indebtedness of low-income countries as an ethical challenge for industrialized market economies', *International Journal of Applied Philosophy*, 4, 3, 1989, pp. 31–8.
65 ibid., p. 36.
66 Lever and Huhne, op. cit., p. 13.
67 Branford and Kucinski, op. cit., p. 135.

68 ibid.
69 Anatole Kaletsky, *The Costs of Default*, New York: Priority Press Publications, 1985.
70 ibid., p. 3.
71 ibid., p. 33.
72 ibid., chs 6 and 7.
73 ibid., p. 46.
74 Branford and Kucinski, op. cit., p. 132.
75 See Jackson, op. cit., pp. 92–3; and Westlake, 'Why a continent suffers in silence', op. cit.

Bibliography

Amin, Samir, 'Underdevelopment and dependency in black Africa', *Social and Economic Studies*, XXII, 1, 1973, pp. 177–96.
—— *Unequal Development: An Essay on the Formations of Peripheral Capitalism*, New York: Monthly Review Press, 1976.
—— *Class and Nation: Historically and in the Present Crisis*, New York: Monthly Review Press, 1980.
Arrow, Kenneth J., 'Why people go hungry', *New York Review of Books*, XXIX, 12, 15 July 1982, pp. 24–6.
Attfield, Robin, *The Ethics of Environmental Concern*, Oxford: Blackwell, and New York: Columbia University Press, 1983.
—— 'Methods of ecological ethics', *Metaphilosophy*, 14, 3–4, 1983, pp. 195–208.
—— 'Value in the wilderness', *Metaphilosophy*, 15, 3–4, 1984, pp. 289–304.
—— 'Development: some areas of consensus', *Journal of Social Philosophy*, 17, 2, summer 1986, pp. 36–44.
—— *A Theory of Value and Obligation*, London: Croom Helm, 1987.
Bahro, Rudolf, *Socialism and Survival*, London: Heretic, 1982.
—— *From Red to Green*, London: Verso, 1984.
—— *Building the Green Movement*, London: Heretic, 1986.
Baker, John, *Arguing for Equality*, London: Verso, 1987.
Baran, Paul, *The Political Economy of Growth*, New York: Monthly Review Press, 1967; first pub. 1957.
Barry, Brian, 'Circumstances of justice and future generations', in R. I. Sikora and Brian Barry (eds), *Obligations to Future Generations*, Philadelphia, PA: Temple University Press, 1978, pp. 204–48.
Bartelmus, Peter, *Environment and Development*, Boston, MA: Allen & Unwin, 1986.
Bauer, P. T., *Dissent on Development*, London: Weidenfeld & Nicolson, 1971.
—— *Equality, The Third World and Economic Delusion*, London: Weidenfeld & Nicolson, 1981.
—— *Reality and Rhetoric: Studies in the Economics of Development*, London: Weidenfeld & Nicolson, 1984.

Baxter, Brian, 'The self, morality and the nation-state', in Anthony Ellis (ed.), *Ethics and International Relations*, Manchester: Manchester University Press, 1986, pp. 113–26.

Beckerman, Wilfred, *In Defence of Economic Growth*, London: Cape, 1974.

Beitz, Charles, *Political Theory and International Relations*, Princeton, NJ: Princeton University Press, 1979.

Bell, Stuart, 'Corporate campaigning', *Links*, 24, 1986, pp. 28–31.

Bennett, Jon, *The Hunger Machine: The Politics of Food*, Cambridge: Polity Press, 1987.

Bideleux, R., *Communism and Development*, London: Methuen, 1985.

Bittner, Rüdiger, 'Maximen', in G. Funke (ed.), *Akten des 4 Internationalen Kant-Kongresses*, Berlin: De Gruyter, 1974.

Blaikie, Piers, *The Political Economy of Soil Erosion in Developing Countries*, London: Longman, 1985.

Bookchin, Murray, 'Social ecology versus "Deep Ecology" ', *Green Perspectives: Newsletter of the Green Program Project*, summer 1987.

—— 'Thinking ecologically: a dialectical approach', *Our Generation*, 18, 2, 1987, pp. 3–40.

Bradley, F. H., *Ethical Studies*, London: Oxford University Press, 1962.

Brandt Commission, *North–South: A Programme for Survival* (the Brandt Report), London: Pan Books, 1980.

—— *Common Crisis North–South: Co-operation for World Recovery*, London: Pan Books, 1983.

Branford, S. and Kucinski, B., *The Debt Squads: The US, the Banks and Latin America*, London and Atlantic Highlands, NJ: Zed Books, 1988.

Brittain, Victoria, 'Fighting brings grim harvest of despair', *Guardian*, 2 January 1991.

Bull, H., *The Anarchical Society*, London: Macmillan, 1977.

Burton, J., 'Back to nature – the financial way', *The Banker*, 138, 754, December 1988, pp. 22–5.

Callicott, J. Baird, 'Animal liberation: a triangular affair', *Environmental Ethics*, 2, 4, 1980, pp. 311–38.

—— 'Animal liberation and environmental ethics: back together again', in his *In Defense of the Land Ethic*, Albany, NY: State University of New York Press, 1989, pp. 49–59.

Charvet, John, *Feminism*, London: Dent, 1982.

Chodorow, Nancy, *The Reproduction of Mothering*, Berkeley, CA: University of California Press, 1978.

Clarkson, Stephen, *The Soviet Theory of Development: India and the Third World in Marxist–Leninist Scholarship*, Toronto: University of Toronto Press, 1978, and London: Macmillan, 1979.

Colletti, Lucio, *Marxism and Hegel*, London: New Left Books, 1973.

Collier, Andrew, 'Scientific socialism and the question of socialist values', in Kai Nielsen and Steven Patten (eds), *Marx and Morality*, Guelph, Ontario: Canadian Association for Publishing in Philosophy, 1981, pp. 121–54.

—— 'Milton Fisk, Marxism and ethics', *Radical Philosophy*, 36, 1984, pp. 20–6.

—— *Scientific Realism and Socialist Thought*, Hemel Hempstead: Harvester Press, 1989.

—— *Socialist Reasoning*, London: Pluto Press, 1990.

Craven, Ian, 'Profit for the poor', *Orbit*, 33, summer 1989, p. 15.

Crocker, David A., 'Toward development ethics', *World Development*, 19, 5, 1991, pp. 457–83.

Devall, Bill, 'A spanner in the woods', *Simply Living*, 2, 12, n.d., p. 43.

Dobb, M., *Theories of Value and Distribution since Adam Smith: Ideology and Economic Theory*, Cambridge: Cambridge University Press, 1973.

Dower, Nigel, *World Poverty: Challenge and Response*, York: Ebor Press, 1983.

—— 'What is development? A philosopher's answer', Glasgow University Centre for Development Studies Occasional Paper Series no. 3, Glasgow: Glasgow University, 1989.

—— 'Philosophy, the environment and sustainable development', *Revista de Filosofia*, Autonomous University of Yucatan, February 1990, pp. 46–57.

Dower, Nigel (ed.), *Ethics and Environmental Responsibility*, Aldershot and Brookfield, VT: Gower, 1989.

Drèze, Jean and Sen, Amartya, *Hunger and Public Action*, Oxford: Oxford University Press, 1989.

Eckholm, Eric P., *Losing Ground: Environmental Stress and World Food Prospects*, Oxford: Pergamon, 1978.

Edelman, Murray, 'The political language of the helping professions', in Michael J. Shapiro (ed.), *Language and Politics*, New York: New York University Press, 1984.

Ellis, Anthony (ed.), *Ethics and International Relations*, Manchester: Manchester University Press, 1986.

Emmanuel, A., *Unequal Exchange*, New York: Monthly Review Press, 1972.

Enderle, G., 'The indebtedness of low-income countries as an ethical challenge for industrialized market economies', *International Journal of Applied Philosophy*, 4, 3, 1989, pp. 31–8.

Enzensberger, Hans Magnus, *The Consciousness Industry*, New York: Seabury Press, 1974.

—— 'A critique of political ecology', *New Left Review*, 84, 1974, pp. 3–31.

Feder, Ernest, 'Latifundia and agricultural labour in Latin America', in Teodor Shanin (ed.), *Peasants and Peasant Societies*, Harmondsworth: Penguin, 1971, pp. 83–97.

—— *Strawberry Imperialism: An Enquiry into the Mechanisms of Dependency in Mexican Agriculture*, The Hague: Institute of Social Studies, 1978.

Feinberg, J., *Social Philosophy*, Englewood Cliffs, NJ: Prentice-Hall, 1973.

Fishkin, James, 'Theories of justice and international relations: the limits of liberal theory', in Anthony Ellis (ed.), *Ethics and International Relations*, Manchester: Manchester University Press, 1986, pp. 1–23.

Fisk, Milton, *Ethics and Society*, Brighton: Harvester Press, 1980.

Fletcher, Joseph, 'Give if it helps, but not if it hurts', in William Aiken and Hugh La Follette (eds), *World Hunger and Moral Obligation*, Englewood Cliffs, NJ: Prentice-Hall, 1977.

Fox, Warwick, 'The deep ecology/ecofeminism debate and its parallels', *Environmental Ethics*, 11, 1, 1989, pp. 5–25.

Frank, André Gunder, *Capitalism and Underdevelopment in Latin America*, New York: Monthly Review Press, 1967.

—— *Latin America: Underdevelopment or Revolution*, New York: Monthly Review Press, 1969.

—— *Crisis: In the World Economy*, New York: Holmes & Meier, 1980.

—— *Crisis: In the Third World*, New York: Holmes & Meier, 1981.

—— *Critique and Anti-Critique*, London: Macmillan, 1984.

Friedmann, Harriet, 'The political economy of food: the rise and fall of the Postwar International Food Order', in Michael Burawoy and Theda Skocpol (eds), *Marxist Inquiries*, Chicago, IL: University of Chicago Press, 1982, pp. 248–86.

Fröbel, Folker, 'The current development of the world economy: reproduction of labour and accumulation of capital on a world scale', *Review*, V, 4, 1982, pp. 507–55.

Fröbel, F., Heinrichs, J. and Kreye, O., *The New International Division of Labour*, Cambridge: Cambridge University Press, 1980.

George, Susan, *How the Other Half Dies: The Real Reasons for World Hunger*, revised edn, Harmondsworth: Penguin, 1977.

—— *A Fate Worse than Debt*, Harmondsworth: Penguin, 1988.

Gilligan, Carol, *In a Different Voice: Psychological Theory and Women's Development*, Cambridge, MA: Harvard University Press, 1982.

Golding, Martin, 'Obligations to future generations', in Ernest Partridge (ed.), *Responsibilities to Future Generations*, Buffalo, NY: Prometheus Books, 1981, pp. 61–72.

Gorz, André, *Ecology as Politics*, Boston, MA: South End, 1980; first French edn, 1975.

Green, R. H., 'Basic human needs: concept or slogan, synthesis or smokescreen?', *Institute of Development Studies Bulletin*, Brighton: Institute of Development Studies, June 1978.

Guha, Ramachandra, 'Radical American environmentalism and wilderness preservation: a Third World critique', *Environmental Ethics*, 11, 1, 1989, pp. 71–83.

Gülap, Haldun, 'Debate on capitalism and development: the theories of Samir Amin and Bill Warren', *Capital and Class*, 28, 1986, pp. 139–59.

Handbook of World Development: The Guide to the Brandt Report, Harlow: Longman, 1981.

Hardin, Garrett, 'Lifeboat ethics: the case against helping the poor', in William Aiken and Hugh La Follette (eds), *World Hunger and Moral Obligation*, Englewood Cliffs, NJ: Prentice-Hall, 1977.

Harriss, Barbara, 'Merchants and markets of grain in south Asia', in Teodor Shanin (ed.), *Peasants and Peasant Societies*, Oxford: Blackwell, 1987.

—— 'Differential female mortality and health care in south Asia', Oxford: Queen Elizabeth House Working Paper 13, 1989.

—— 'Intrafamily distribution of hunger in south Asia', in Jean Drèze

and Amartya K. Sen (eds), *Entitlement and Well-being*, Oxford: Clarendon Press, 1991, pp. 351–424.

Heilbroner, Robert, *An Inquiry into the Human Prospect*, London: Calder
& Boyars, 1975.

Hill, Thomas, 'Servility and self-respect', *Monist*, 57, 1973, pp. 87–104.

Höffe, Otfried, 'Kants Kategorischer Imperativ als Kriterium des Sittlichen', *Zeitschrift für Philosophische Forschung*, 31, 1977, pp. 354–84.

Howard, Stuart, 'When the bosses are international, we've got to be
international too', *Links*, 24, 1986, pp. 26–7.

Hughes, Alex, 'Corporate killers: Union Carbide in India', *Links*, 24,
1986, pp. 16–19.

Hume, David, *A Treatise of Human Nature*, ed. L. A. Selby-Bigge,
Oxford: Clarendon Press, 1964.

Hunt, Geoffrey, 'Gramsci, civil society and bureaucracy', *Praxis International*, 6, 2, 1986, pp. 206–19.

—— 'Two methodological paradigms in development economics', *The
Philosophical Forum*, XVIII, 1, 1986, pp. 52–68.

—— 'The development of the concept of civil society in Marx', *History
of Political Thought*, VIII, 2, 1987, pp. 263–76.

—— 'Antonio Labriola, evolutionary Marxism and Italian colonialism',
Praxis International, 7, 3–4, 1987–8, pp. 340–59.

—— Critical review of Peter Bartelmus, *Environment and Development*,
(Boston MA: Allen & Unwin, 1986), *Explorations in Knowledge*, V, 1,
1988, pp. 52–6.

—— 'Hegel and economic science', in B. Cullen (ed.), *Hegel Today*,
Aldershot: Avebury, 1988, pp. 61–87.

Jackson, Ben, *Poverty and the Planet: A Question of Survival*, Harmondsworth: Penguin, 1990.

Jaggar, Alison, *Feminist Politics and Human Nature*, Brighton: Harvester
Press, 1983.

Jenkins, Robin, *Exploitation*, London: Paladin, 1971.

Kagan, Shelly, *The Limits of Morality*, Oxford: Oxford University Press,
1989.

Kaletsky, A., *The Costs of Default*, New York: Priority Press Publications, 1985.

Keohane, R. O. and Nye, J. S. (eds), *Transnational Relations and World
Politics*, Cambridge, MA: Harvard University Press, 1970.

Kittay, Eva Feder and Meyers, Diana T. (eds), *Women and Moral Theory*,
Totowa, NJ: Rowman & Littlefield, 1987.

Komarov, Boris, *The Destruction of Nature in the Soviet Union*, London:
Pluto Press, 1981.

Körner, P., Maass, G., Siebold, T. and Tetzlaff, R., *The IMF and the
Debt Crisis*, London and Atlantic Highlands, NJ: Zed Books, 1987.

Kothari, Rajni, 'Environment and alternative development', *Alternatives*,
V, 1979–80, pp. 427–75.

Laclau, Ernesto, 'Feudalism and capitalism in Latin America', *New Left
Review*, 67, 1971, reprinted in his *Politics and Ideology in Marxist Theory*,
London: Verso, 1979.

Lappé, Frances Moore and Collins, Joseph, *Food First: Beyond the Myth of Scarcity*, Boston, MA: Houghton Mifflin, 1977.

Lever, H. and Huhne, C., *Debt and Danger: The World Financial Crisis*, Harmondsworth: Penguin, 1987.

Limqueco, Peter and McFarlane, Bruce (eds), *Neo-Marxist Theories of Development*, New York: St Martin's Press, 1983.

Linear, Marcus, *Zapping the Third World: The Disaster of Development Aid*, London: Pluto Press, 1985.

Lloyd, Genevieve, *The Man of Reason: 'Male' and 'Female' in Western Philosophy*, London: Methuen, 1984.

Locke, John, *An Essay Concerning Human Understanding*, ed. Peter Nidditch, Oxford: Clarendon Press, 1975.

Luban, D., 'The just war and human rights', *Philosophy and Public Affairs*, 9, 2, 1980, pp. 160–81.

Luper-Foy, Steven (ed.), *Problems of International Justice*, Boulder, CO: Westview Press, 1988.

MacIntyre, Alasdair, *A Short History of Ethics*, London: Routledge & Kegan Paul, 1967.

—— *After Virtue*, London: Duckworth, 1981.

—— *Is Patriotism a Virtue?*, Lawrence, KA: Philosophy Department, University of Kansas, 1984.

McMillan, Carol, *Women, Reason and Nature*, Oxford: Blackwell, 1982.

Marx, Karl, *Grundrisse*, Harmondsworth: Penguin, 1973.

—— *Early Writings*, Harmondsworth: Penguin, 1975.

—— *Capital*, vol. 1, Harmondsworth: Penguin, 1976.

Marx, Karl and Engels, Frederick, *Collected Works*, vol. 5, London: Lawrence & Wishart, 1976.

Massachusetts Institute of Technology, *Man's Impact on the Global Environment: Assessment and Recommendations for Action*, Cambridge, MA: MIT, 1970.

Meier, G. M. (ed.), *Leading Issues in Development Economics*, Oxford: Oxford University Press, 1964.

Meillasoux, C., 'Development or exploitation: is the Sahel famine good business?', *Review of African Political Economy*, I, 1, 1974, pp. 27–33.

Mill, John Stuart, *Utilitarianism, On Liberty, Essay on Bentham*, London: Collins/Fontana, 1962.

Moore, G. E., *Principia Ethica*, Cambridge: Cambridge University Press, 1903.

Naess, Arne, 'The shallow and the deep, long-range ecology movements; A summary', *Inquiry*, 16, 1973, pp. 95–100.

—— 'Sustainable development and the deep, long range ecological movement', *The Trumpeter*, 5, 4, 1988, pp. 138–42.

Nagel, Thomas, *Mortal Questions*, Cambridge: Cambridge University Press, 1979.

Nicholson, Linda, 'Feminism and Marx: integrating kinship with the economic', in Seyla Benhabib and Drucilla Cornell (eds), *Feminism as Critique*, Cambridge: Polity Press, 1987.

Nielsen, Kai, 'Global justice, capitalism and the Third World', *Journal of Applied Philosophy*, 1, 2, 1984, pp. 175–86.

—— *Equality and Liberty: A Defense of Radical Egalitarianism*, Totowa, NJ: Rowman & Allanheld, 1985.

—— *Marxism and the Moral Point of View*, Boulder, CO: Westview Press, 1988.

—— *After the Demise of the Tradition: Rorty, Critical Theory, and the Fate of Philosophy*, Boulder, CO: Westview Press, 1991.

Noddings, Nell, *Caring*, Berkeley, CA: University of California Press, 1984.

Norman, Richard, 'Liberty, equality, property', *Aristotelian Society*, supplementary volume, LV, 1981, pp. 193–209.

Okin, Susan Moller, *Women in Western Political Thought*, Princeton, NJ: Princeton University Press, 1979.

—— 'Justice and gender', *Philosophy and Public Affairs*, 16, 1987, pp. 42–72.

O'Neill, Onora, *Faces of Hunger: An Essay on Poverty, Justice and Development*, London: Allen & Unwin, 1986.

—— 'The moral perplexities of famine and world hunger', in Tom Regan (ed.), *Matters of Life and Death: New Introductory Essays in Moral Philosophy*, 2nd edn, New York: Random House, 1986, pp. 294–337.

—— 'Ethical reasoning and ideological pluralism', *Ethics*, 98, 1988, pp. 705–22.

—— *Constructions of Reason: Explorations of Kant's Practical Philosophy*, Cambridge: Cambridge University Press, 1989.

Parsons, H. L. (ed.), *Marx and Engels on Ecology*, Westport, CT: Greenwood Press, 1977.

Passmore, John, 'The treatment of animals', *Journal of the History of Ideas*, 36, 1975, pp. 195–218.

Pateman, Carole, *The Sexual Contract*, Cambridge: Polity Press, 1988.

Pearce, David, Markandya, Anil and Barbier, Edward B., *Blueprint for a Green Economy* (the Pearce Report), London: Earthscan, 1989.

Pfeiffer, Raymond, 'The responsibility of men for the oppression of women', *Journal of Applied Philosophy*, 2, 1985, pp. 217–29.

Politics for Life: The Green Party Manifesto, London: Green Party, 1985.

Porritt, Jonathon, *Seeing Green*, Oxford: Blackwell, 1984.

Postow, B. C., 'Economic dependence and self-respect', *The Philosophical Forum*, 10, 1978–9, pp. 181–201.

Prentis, Steve, *Biotechnology: A New Industrial Revolution*, London: Orbis, 1984.

Programme of the German Green Party, trans. of 2nd German edn, preface by Jonathon Porritt, London: Heretic, 1983.

Rawls, John, *A Theory of Justice*, Cambridge, MA: Harvard University Press, 1971, and Oxford: Clarendon Press, 1972, and Oxford University Press, 1973.

—— 'Justice as fairness: political not metaphysical', *Philosophy and Public Affairs*, 14, 1985, pp. 223–51.

Richards, David A. J., 'International distributive justice', in Roland J. Pennock and John W. Chapman (eds), *Nomos*, XXIV, New York: New York University Press, 1982, pp. 275–95.

Rodman, John, 'The liberation of nature', *Inquiry*, 20, 1977, pp. 83–145.

Rosenstein-Rodan, P. N., 'Problems of industrialization of eastern and south-eastern Europe', *Economic Journal*, 1943, pp. 204–7.

Routley, Val and Routley, Richard, 'Human chauvinism and environmental ethics', in Don Mannison, Michael McRobbie and Richard Routley (eds), *Environmental Philosophy*, Canberra: Australian National University, 1980, pp. 96–189.

Ruddick, Sara, 'Remarks on the sexual politics of reason', in E. F. Kittay and D. T. Meyers (eds), *Women and Moral Theory*, Totowa, NJ: Rowman & Littlefield, 1987, pp. 237–60.

—— 'Maternal thinking', in her *Maternal Thinking: Towards a Politics of Peace*, Boston, MA: Beacon Press, 1989, pp. 13–27.

Sachs, Ignacy, 'Environment and development revisited', *Alternatives*, VIII, 1982, pp. 369–78.

Sandel, Michael, *Liberalism and the Limits of Justice*, Cambridge: Cambridge University Press, 1982.

Sartre, Jean-Paul, *The Transcendence of the Ego*, New York: Noonday, 1957.

Scott, Alison, 'Industrialization, gender segregation and stratification theory', in Rosemary Crompton and Michael Mann (eds), *Gender and Stratification*, Cambridge: Polity Press, 1986, pp. 154–89.

Sen, Amartya K., *Poverty and Famines: An Essay on Entitlement and Deprivation*, Oxford: Clarendon Press, 1981.

—— *Resources, Values and Development*, Oxford: Blackwell, and Cambridge, MA: Harvard University Press, 1984.

—— 'Gender and co-operative conflicts', Working Paper of the World Institute for Development Economics Research (WIDER), Helsinki: United Nations University, 1987.

Shiva, Vandana, 'Recovering the real meaning of sustainability', in David E. Cooper and Joy A. Palmer (eds), *The Environment in Question: Ethics and Global Issues*, London and New York: Routledge, 1992, pp. 187–93.

Shue, Henry, 'Exporting hazards', in Peter G. Brown and Henry Shue (eds), *Boundaries: National Autonomy and Its Limits*, Totowa, NJ: Rowman & Littlefield, 1981, pp. 107–45.

—— *Basic Rights: Subsistence, Affluence and US Foreign Policy*, Princeton, NJ: Princeton University Press, 1980.

—— 'The interdependence of duties', in Philip Alston and K. Tomasevski (eds), *The Right to Food*, Dordrecht: Nijhoff, 1984.

Sidgwick, Henry, *The Methods of Ethics*, 7th edn, London: Macmillan, 1907.

Singer, Peter, 'Famine, affluence and morality', *Philosophy and Public Affairs*, 1, 1971–2, pp. 229–43.

—— *Animal Liberation: A New Ethic for Our Treatment of Animals*, London: Cape, 1976.

—— 'Reconsidering the famine relief argument', in Peter G. Brown and Henry Shue (eds), *Food Policy*, New York: Free Press, 1977, pp. 36–53.

—— *Practical Ethics*, Cambridge: Cambridge University Press, 1979.

—— *The Expanding Circle*, Oxford: Oxford University Press, 1981.

Solodnikov, V. G., *Some Problems of Economic and Social Development of Independent African States*, Moscow, 1967.

Southwick, Charles H. (ed.), *Global Ecology*, Sunderland, MA: Sinauer, 1985.

Spretnak, C. and Capra, F., *Green Politics*, London: Paladin, 1985.

Sprigge, T. L. S., *The Rational Foundations of Ethics*, London: Routledge, 1988.

Stewart, F., 'Basic needs strategies, human rights, and the right to development', *Human Rights Quarterly*, 11, 1989, pp. 347–74.

Stiehm, Judith Hicks, 'The unit of political analysis: our Aristotelian hangover', in Sandra Harding and Merrill B. Hintikka (eds), *Discovering Reality: Feminist Perspectives on Epistemology, Metaphysics, Methodology and Philosophy of Science*, Dordrecht: Reidel, 1983.

Streeten, Paul, *Basic Needs*, Washington, DC: International Bank for Reconstruction and Development (World Bank), 1977.

Streeten, Paul, *et al.*, *First Things First: Meeting Basic Needs in Developing Countries*, Oxford: Oxford University Press, 1981.

Sunkel, Osvaldo, 'Transnational capitalism and national disintegration in Latin America', *Social and Economic Studies*, XXII, 1, 1973, pp. 132–76.

—— 'The transnational corporate system', *Links*, 24, 1986, pp. 7–9, reprinted from the *CTC Reporter*, autumn 1985.

UNICEF, *The State of the World's Children 1989*, Oxford: Oxford University Press, 1989.

—— *The State of the World's Children 1990*, Oxford: Oxford University Press, 1990.

United Nations, *Declaration on the Right to Development*, New York: United Nations, December 1986.

Vidal, John, 'Long shadows over a parched land', *Guardian*, 18 January 1991.

Vincent, R. J., *Human Rights and International Relations*, Cambridge: Cambridge University Press, 1986.

Vroey, M. de, 'The transition from classical to neo-classical economics: a scientific revolution', in W. J. Samuels (ed.), *The Methodology of Economic Thought*, New Brunswick, NJ: Transaction Books, 1980.

Wallerstein, Immanuel, *The Modern World System*, vol. 1, New York: Academic Press, 1974.

—— *The Capitalist World Economy*, Cambridge: Cambridge University Press, 1980.

Walzer, Michael, *Spheres of Justice: A Defence of Pluralism and Equality*, Oxford: Martin Robertson, 1983.

Warren, Bill, *Imperialism: Pioneer of Capitalism*, London: New Left Books, 1980.

Westlake, M., 'Recession puts the brakes on recovery', *Guardian*, 4 February 1991.

—— 'Why a continent suffers in silence', *Guardian*, 5 February 1991.

Williams, Bernard, *Moral Luck*, Cambridge: Cambridge University Press, 1981.

—— *Ethics and the Limits of Philosophy*, London: Fontana, 1985.

Wimmer, Ernst, 'Ideology of the "new social movements" ', *World Marxist Review*, 28, 7, 1985, pp. 36–44.

Woodhouse, E. J., 'Re-visioning the future of the Third World: an ecological perspective on development', *World Politics*, XXV, 1, 1972, pp. 1–33.

World Bank, *World Debt Tables 1990–91*, vol. 1, *Analysis and Summary Tables*, and vol. 2, *Country Tables*, Washington, DC: World Bank, 1990.

—— *World Development Report 1990*, Oxford: Oxford University Press, 1990.

World Commission on Environment and Development, *Our Common Future* (the Brundtland Report), Oxford: Oxford University Press, 1987.

Zjilstra, Jasper, 'Rainforest reality', *Orbit*, 33, summer 1989, p. 16.

Index